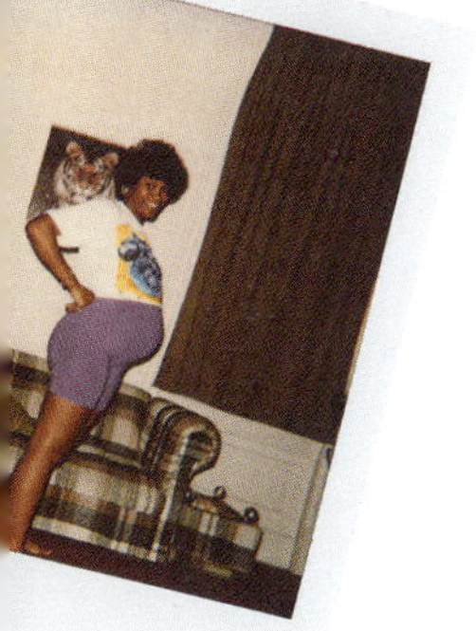

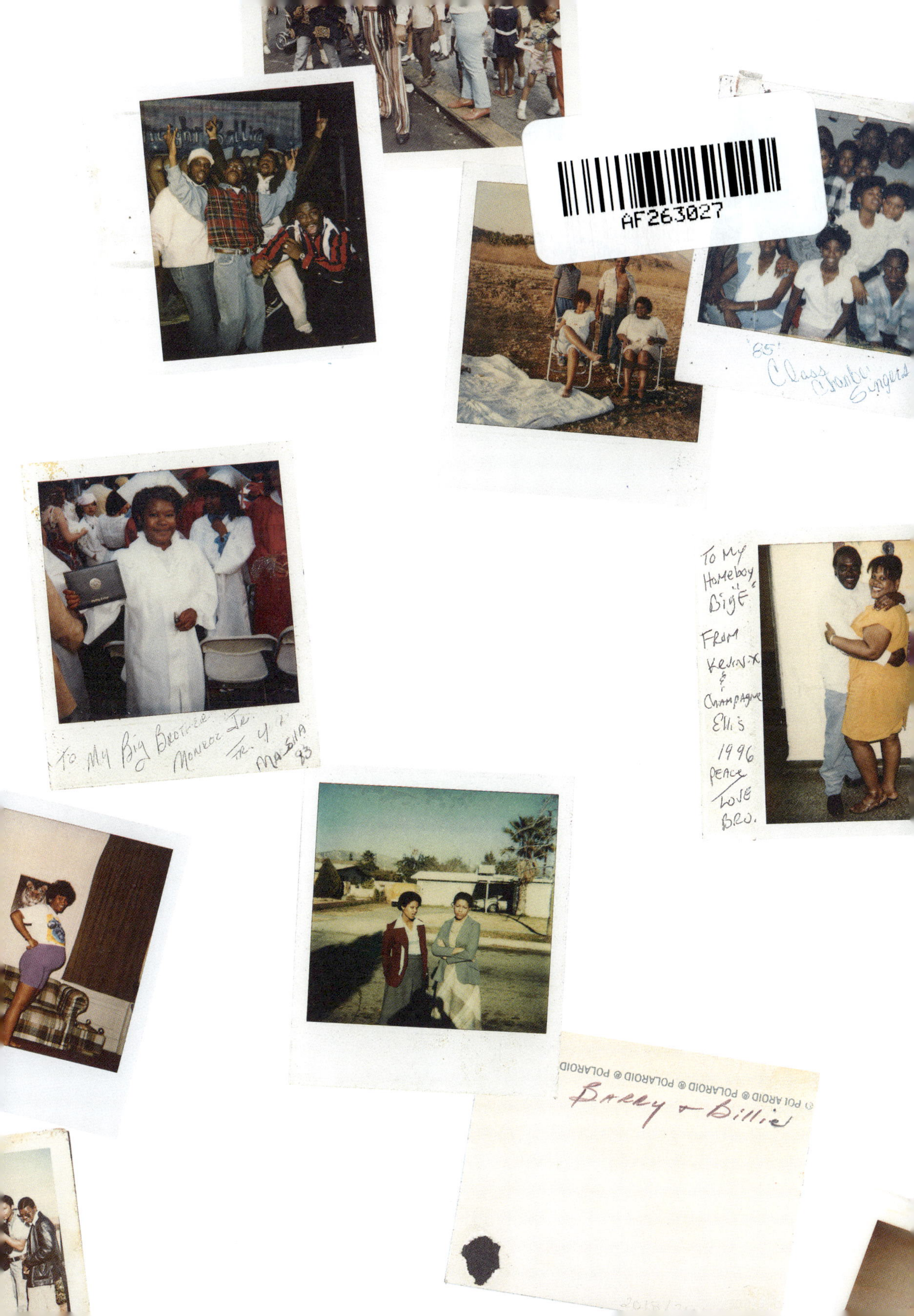

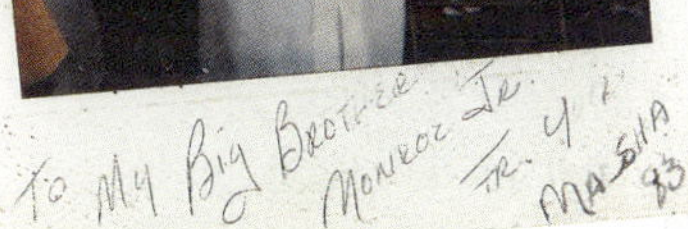

To My Big Brother Monroe Jr.
Tr. 4 Masha
83

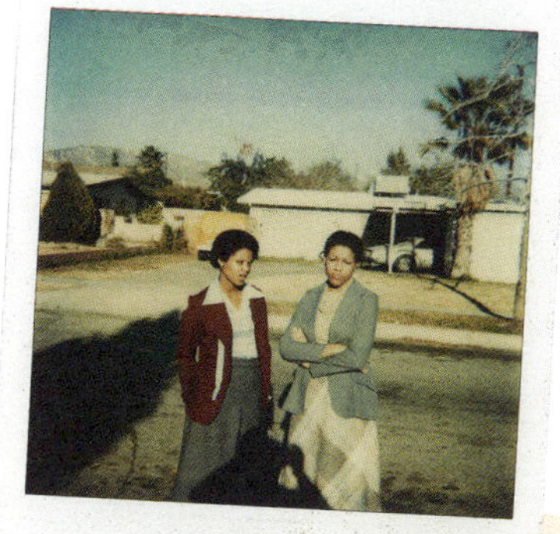

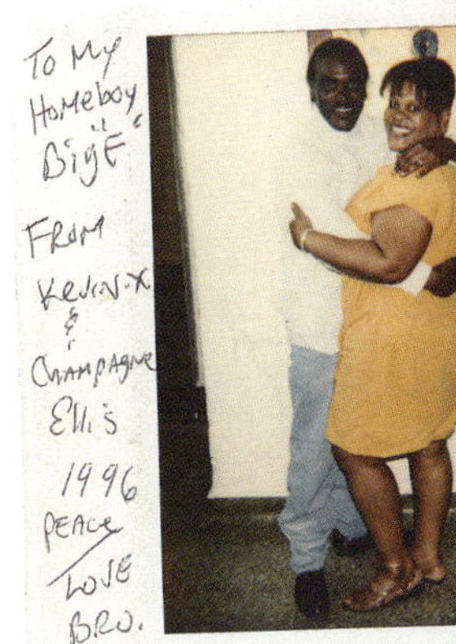

To My
Homeboy
Big "E"
From
Kevin X.
&
Champagne
Ellis
1996
Peace
Love
Bro.

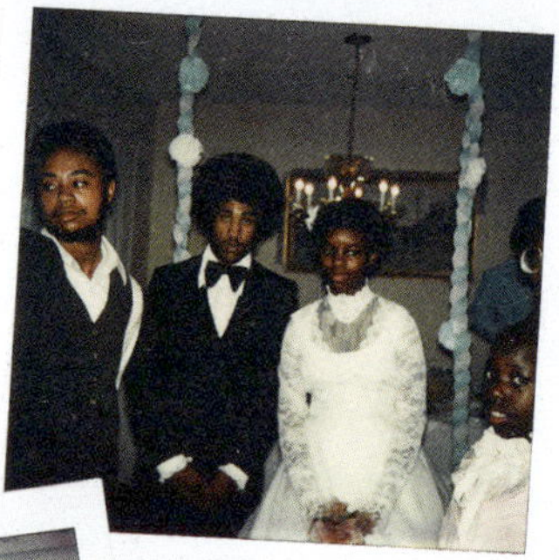

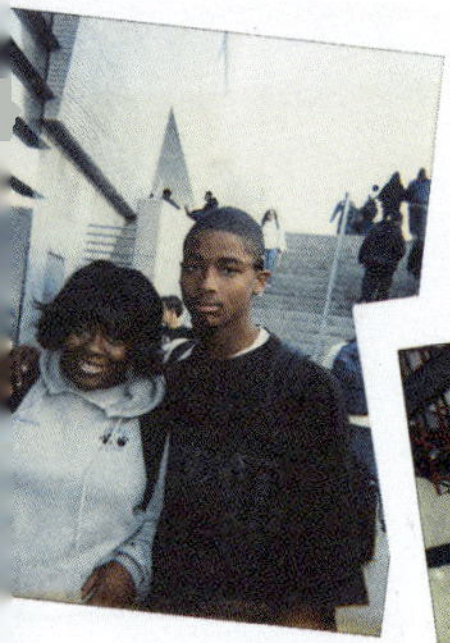

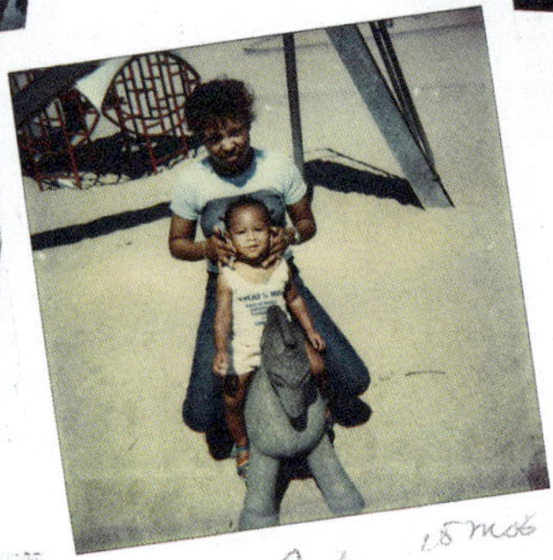

Alondra Park
Sept. 9, 1979   28 mos

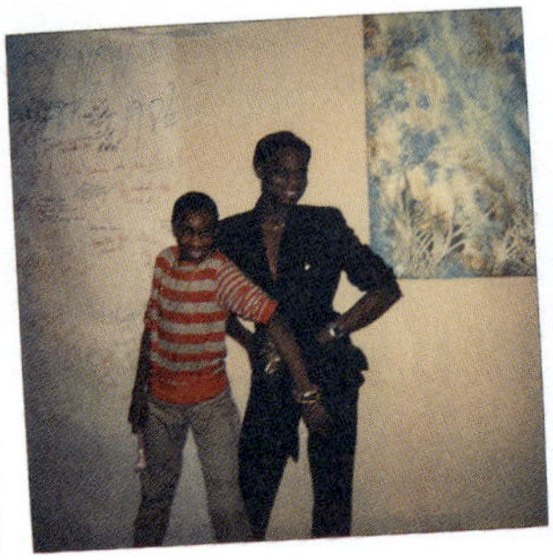

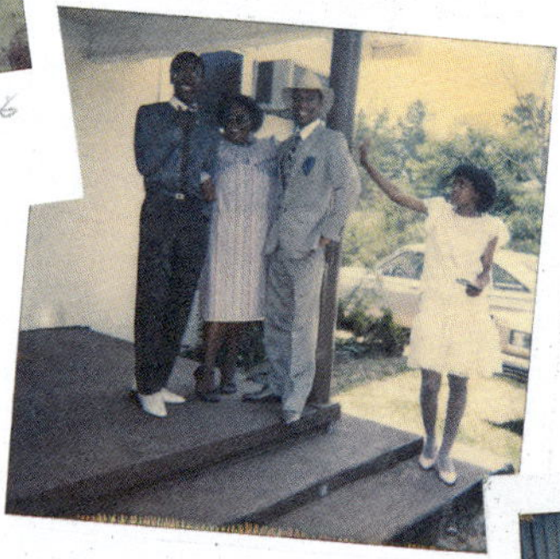

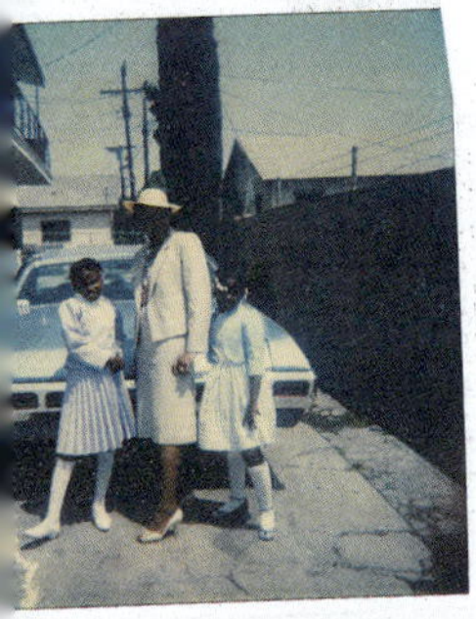

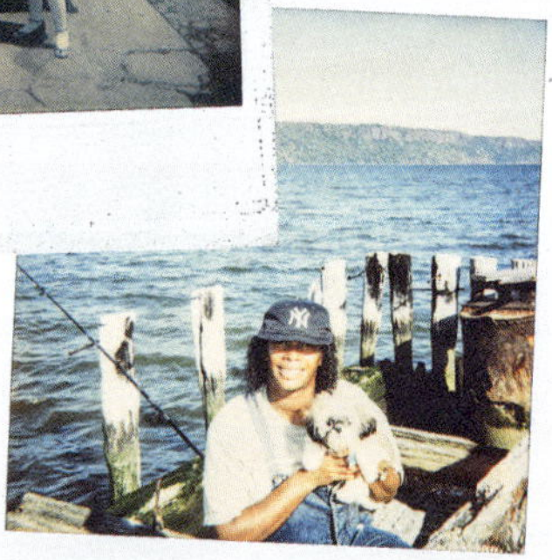

Grace & Peas on the
Hudson River.   10.7.97

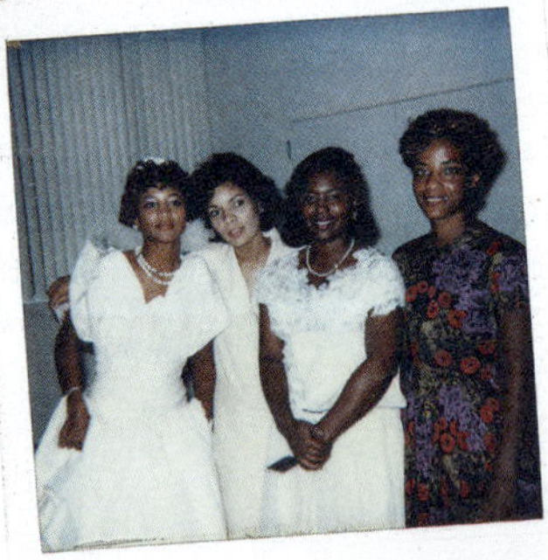

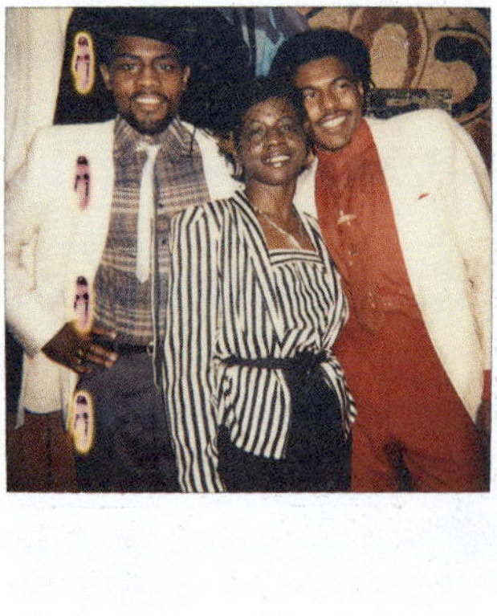

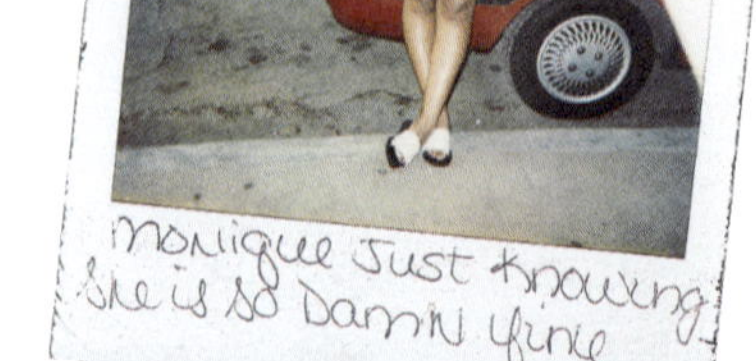

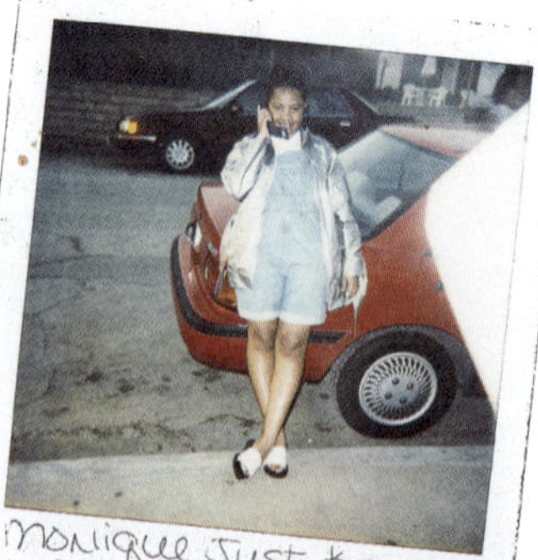

Monique Just Knowing
She is So Damn Fine

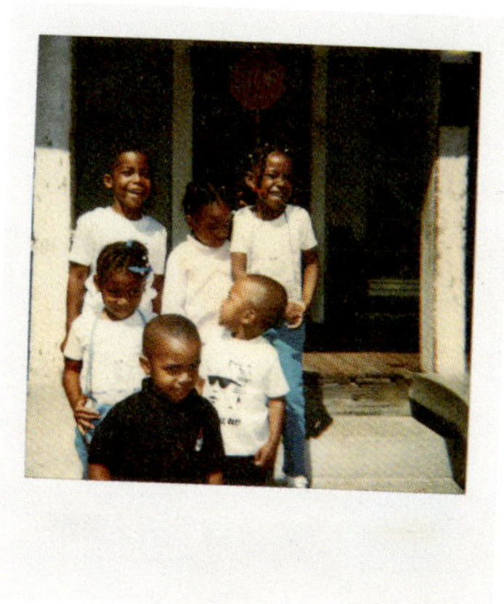

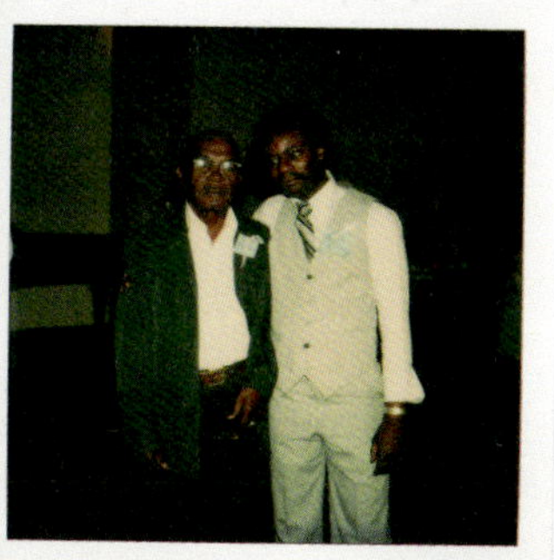

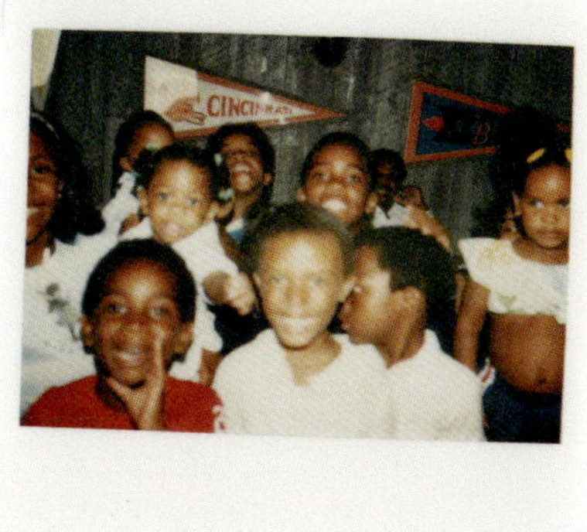

WHAT MATTERS MOST

Photographs of Black Life

Art Gallery of Ontario
DelMonico Books • D.A.P.
New York

Edited by Zun Lee and Sophie Hackett

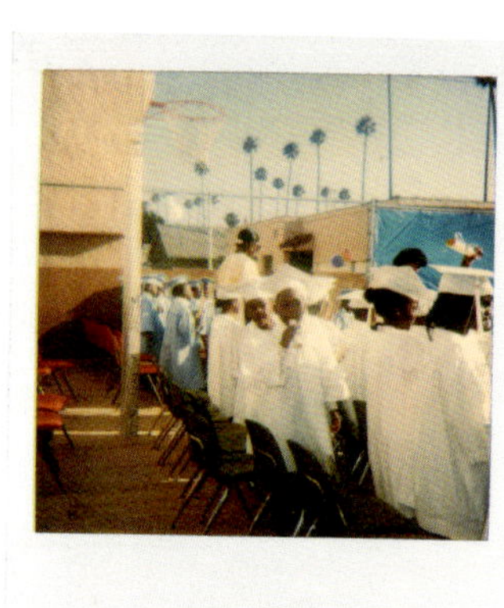
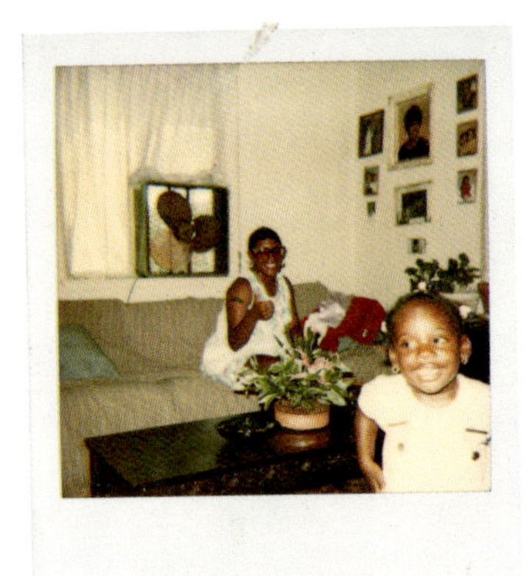
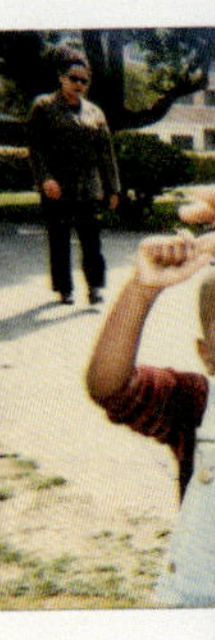
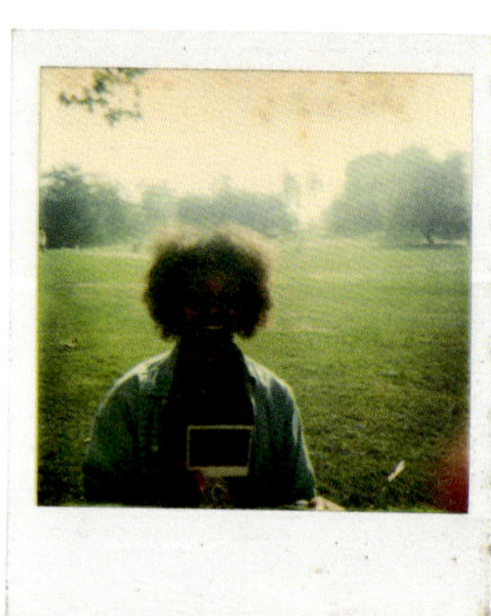
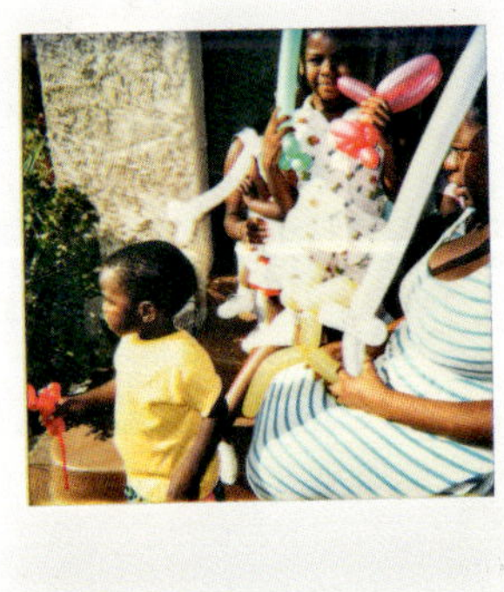
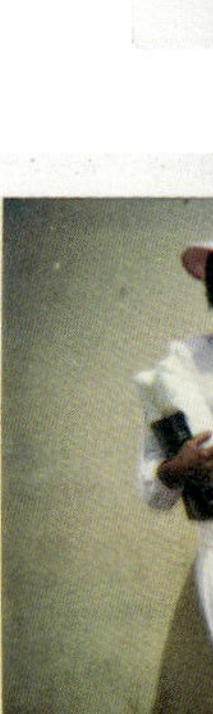
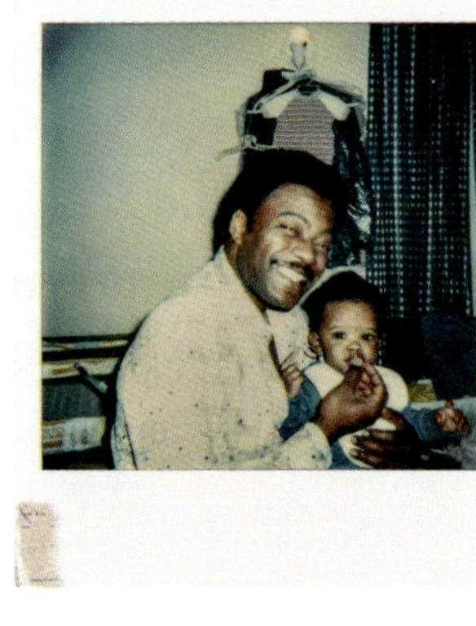
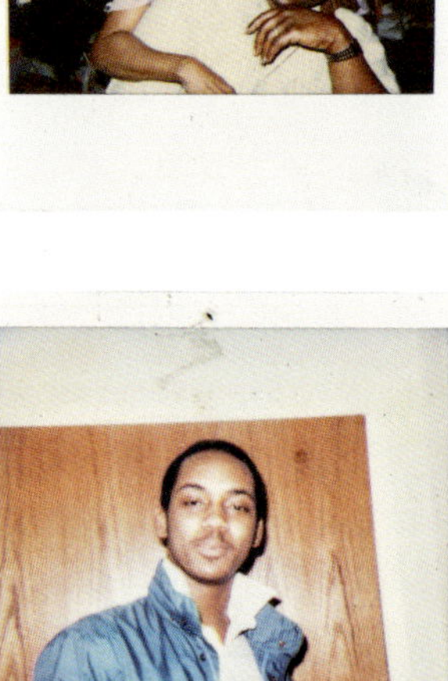
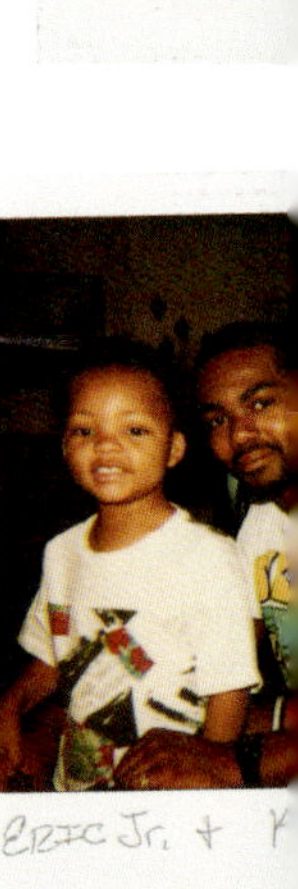
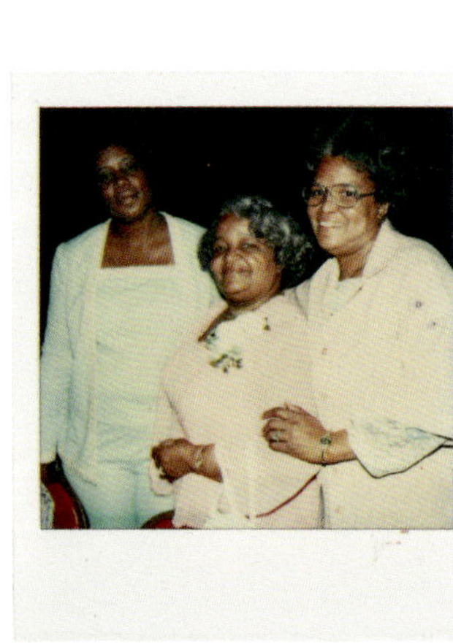
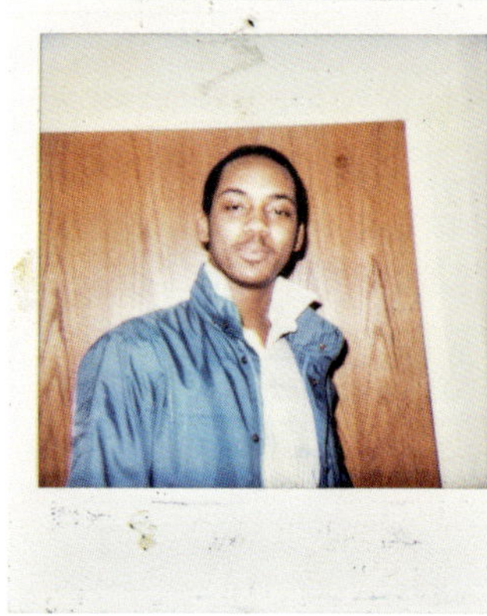
ERIC Jr. + K

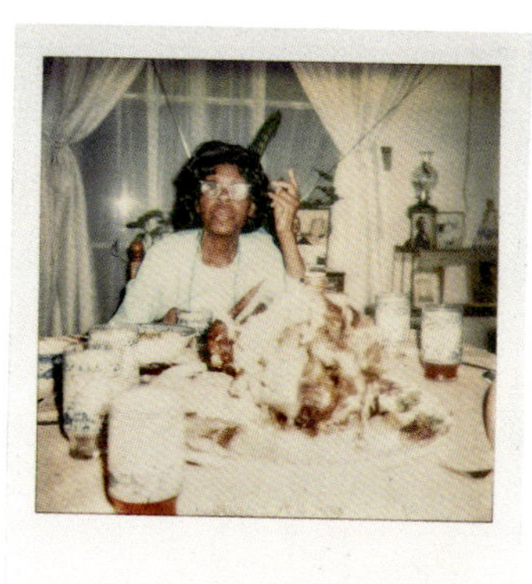

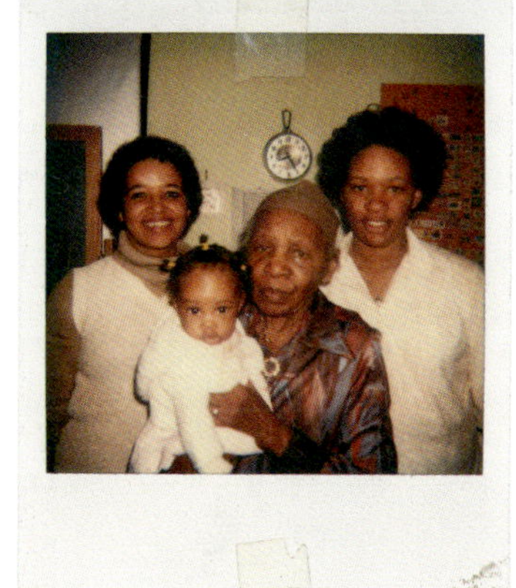

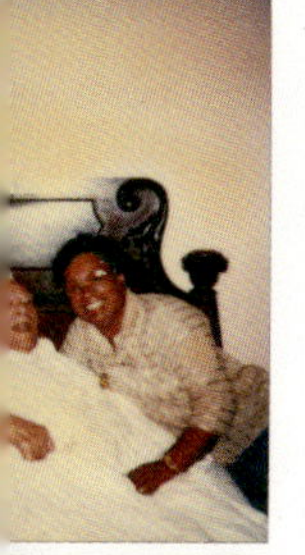

*Black Aliveness
as sane, wild,
alert, infinite,
and forever.*

—Ronaldo V. Wilson

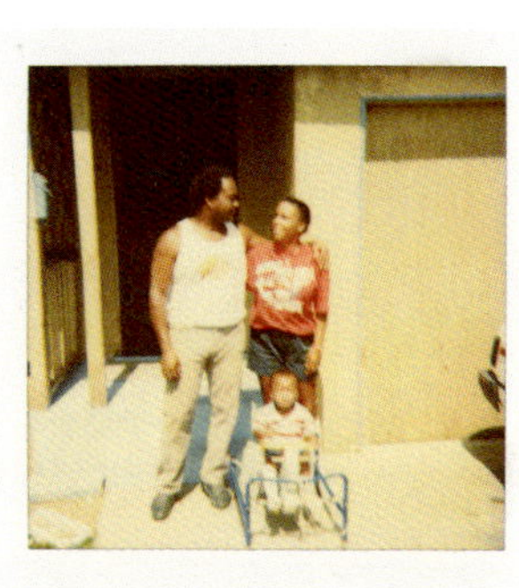

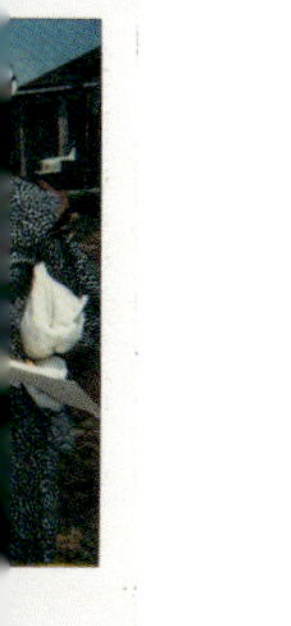

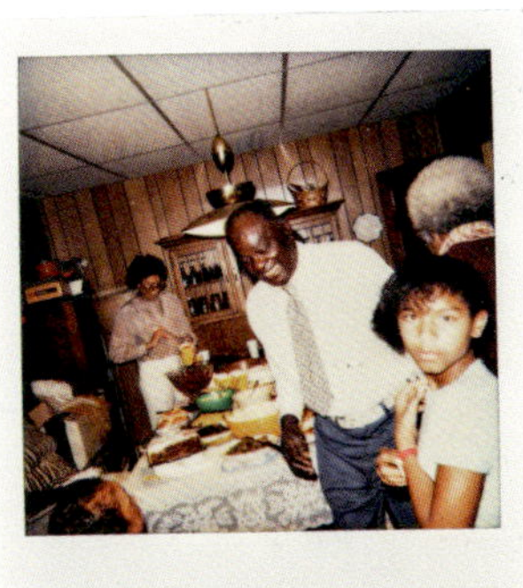

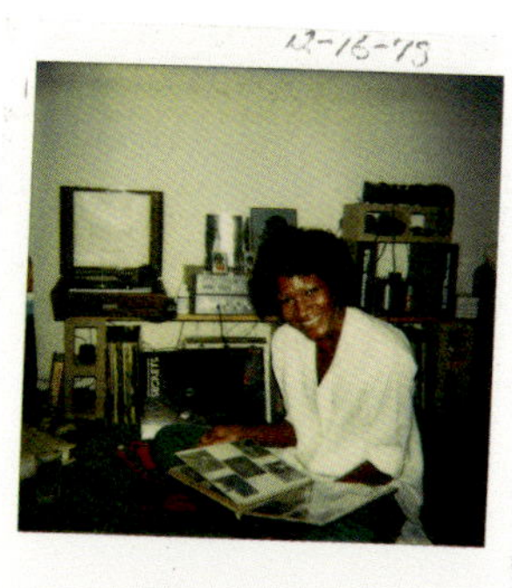

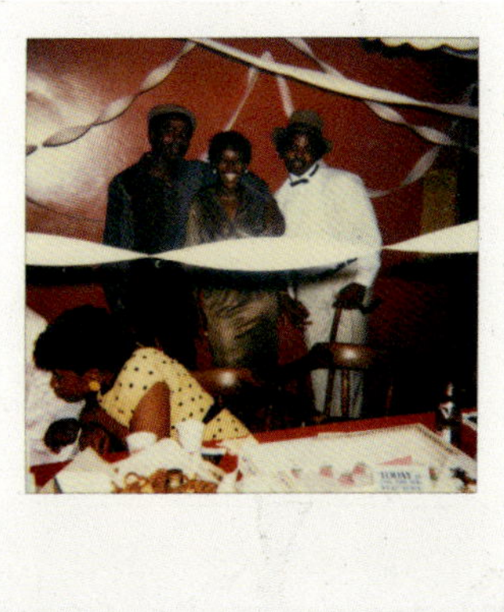

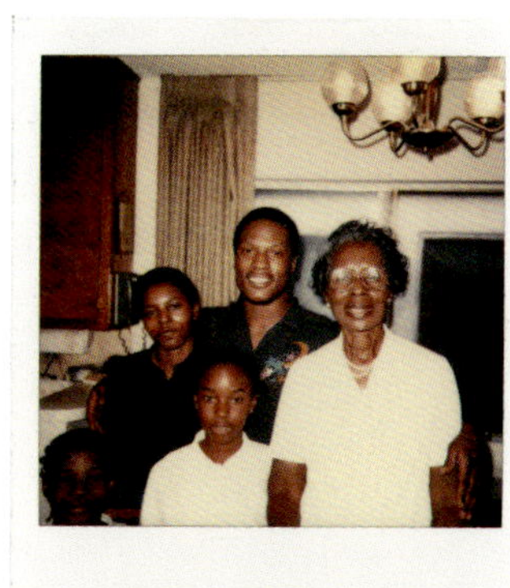

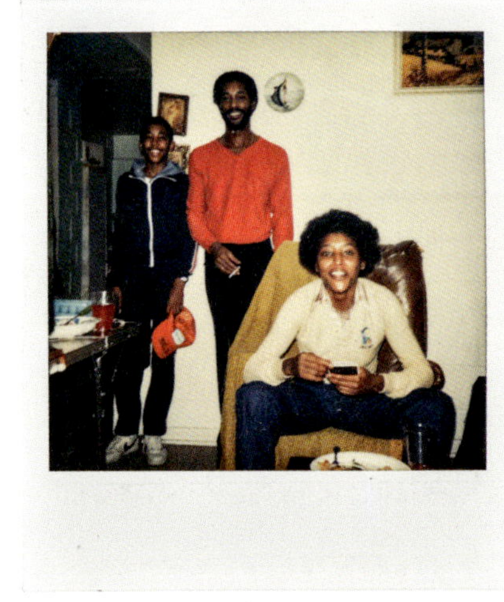

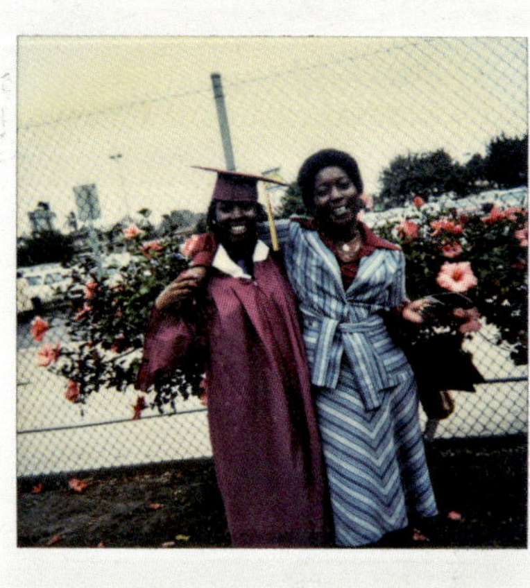

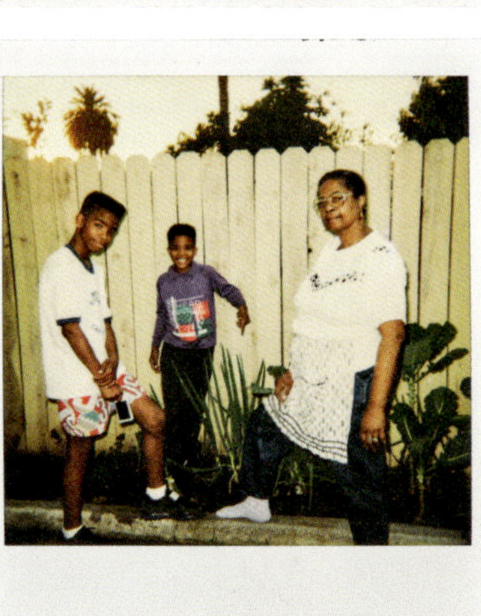

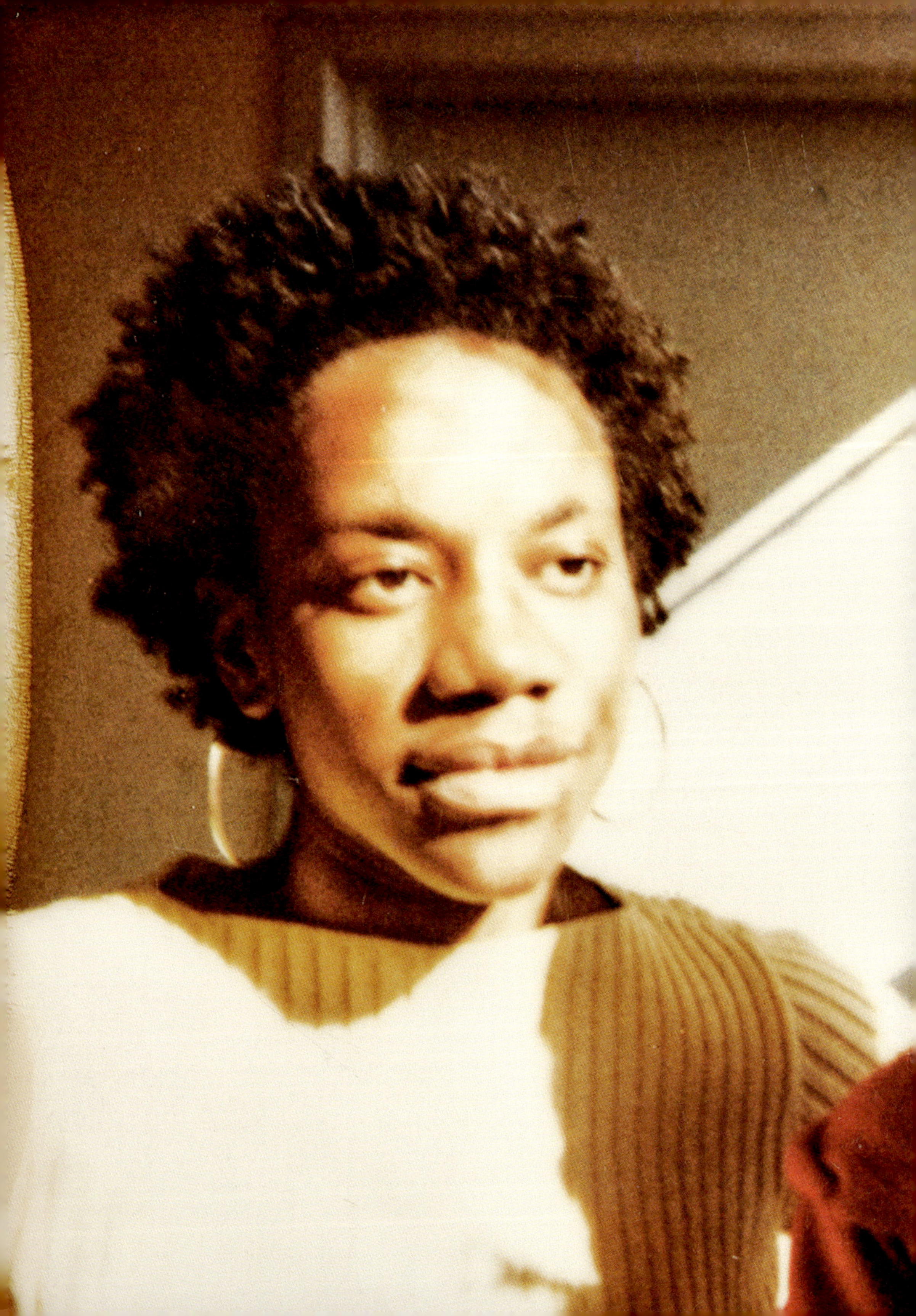

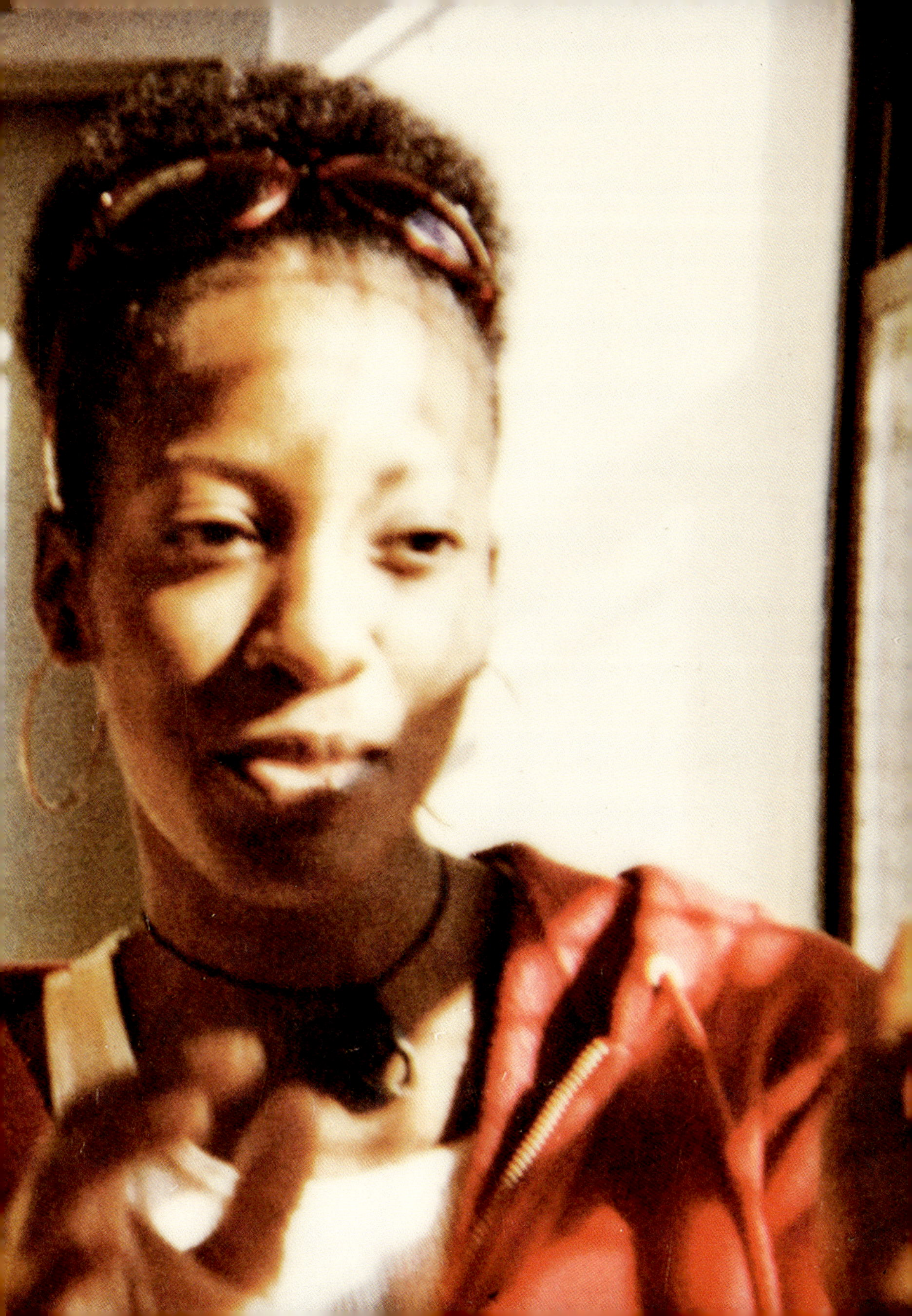

Director's Foreword

STEPHAN JOST
Michael and Sonja Koerner Director, and CEO

From 2012 to 2018, artist and educator Zun Lee sought out Polaroid prints that showcased the lives of Black Americans. Scouring online auctions and yard sales, Lee amassed more than four thousand family photographs dating from the 1950s to the 2000s to create what he has dubbed the *Fade Resistance* collection. This collection, which was acquired by the AGO in 2018, is at the heart of *What Matters Most: Photographs of Black Life*, an exhibition co-curated by Lee and the Gallery's Curator of Photography, Sophie Hackett.

These snapshots offer us intimate glimpses of ordinary people: listening to music, crossing the stage at graduation ceremonies, dressing up, exchanging rings, blowing out birthday candles, raising children. In these moments, paused in photographs, the everyday takes on an extraordinary sheen. Lee is deeply invested in preserving Black American heritage and community rituals, not as part of the past, but as expressions of the present. His attention to and care for these humble objects draw attention to a rich, visual record of Black self-representation and subjectivity over time. Indeed, as we at the AGO strive to feature more Black artists and subjects—a project that has become ever more urgent as we have witnessed both the senseless acts of anti-Black violence in recent years and the attendant rise of the Movement for Black Lives—we are committed to ensuring that Black communities see themselves and their experiences reflected in major exhibitions such as this one.

We deeply appreciate the lead support of David W. Binet, the generous support of Martha LA McCain, and the additional assistance of Cindy & Shon Barnett, all of whom have shown tremendous enthusiasm for the *Fade Resistance* collection and the exhibition it inspired, as well as for the related program *Ways of Caring*.

I am deeply appreciative of staff across the gallery whose efforts were instrumental in making this exhibition possible, especially Sophie Hackett, Research & Collections Assistant Emily Miller, and Project Manager Hillary Taylor. Thanks to Julian Cox, Chief Curator and Deputy Director; Jessica Bright, Chief, Exhibitions, Collections & Conservation; Production Manager Malene Hjørngaard; Production Assistant Evelyn Quinn; and designers Aleksandra Grzywaczewska and Tara Keens-Douglas. This exceptional publication is the result of the combined efforts of Publishing Manager Jim Shedden and his department and the design acumen of Brian Johnson, Silas Munro, and Randa Hadi at Polymode Studio, as well as our superlative contributing authors Dawn Lundy Martin, Fred Moten, and Stefano Harney, who, with Hackett and Lee, provided sage and moving reflections that amplify the power of this work. And finally, I am profoundly grateful to Zun Lee, not only for his work as a co-curator and co-editor, but also for entrusting the AGO to care for and present his collection in a way that respects the complex dynamics contained in these photographs and honours the people who brought them into being.

Black Aliveness in Flight

Black Aliveness as sane, wild, alert,
infinite, and forever.

—Ronaldo V. Wilson

DAWN LUNDY MARTIN What the invitation to see something or someone allows, and what it doesn't allow. When the invitation—if it is indeed an invitation—suggests a pushing out and a pushing against. Against what? Against the invitation itself? We can posit that the invitation was not given, but instead taken and taken up through no one's fault; we can posit that the so-called "invitation" was produced by the accident of misplacing something that was once, at least for a moment, dear. One way of looking is also an intervention within the lives of people we do not know and their intimate experiences. One meaning of intervention is "a coming between"— in this case, a visual coming between the instant photograph and its intended audience, a slippage made possible by temporal and social displacement. You lose your wallet, let's say, because you lost your house because you lost your neighborhood because you're lost now. This is all to say *Fade Resistance*, Zun Lee's collection of thousands of Polaroids featuring Black people as the primary subjects, resists transparency as much as it reveals something ineffable about Black life.

The magnificence of being at once intensely familiar and entirely alien. *I ain't been where you been but I know what you know.*

A great many of the photographs in this collection exhibit
a kind of wholesomeness of Black family life—holidays, just-
born babies, family reunions, graduations, people and new
cars, snapshots of everyday life. A woman lies on a sofa
talking into a red telephone receiver. Two middle-aged men
play cards on Thanksgiving, 1985. A father gives his son
his first haircut in a kitchen. A girl in a white dress sits at
a white piano. Even cool cats, ya dig, sign photos "To Dad
with Love." Like all worthwhile archives, this one refuses
wholeness, but instead points us toward what's outside
of the frame and in its corners/off center, what's missing,
and what's singular. It's in these fissures, peripheries, and
striking singularities where one might glimpse what I think
of as a Black understanding.

In one photo, a fit young man stands, naked, in front of a
row of bathroom sinks and mirrors. The top arch of his
bare ass is visible. His muscular back draws our attention
toward the vertical dip of his spine. Although he's facing
away from the camera, we see his face in the mirror taking
in both the photographer and the viewer outside the frame:
us. He leans on one of the sinks in the space, which appears
to be either barracks or a locker room. His mouth is parted
rather seductively, as if caught not entirely by surprise in
his birthday suit. What strikes me about the photo is how

the double image—what the mirror reflects and the mirror image itself—approximates the complicated notion of what Blackness might be if Blackness were something that could be named, foreclosed, known. A kind of *ars poetica* for the collection, this image untangles the role of the Black subject from its tight historical knot and examines the role of snapshot instant photography in (un)determining that role. This image invents itself. If as, Leslie Marmon Silko writes, "A photograph is a passageway," and "some photographs are dead ends," then this photograph is a knife slicing the passageway open so that we encounter a pitch in the *visual frequency* and become unsure of our footing.

In Tina Campt's lexicon "frequency" is a term used to "account for the impression images leave on us, their impact and how they move us." The term also has to do, as Campt notes, with the rate at which something occurs, its vibrational quality. The visual frequency in the case of Lee's found collection of Black life Polaroids matters as a gesture toward the vibrational impact of how we're able to visually metabolize the volume of images. A fluttering overwhelms the sensorium. A fluttering mystifies any relationship between the object and the gaze, even if you are the object of your own gaze. Does it—the object—fly away?

We were not intending to be the object of the white gaze and yet here we are. Now that we're here, see us captured in vibrational aliveness. The Black aliveness that interests me is the *don't look this way* kind, the *what you lookin at* kind, the *neutral innocence nobody ever gave us* kind, the kind that's operational by flight. "Lines of flight are the bolts of pent-up energy that break through the cracks in a system of control and shoot off on the diagonal. By the light of their passage, they reveal open spaces beyond the limits of what exists." That's philosopher Tim Rayner's excellent summary of Gilles Deleuze and Felix Guatarri's notion of "ligne de fuite," which theorizes a possibility for escape when there appears to be none. Deleuze and Guatarri, he says "link human creativity to flight." My Black understanding is attendant to flight as creative energy as much as it takes up that creative energy in terms of resistance.

My Black understanding emerges from two instant photographs I borrowed from my mother's family album. I make an offering to the archive, a coming between the coming between. The "I" becomes a willing subject, sliding its way in. What difference does it make when "I" enter the visual frequency? What do I know?

What remains when the photograph fades:

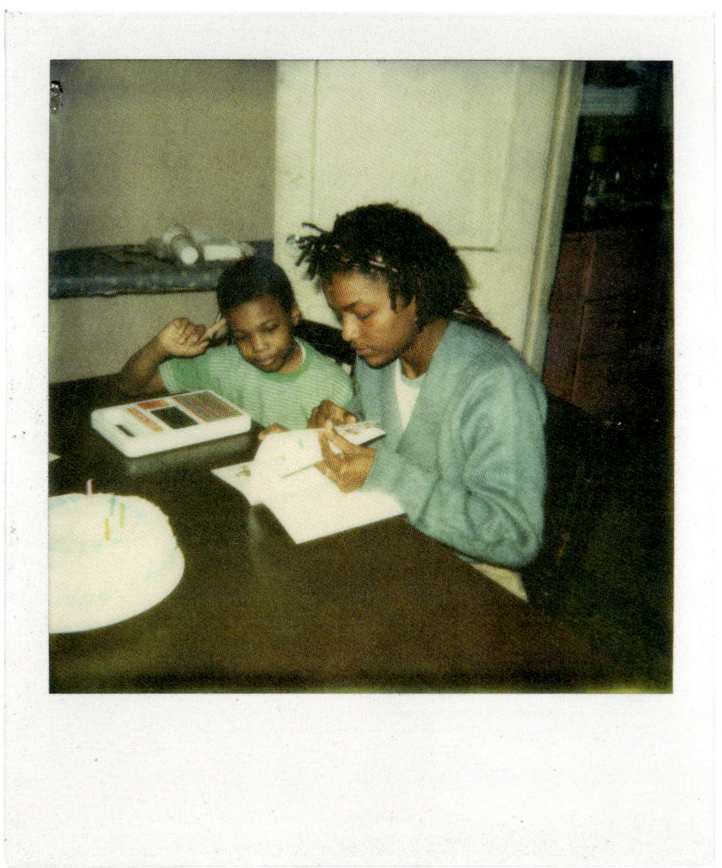

Little Khalil & Me. Image courtesy of Dawn Lundy Martin.

Little Khalil & Me

Little Khalil, as we call him, is my first cousin once removed, basically, my cousin Khalil's son. Khalil was renamed Khalil when his parents joined the Nation of Islam. His birth name is Allen, "Al" for short. The name on Little Khalil's birth certificate is Carlos. That's the name he uses now, Carlos, but almost everyone in the family still calls him Little Khalil. He spent lots of time over at my parents' house, because his parents—Big Khalil and his girlfriend Cookie—abandoned him, just up and left. He lived with his grandparents full-time, Little Khalil—with my mother's sister Shirley, whose Muslim name is Sakena, and her husband Jimmy, or Jamil. On this day, Little Khalil's seventh or eighth birthday, I'm trying to help him understand how to use some digital device for children. I was in college at the time—I can tell by my hair. So it must be summer. If it's summer, my job is driving an ice-cream truck. It's a cool biz that my mother heard about on the radio where you rent a truck for the summer, buy the ice cream wholesale, and mark it up tenfold. The company assigns you a route. Some days, I take Little Khalil out with me on the truck and we eat snow cones, *Ghostbusters*

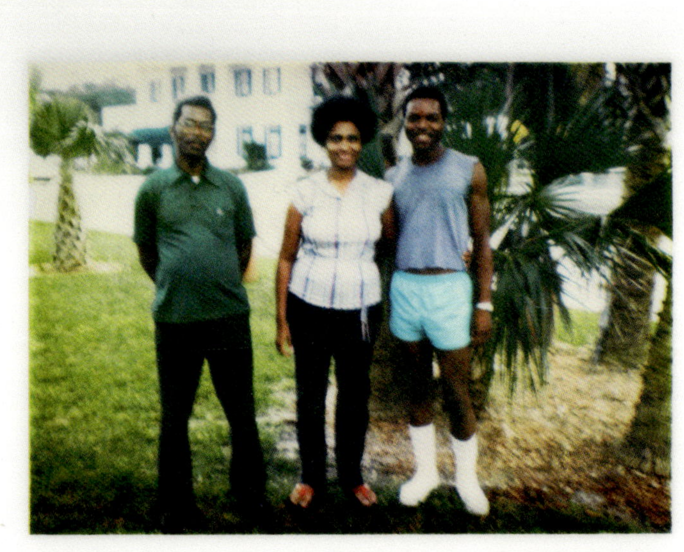

Dad (Andrew), Andrew Jr. & wife—Florida (maybe Jacksonville, maybe Daytona Beach). Image courtesy of Dawn Lundy Martin.

popsicles, Creamsicles, and Good Humor Chocolate Éclair
bars until we feel sick. I force him to memorize Robert
Frost's "The Road Not Taken" as penance. If it's the summer
of the ice-cream truck I'm making lots of easy ice-cream
money and living with my boyfriend, Mark—even though
I suspect I'm gay.

Andrew Martin is my father. Or was. Or is. Or was, in the
sense that he was married to my mother until he died at the
age of seventy-eight, and that he raised me. Long before
I was born, and long before he met my mother, Andrew was
married to another woman, Edna, who divorced him some
years after she gave birth to two boys—Andrew Jr. and
Gregory. None of us who remain can remember Andrew Jr's
wife's name. Note the physical distance between Andrew and
Andrew Jr. as they pose for the photograph. Note Andrew's
arms tucked behind his back (he always stood like that), and
his almost imperceptible smile. You might have had to know
him to notice that smile. There are very few photographs of
my father in our family albums. I have not seen Andrew Jr.
in over forty years. When I look at this photo, what I imagine
is Dad's arm draped over Andrew Jr.'s shoulder. Years later,
Andrew Jr. will walk out of the home he shares with his wife
and sons to buy cigarettes and he will not return. He will not
attend Dad's funeral. I do not remember his voice. In fact,
this photo is my only memory of Andrew Jr. even though
I was not there.

I pinch the photos on August 24, 2021, Mom's eighty-eighth
birthday. We have just returned from a laboured trip during
which she received her first pedicure in almost two years.
She is hobbled by old age and arthritic pain, a bodily return
to a generational story she has told many times about her
Aunt Kizzy, whose entire body was so plagued by arthritis
she could not be touched. The photograph—the instant
photograph of Black life—might be like the bodies of my
mother and Aunt Kizzy—a refusal of the haptic ("you can't
touch this"), and in that refusal, an alternate possibility for
(un)knowing, or something we might call flight.

After wind was water
After we were water
When water subsumed
When the thing that was was water
When our arms were water, our
gesture's flower
Our gestures bloom
When it was
When we were
When water was not
When we subsumed water
When we shivered into flame

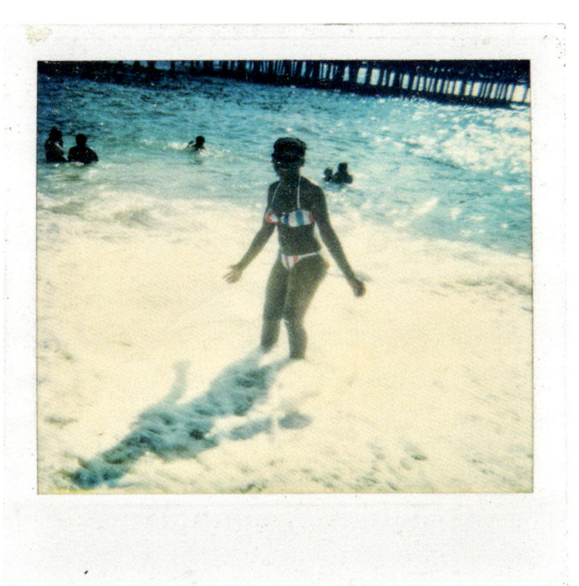

Fade of the Black Family Photograph

STEFANO HARNEY & FRED MOTEN

In our societies—the societies of real subsumption—art is a malignant fetish.

Art is supposed to function as a totem that helps us make sense of our immensely complex and far-ranging social situations. Art is meant to work as a ceremony to conjure a vision of how we live together.

But this fetish of art is constantly doubled by another: the fetish of the commodity. Just when someone finally feels the presence of one, then comes the chill of the other.

One could liken it to the syncretic Catholic saints. One kneels to pray in front of this saint, only to end up worshipping an African god. Yet this analogy does not work because only a visiting Pope is trapped by this syncretism. The worshippers are released.

It is more like praying to a syncretic blue-eyed devil. You kneel to pray for humanity, only to end up worshipping white supremacy.

Since the fetish of art is doubled by the fetish of the commodity, one is always seeing double or hearing something else. Things look a little blurry until we can feel that the fetish of the commodity has also brought its twin; but its twin is flesh, not art.

Thus, the fetish of art is continually destabilized by its
malignancy, even as the fetish of the commodity suffers its
own fleshly metastasis. We're held in constant shudder.

This is perhaps nowhere truer than in the art of photography.

This intense destabilization is not a result of the demotics
of the art form, nor is it directly caused by the simulacrum
adhering to photography, nor even the uncanny that hangs
around it.

The destabilization comes from the fact that with
photography, the frame comes first.

Everyone who takes a photograph knows this intuitively.
And everyone who views a photograph cannot help but think
someone or something has been caught in this frame.

Paintings or sculptures seem to emerge from the centre,
moving outward toward what will be their frames. This
occurs even more so with video and performance, where
duration seems to create the frame.

But with photography, the framing appears to us as an act of
separation, an act of focus, and an act of isolation.

Could this ever be any truer than with the Polaroid? We hold the frame first, and wait for what is held in it, what has been captured.

Could we not then say that all photography is portraiture?

In other words, does the priority of the frame not naturalize for us a separate unit that is as it should be? Does the frame's primacy not individualize what it sees? Does everyone not become "a sitter" through the prior imposition of the frame?

This tendency of all photography toward portraiture is also of course the tendency of all photography toward the universe of subject and object.

And therefore, from portraiture it is a short step to the subject reaction.

Who is this sitter, we ask, caught in the frame? We have the simultaneous sense that this sitter belongs in the frame as the proper unit of viewing, while, as a subject, this sitter should not be framed.

This subject reaction—this effort at restoration, repair, or reconciliation—is intensified the more the portrait appears framed, captured, or portrayed (the latter a word that did not come into use until the nineteenth century, centuries after the word "portraiture").

Thus, this unit of photography as portrait appears to us as the same unit, the unit of the subject—however constrained, that is the unit of rights. Of all the art forms, photography is the one most susceptible to a discourse of rights, for good reason. The right it most invokes is the right to ownership.

Is there any wonder that throwing away family photographs seems like a violation to us? It is as if the subjects held there are then abandoned as well, the result of a general disposability that we know as "being-owned." If the subject reacts to being-owned by claiming ownership, there can't be any wonder. The claim itself becomes our own when we can't own in being-owned. That claim is given, and portrayed, in the family photo, which seems to hold the fate by which it is held: that it is and that it will be taken.

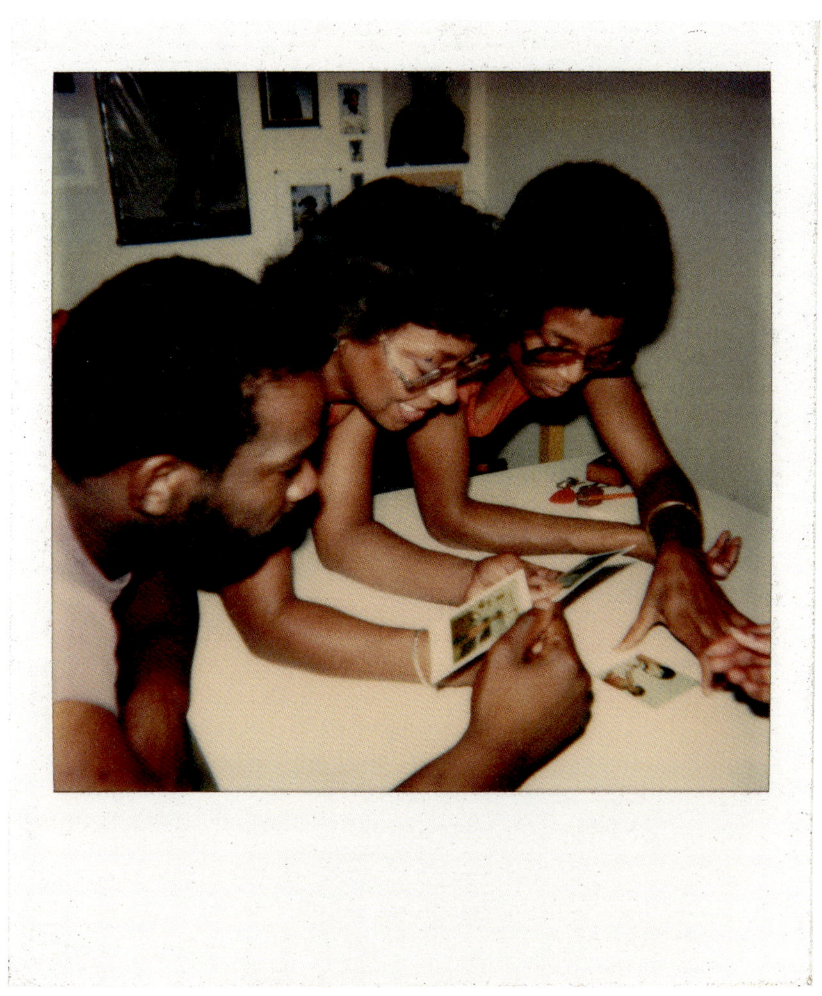

All photography is portraiture, perhaps especially when the figure of the sitter does not seem to be there, because that is when the photograph must be repatriated by its viewer. It must be resituated again in interpersonal relations. Every object has its subject, somewhere, just as everything that can be owned has its owner, somewhere. Love comes to everyone.

As we stand in front of the photograph, we restore in our subject reaction not our subject, nor the sitter, nor the lost object's home. We restore the syncretism, the malignant fetish. We are now framed and emerge within our frame with all naturalness.

But what if we did not resist the priority of the frame in photography? What if we did not react to its framing, either by trying to restore what is inside it, or by longing for what is outside of it? What if the frame could become a means that did not compel us to complete its ends? Perhaps this would allow for an expansion of means in the photograph, and for photography to be a practice of means that resists the ends of gaze and image.

It's a hard gift by which we are given to think of the black family photograph. As with all gifts, what is given—and the giving itself—are more than anyone's to give and more than one. In sharing, something like nothing is shared, some shard of the violence of give and take. That's the chemistry of the black family photograph. The Polaroid develops in sight as it fades to touch. Existence insists upon this blur of wound and blessing. In the interface, we fall in love with how a general, generative, anti-familial, anti-private economy emerges in recess, at and as the material expense of spirit. It's the aspiration of our dying breath, the substance of being unseen in always being seen, which, secretly, selflessly, we see with ourselves, not seeing ourselves but seeing something more in seeing with, as if seeing with were all, as if all were just that practice, just how we do on Sunday evenings, evidently.

Look at mama'n'em. Look at mama's play mama, who carried you around when you were a baby, as if you were her baby, because you were. Now you carry her in how you carry yourself. You favour her, as an effect of carrying. Are you carried away? Can you almost see? When you hold her in your hand, you're all we have. All that gets passed from hand to hand at the serial kitchen table. All we really have are all these variations on how could I let you get away, in open trio, in profile, in abandon through abandonment—our own only in unowning, all unaware of being seen in a future of being shown, one hand withdrawn, another hand awaiting.

Here's a photograph of what looks like a family sitting at a table looking at what looks like a bunch of family photographs. The family is well-photographed, as the wall attests. This chain of viewing (looking, looking like, seeing with, seeming, unseaming) is a chain of handing. There's violence in being held on the verge of being hidden. Being treasured is all but being lost. Nothing found in being sought. Common breath is gone and we can't reconstruct it. And anyway, what's this presumption of family, and its rights and its brokenness, all of which are confirmed in the snapshot's uncanny, untimely career? Can there be such a thing as a black family photograph? Should there be? What happens when certain privileges that might accrue through familiarity are exploited, circulated, and claimed by strangers? We can't know what losses recur in that review, or in this one. At the same time, we know what happens, and what has happened, and what will happen, when family and its rights are left in shards. At the same time, what happens when what happened to the family, and what accrues in the denial of what happened, is shared? Whatever happens, whatever's happened, these photographs are stolen. If I told you I love you, pretty baby, would it make up for what they say? If I hold you and shield you, darling, will you linger awhile today? Borne and born in a continuing mission to steal away, the photograph is commissioned against, but also under, the terms of a contract of civil butchery. Held out, held back, shard, shielded—the chemistry of stolen moments is our true and terrible and beautiful black share.

See, somehow, the photograph got away from whoever took it, and from whoever held it, and from whomever they held it for in the hope that the stolen moment wouldn't fade. Surely, whoever's in the photograph held it that very night, uncaptured. Now, it's gone in our beholding because someone who held them in regard had to let it go. And shit never just happens like that. Something happened.

If it seems like something happened, it's because something always does and has. Something always happens because something happened. The interminable flash and unending moment of being stolen, and here we are, gone.

The photograph that is given and/or thrown away, handed down and out onto the street, unpreserved and unprotected in the family's varied and sustained nuclear winter, and relegated to nurture's absence is also dispersed and sown against the deadly logic of the heirloom. It is the inheritance of the inheritable and all their kin that they can only all but inherit. If they bear every element of severe tragedy and bright enjoyment—which being held, however carefully, by the museum can only surreptitiously intensify—they do so as unnatural objects whose unfree radicality bears generative and degenerative chance. Insofar as we have to accept that, we have to act like we choose to accept that. This is the substance of the photograph, which has been taken. This is the family photograph of the taken, the held, the handed. It's all we have to hand, and here it is, and here we are, gone.

Maybe there's an experimental play of the museum by those whom the museum will have put on display, which disperses the museum as a mechanism for disbursement. Is *Fade Resistance* an exhibition or a depth charge, neither given nor ungiven as impossible inhibition but, rather, foregiven in and as a demonstration of explosive modesty? Zun Lee can no longer carry (the mass, black, infractive universe, carried and radiated by) those photographs alone. The photographs can't be carried like that and we have to want to want to say they don't want that, anyway. They don't want to be kept. They don't want to be collected. It's just that our experiment is held under the duress of the general experiment in which we're held. Its condition is genocide, and having no choice, because we have no choice, we practice acting as if we've chosen to relinquish choice in favour of common renewal of the preferential option for collective, uncollectible care, which is the curate's—and not the curator's—shar'd portfolio and shade. The curatorial anomaly, this contranymic contradiction, is exacerbated in militant preservation. The intrafacial fade of alchemical, incoordinate hand and eye (and nose and ear and tongue), and here we are, gone.

An offer of the murmur and murder of the black family photograph—its gathering soar and plunge and loss and more—is made by we who cannot help but care. In terrible medium and atmosphere and solution, and in that withdrawal in offering that they condition, can we produce and discover an immediate and absolute ignition? There might be another star, and in sharing breath and touch in sight, the broken family shares something else. The refusal to be owned of those who are refused the right to own, which is borne as irreducibly social existence, insists unto the end of the family, the human, the image, and the gaze, all of which are brutalized and brutalize in owning and being-owned; the refusal insists unto the advent of animated, animative seeing-with, which is felt and passed, by all who recognize their kin, from breath to breath and hand to hand, until the photographs themselves withdraw in handing, fade into resistance.

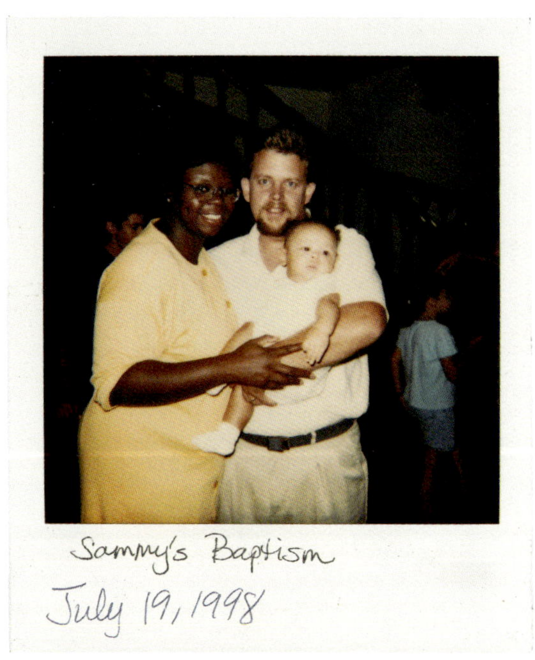

Sammy's Baptism
July 19, 1998

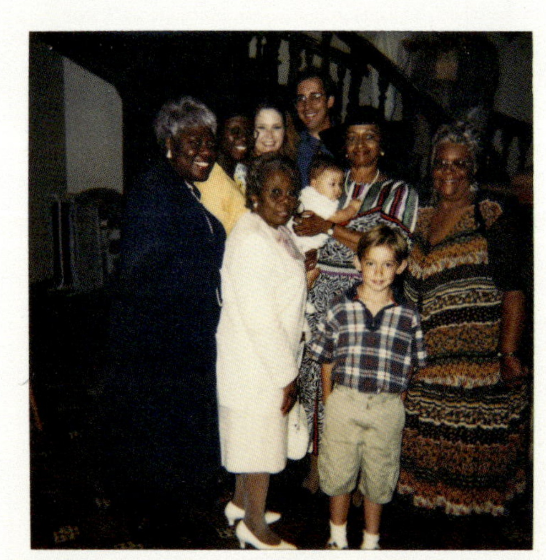

GiGi Rose, Gran Barbara, Mommy,
Aunt Nora, Uncle Matt, Aunt Jackie,
Aunt Juanita, Logan & Sammy

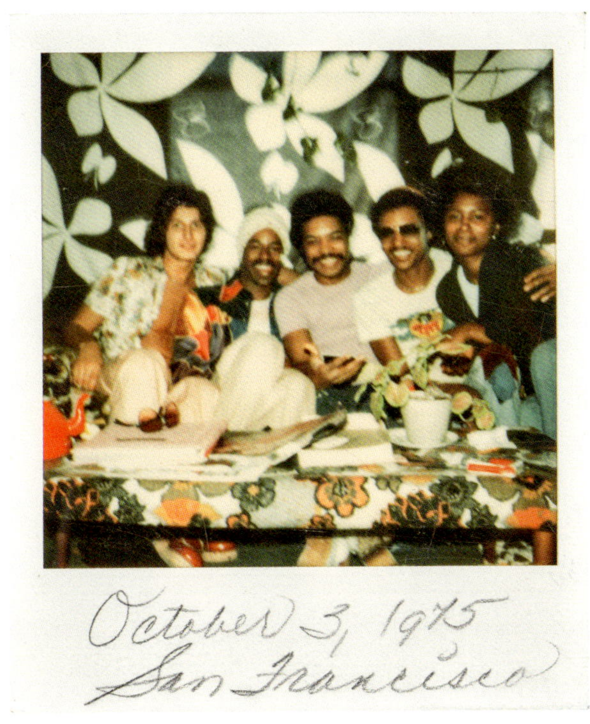

October 3, 1975
San Francisco

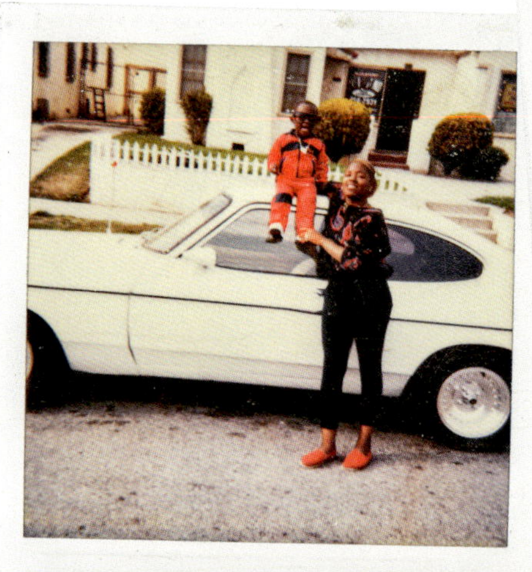
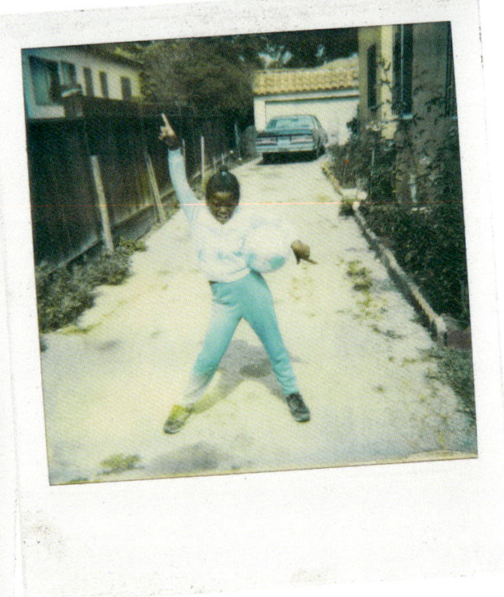
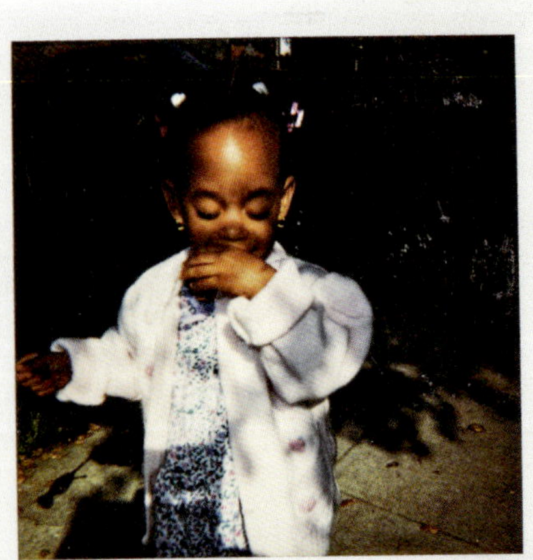
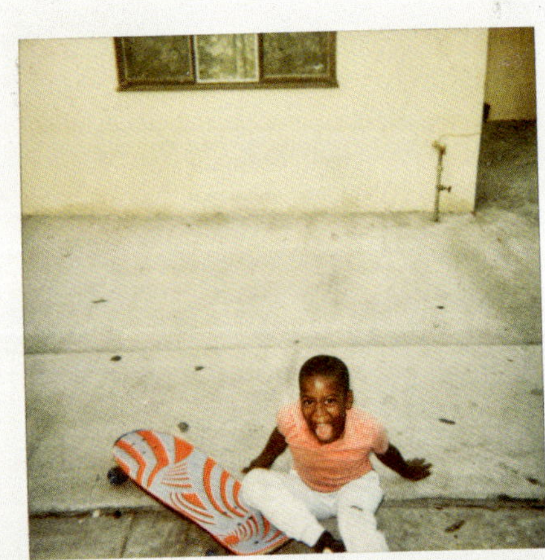
age
6
6/19/88

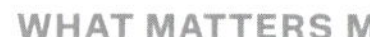

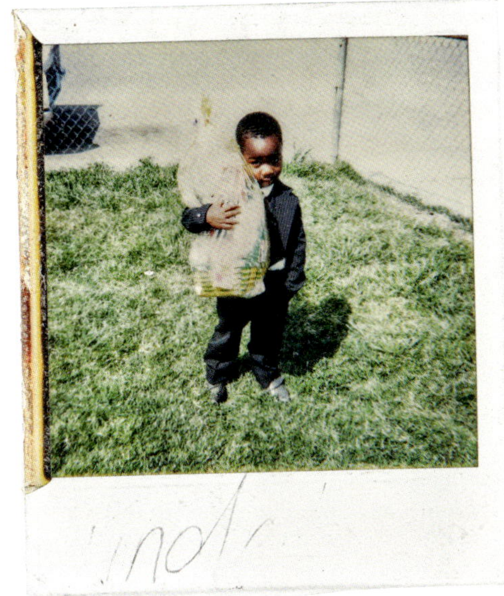

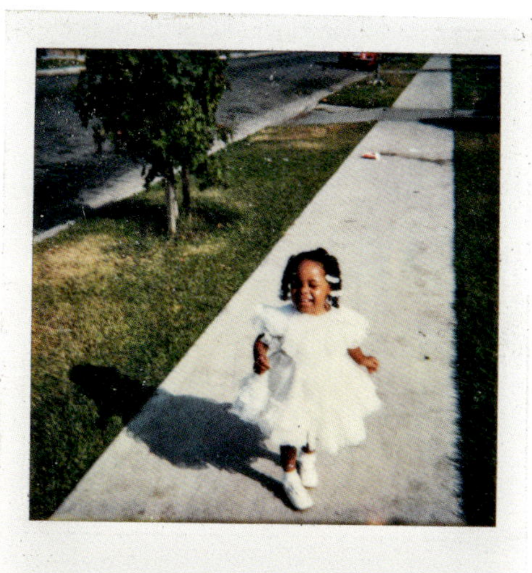

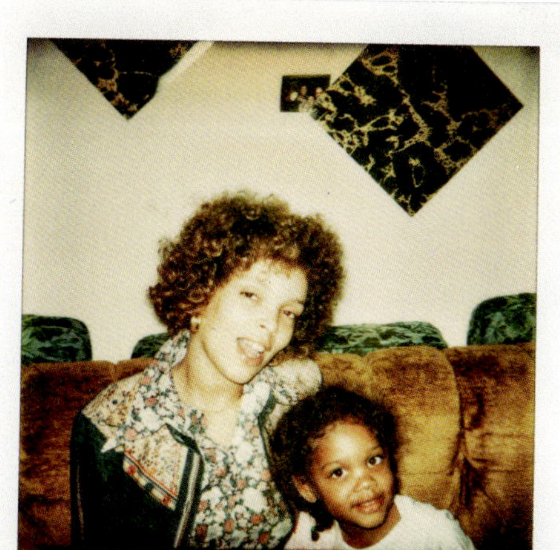

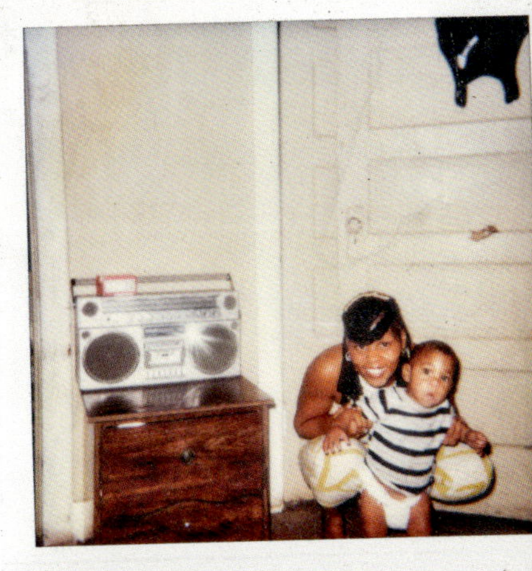
NEICY, DONTE

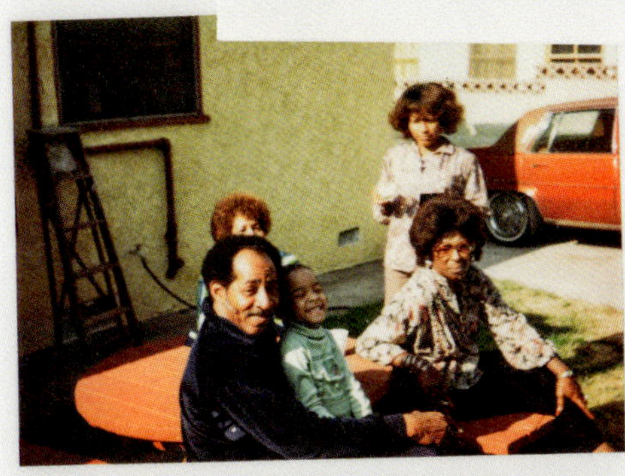

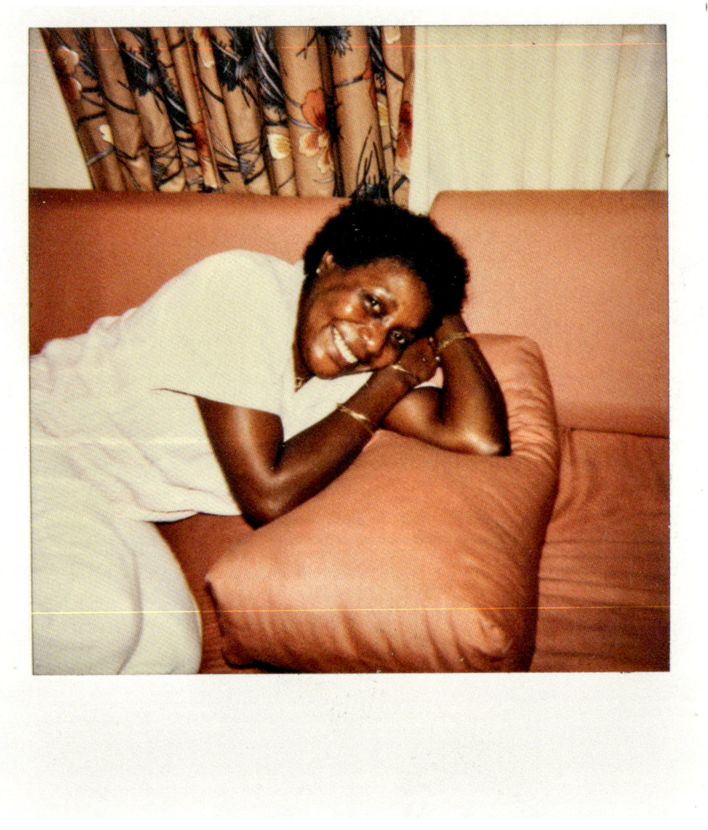

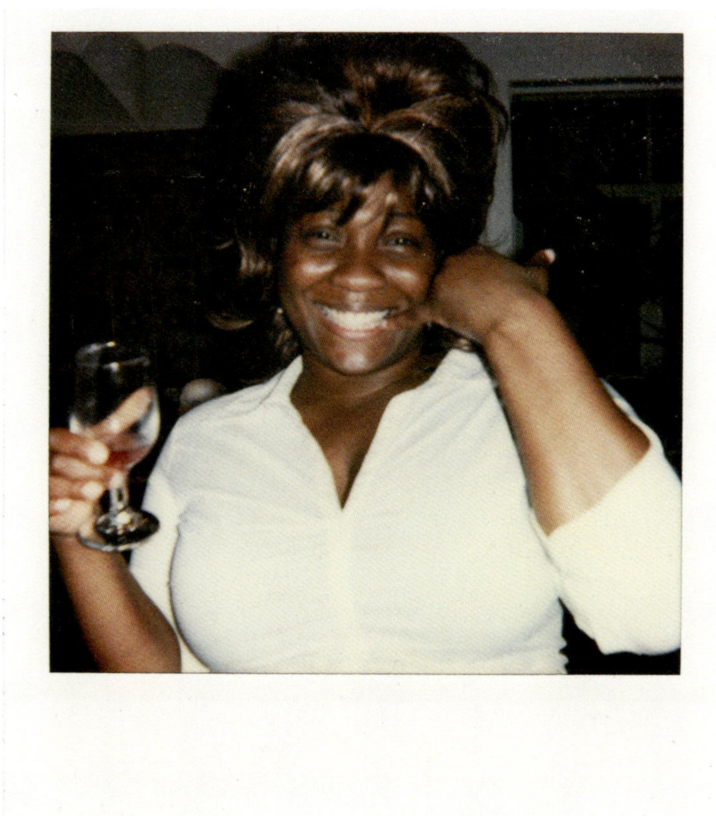

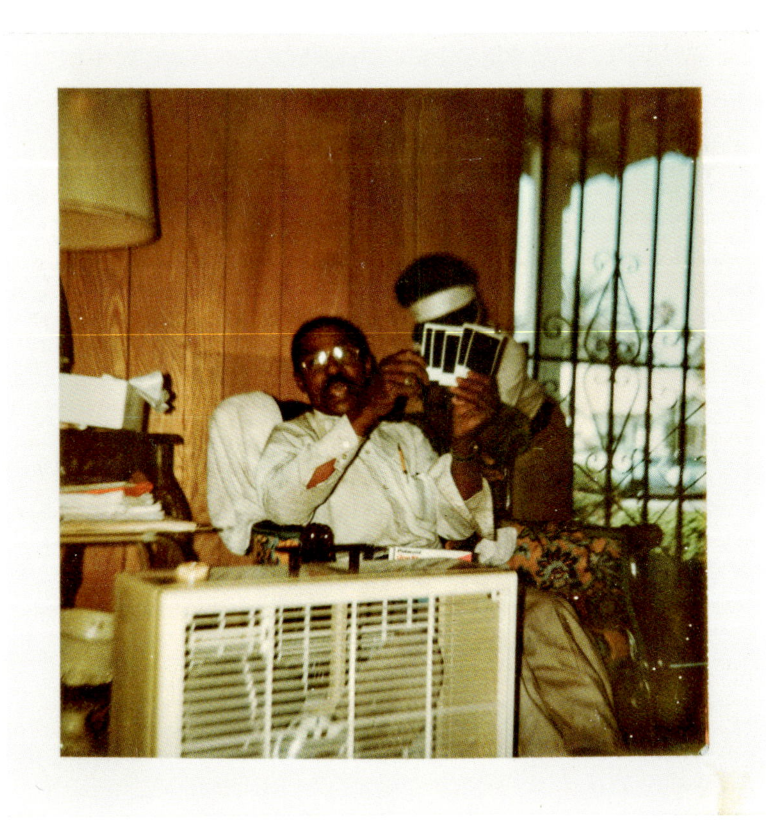

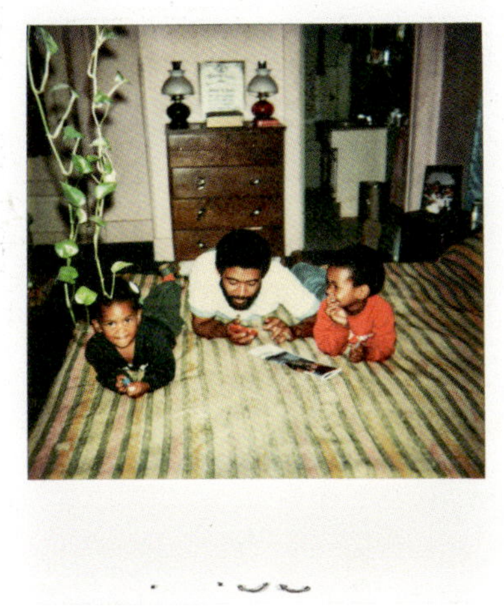

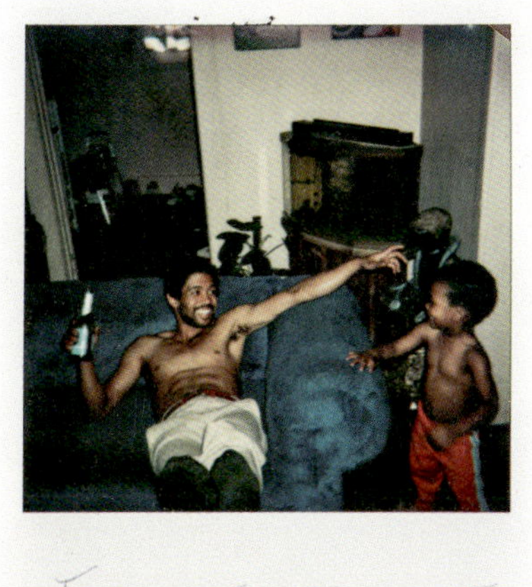

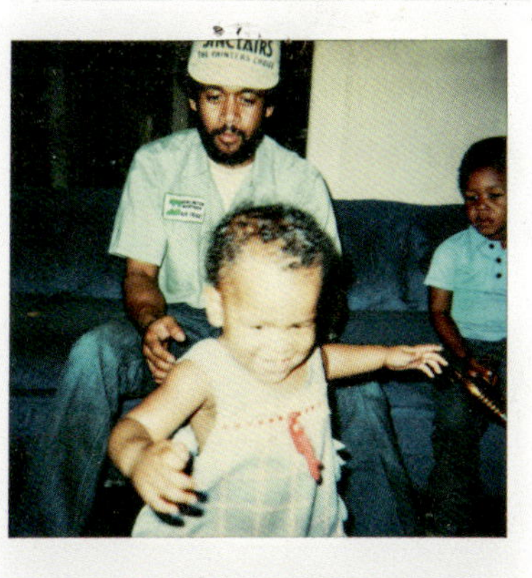

10-11-78

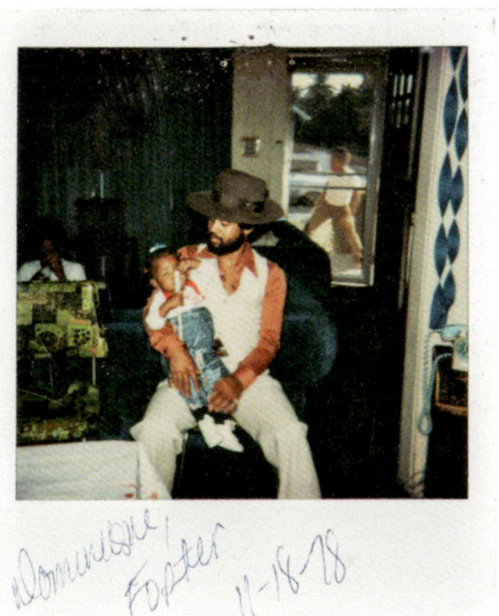

Dominique
Foster 11-18-78

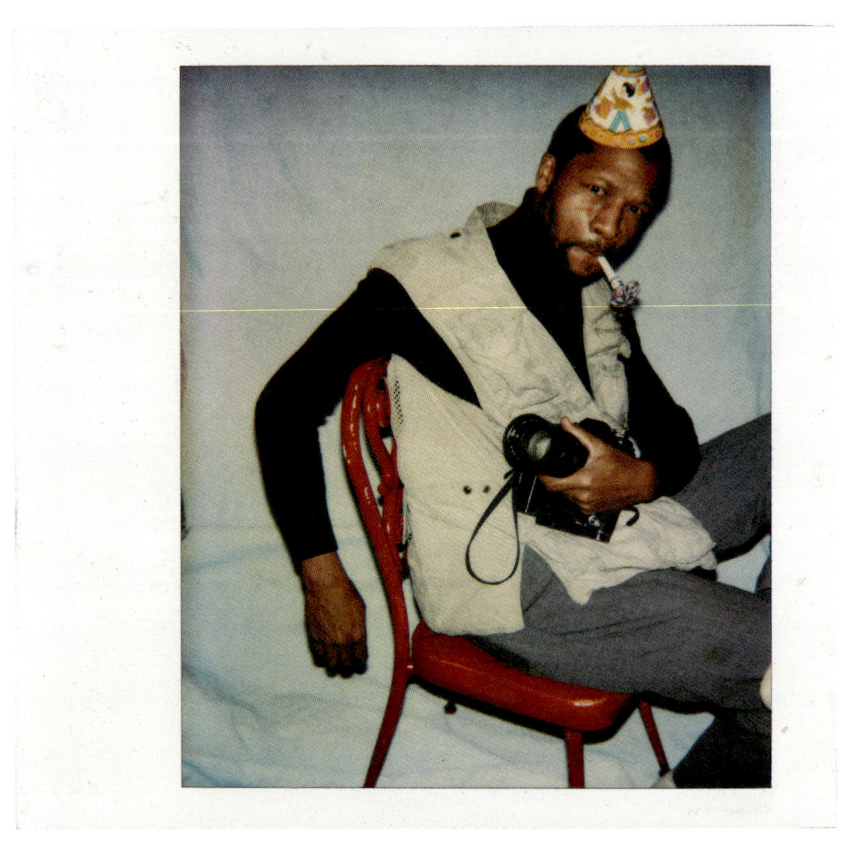

No one weeps, a day's decolletage plunges us into what desire leaves in the wake of a radiant abyss, Black light—oxymoron of our being— voluminous shape, any shade of Blackness, body body. A rose pressed between teeth. This wild intercourse: stillness. I dive into the white frame, my hair alive with a young newness of becoming JD Lighting Jay Birthday Cake Candles 1982. Where are we now? How could we know anything else but this textured comforter, fingers trace its web-white cracks, its shadow stains from the wear of existence.

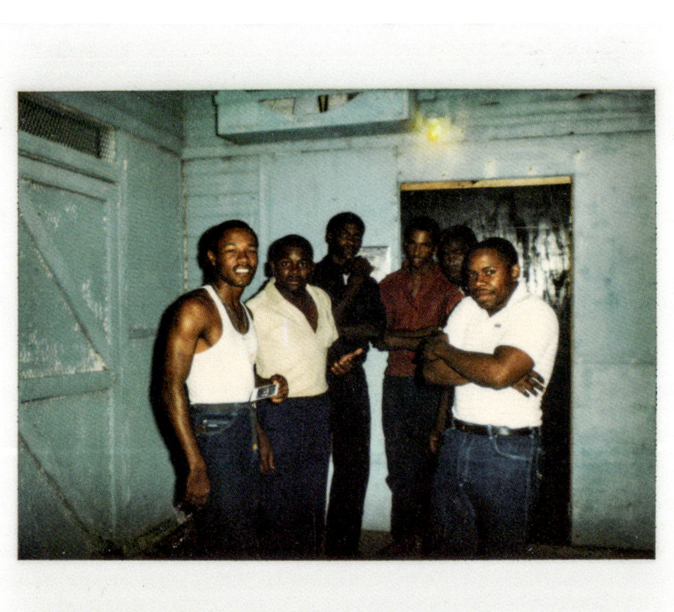

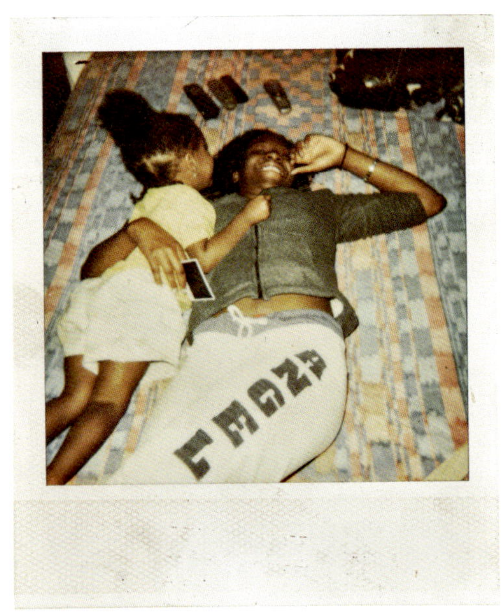

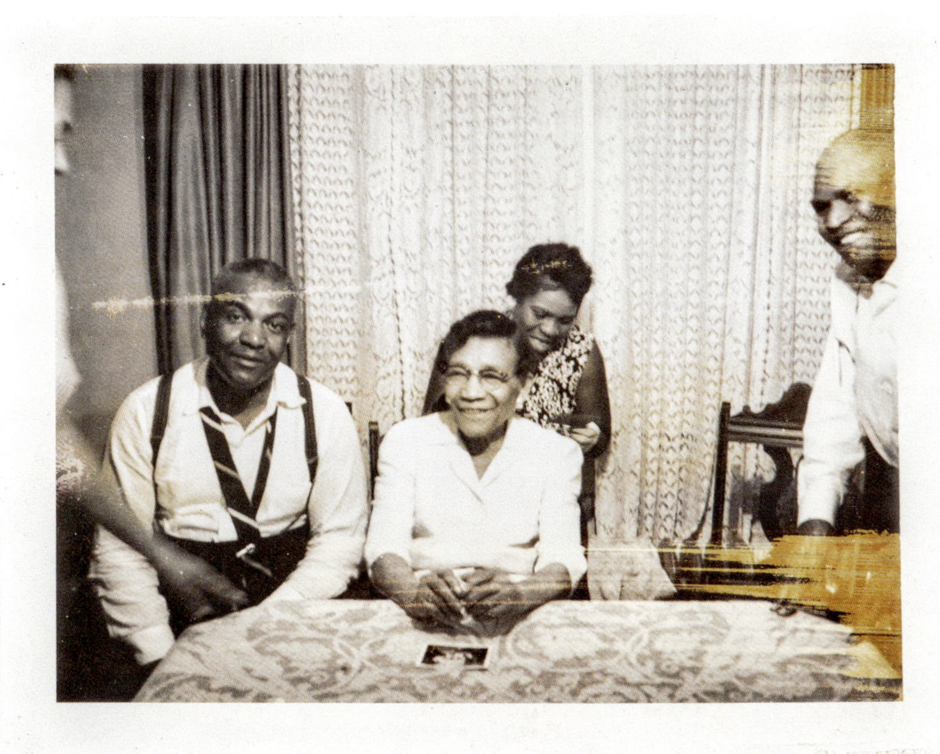

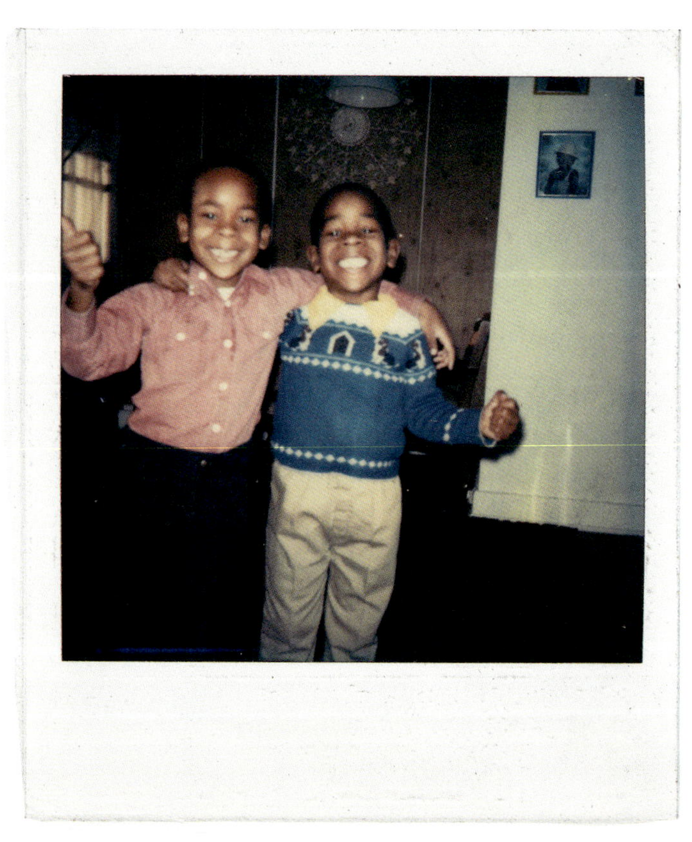

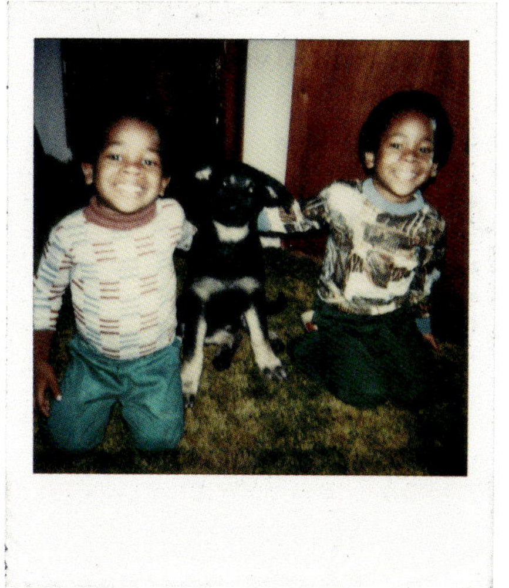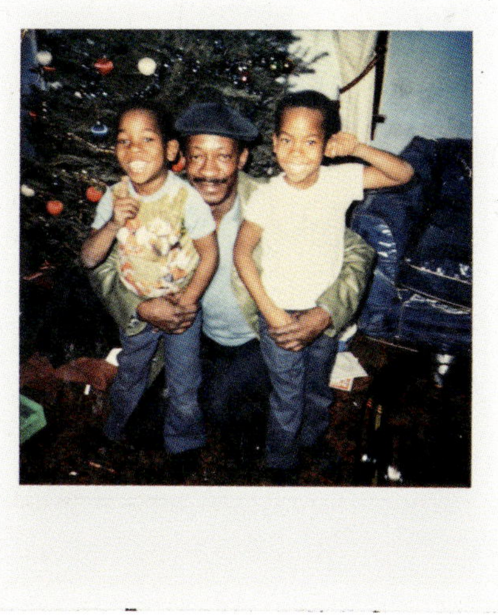

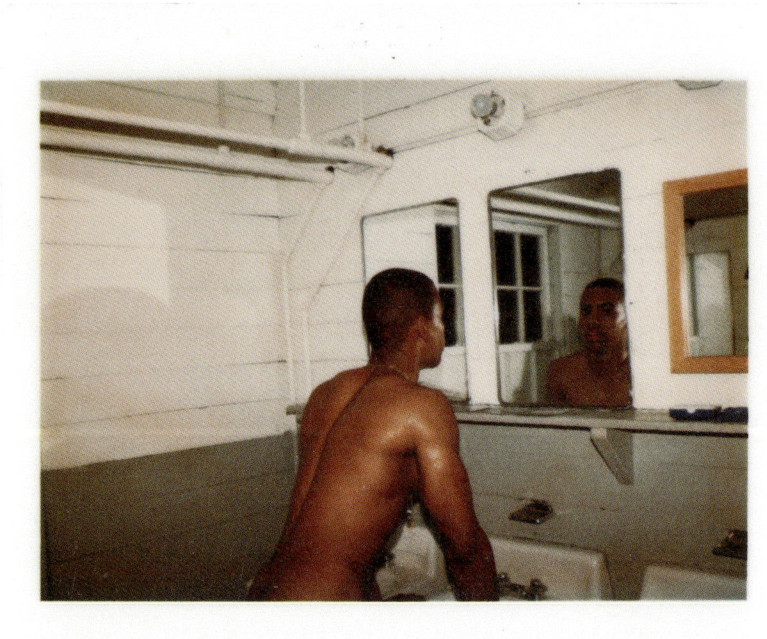

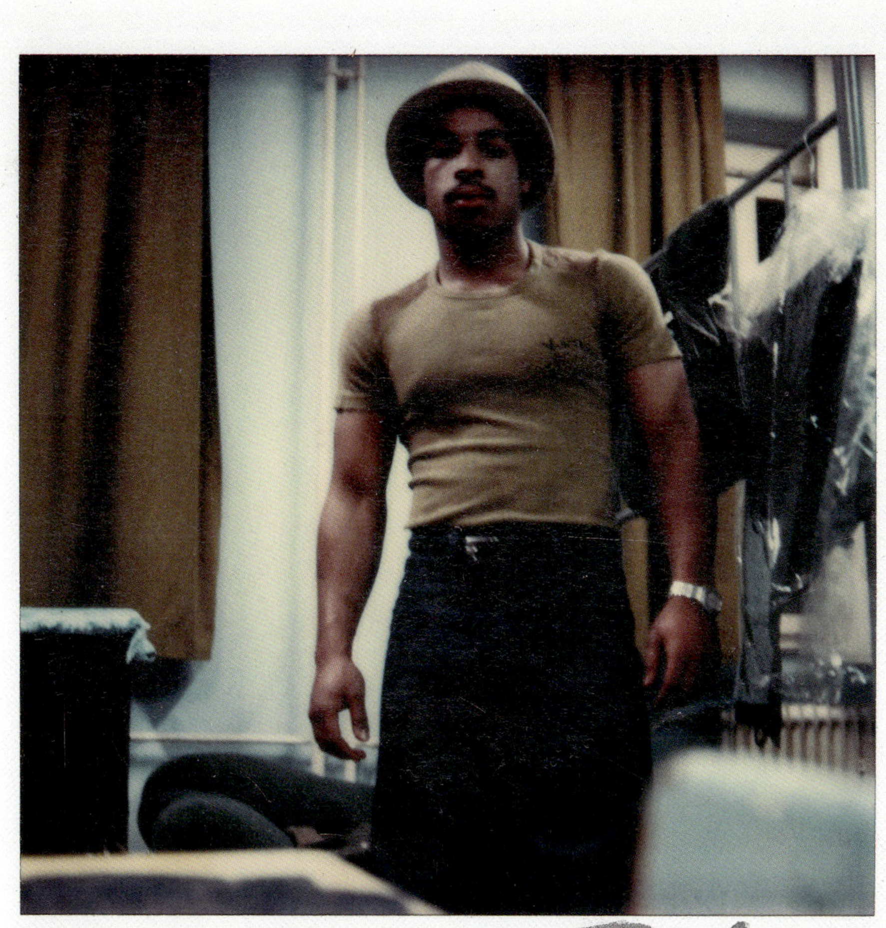

12-16-77, To Dad.
Love. Butch

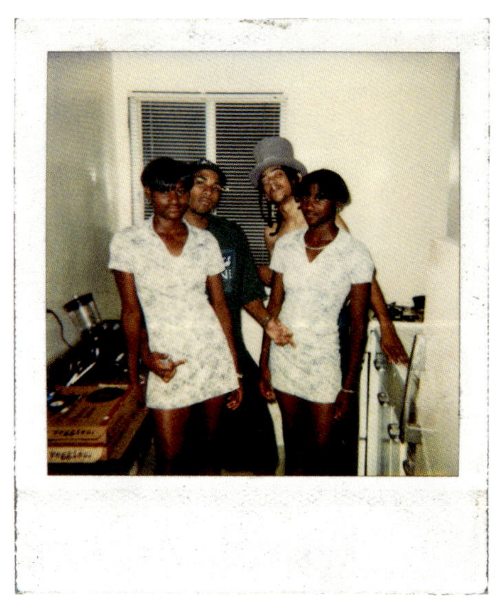

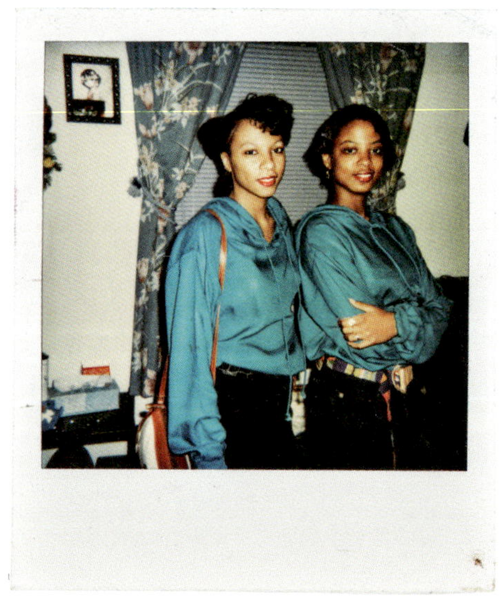

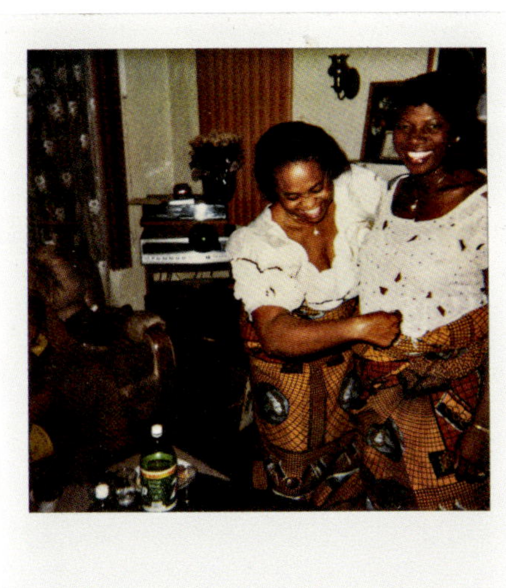

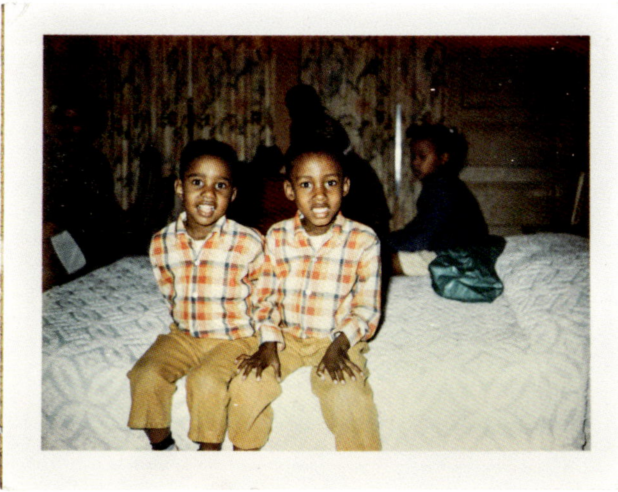

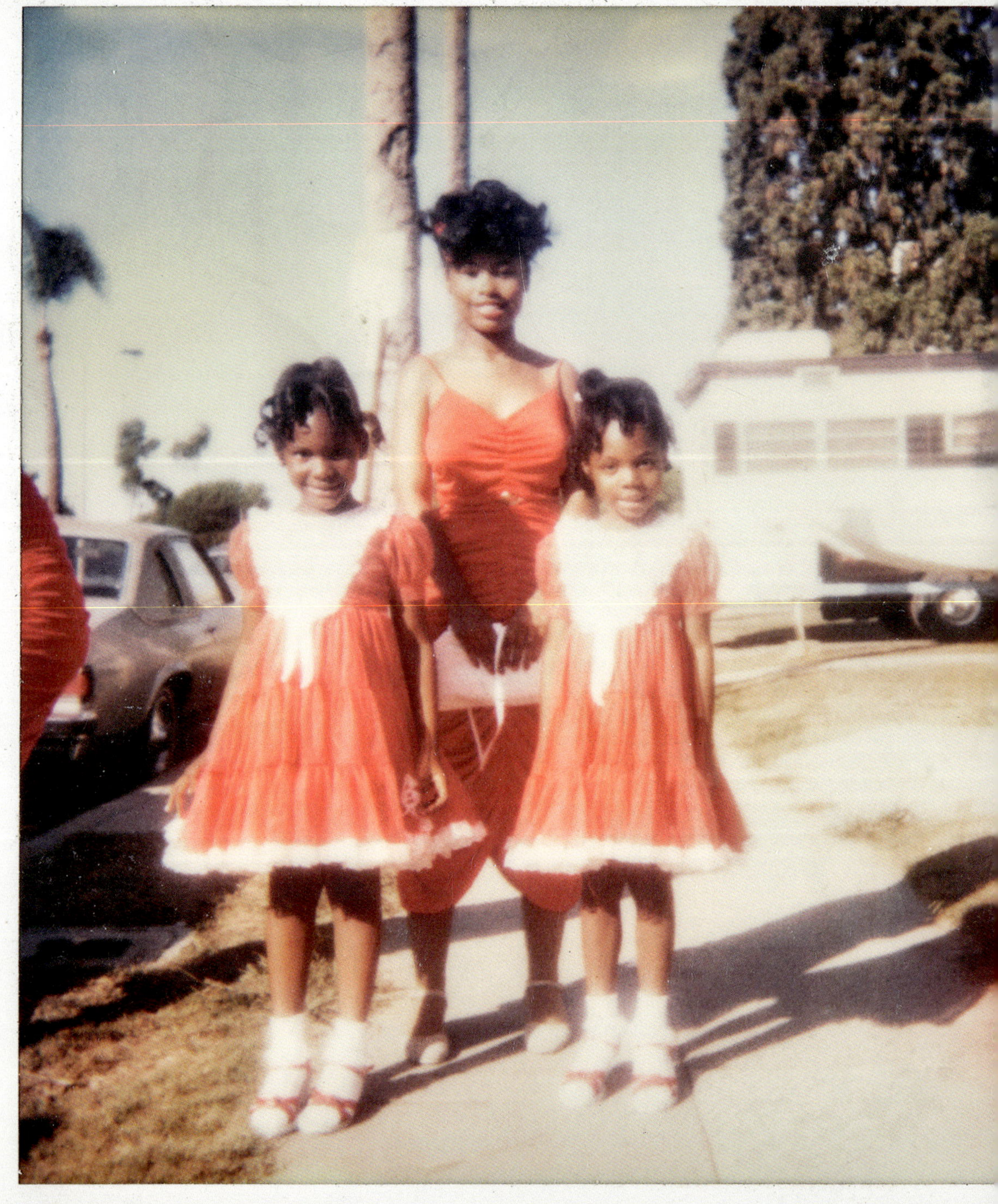

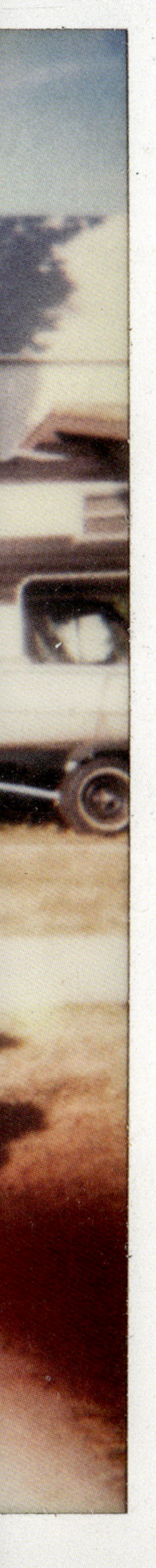

Photographs of Black Life

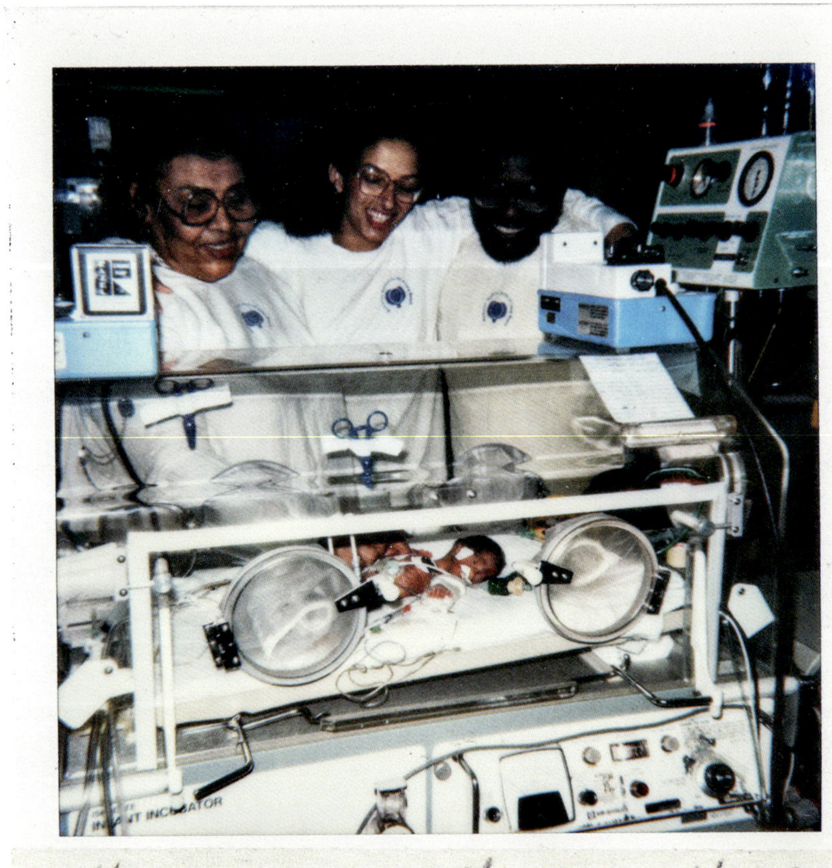

Geoffrey — Grandma Hall
Mother &
5-13-84   Dr. BASU

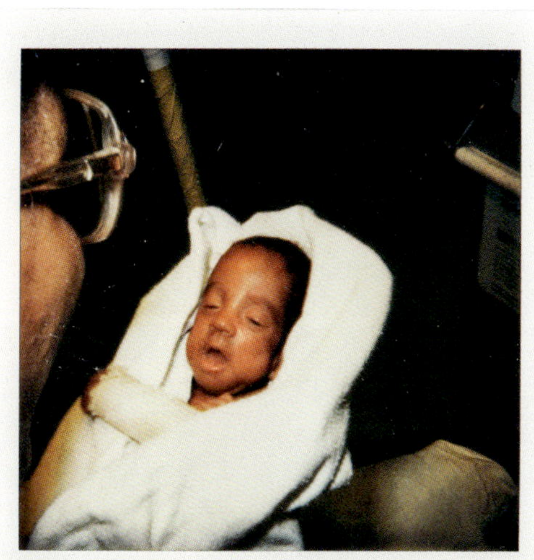

GEOFREY   7-8-84
62 days old (62)
1180 gms = 2 lbs 9½ oz.

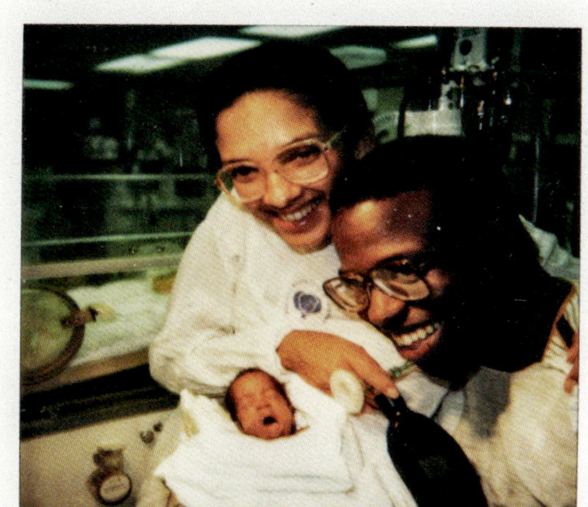

ASHLEY, mom & DAD
7-9-84   9 weeks old

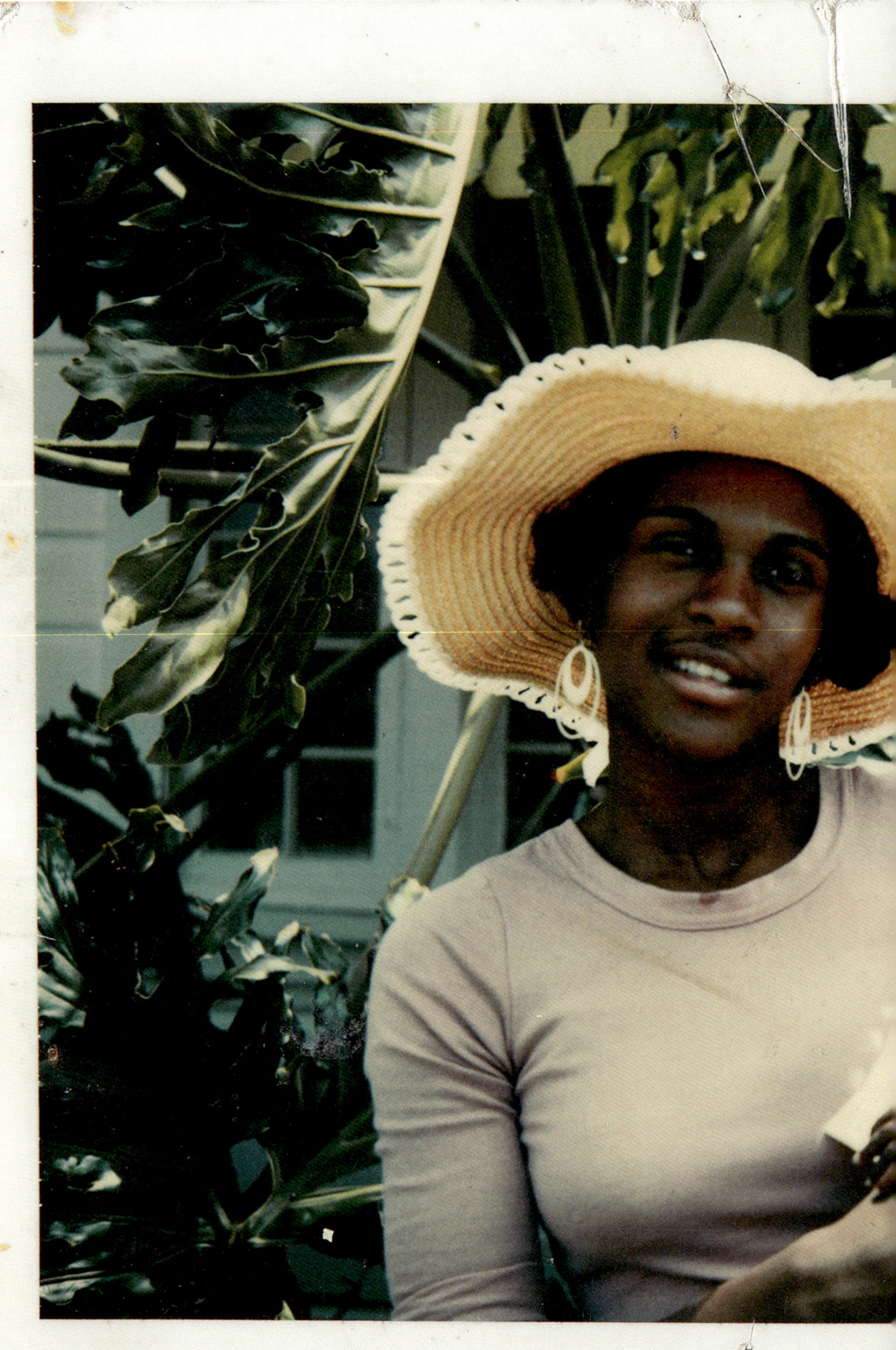

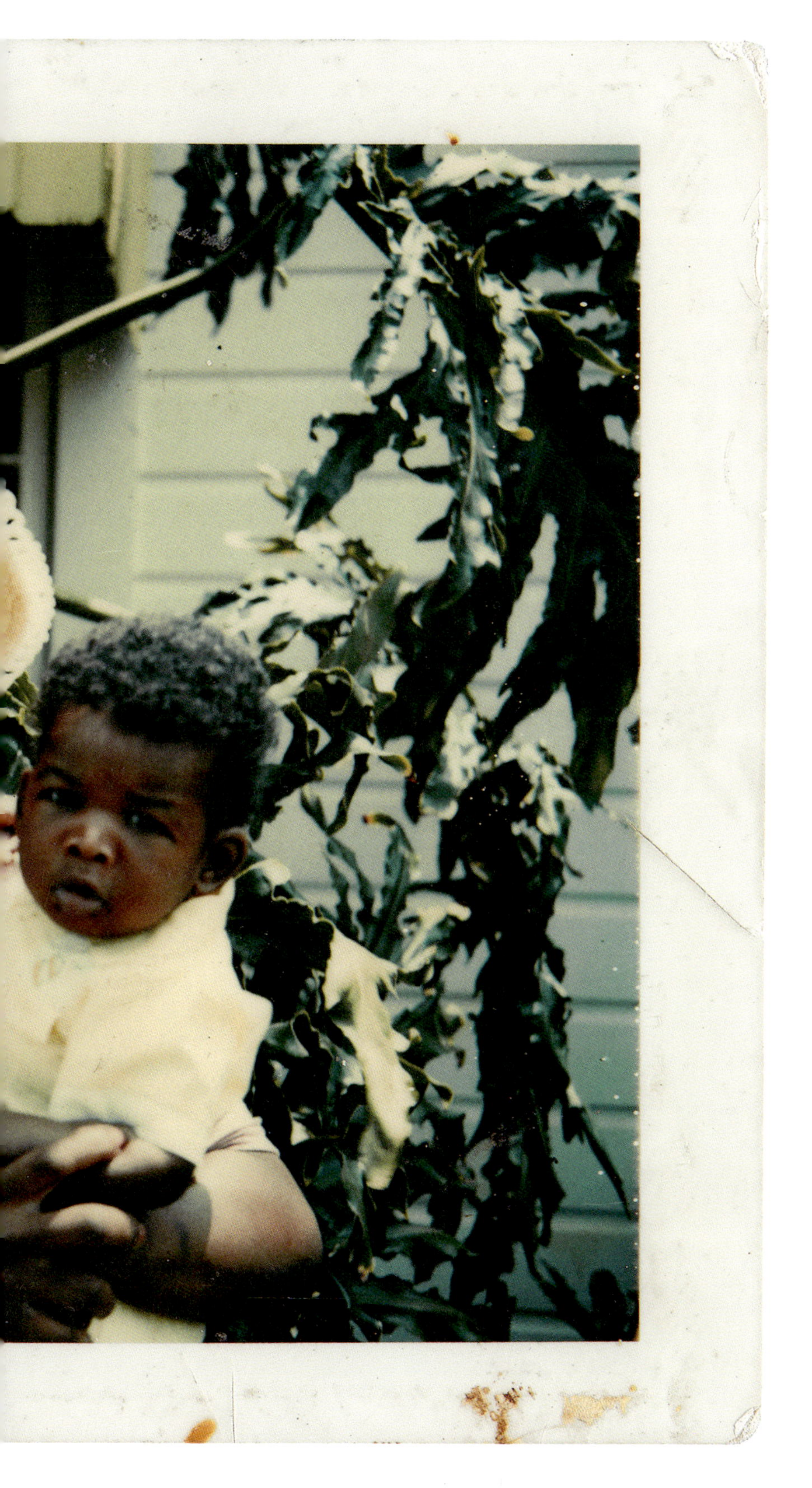

Now, you enter submissively, bowing
to qualities of light velvet as skin,
interiors transport, of a strobe-light
world, the word an imagined form of
being, Black pose, stray keys come
about, smear of dissidence in Rolling
Stones and hand gestures, no nation
mask, glimpse gaze out, a counterpoint
to Christina Sharpe's anti-Black
weather. Frame what cannot be
captured, what cannot be contained in
the tattered corners, Scotch-tape
residue. What vestiges of waters remain
untraceable when it's not you and nem,
but me and nem. Could be roil. As in,
we got a dog. How you exit the stage.

Otha and Pam   Herman Desiree
R-28-75   Dec 28, 95

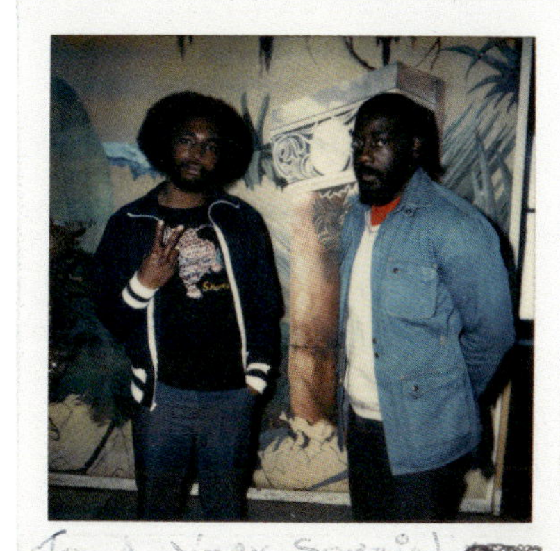
To a very special
woman — From The
Prince — Bright Days Ahead

Evan (Gloria's son) Xmas '84
12-21-84

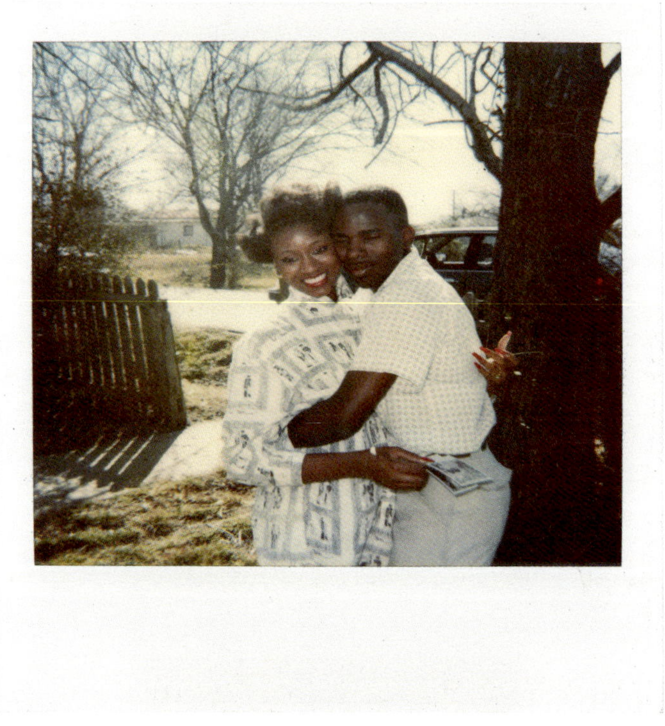

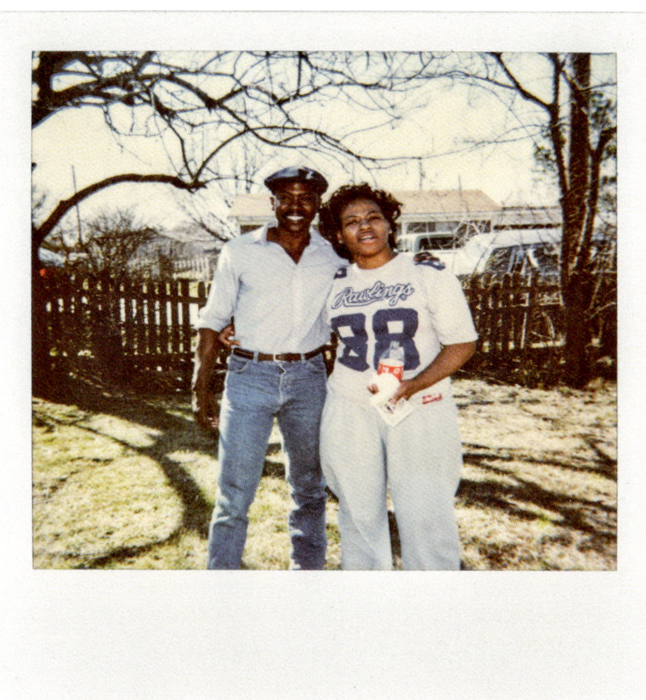

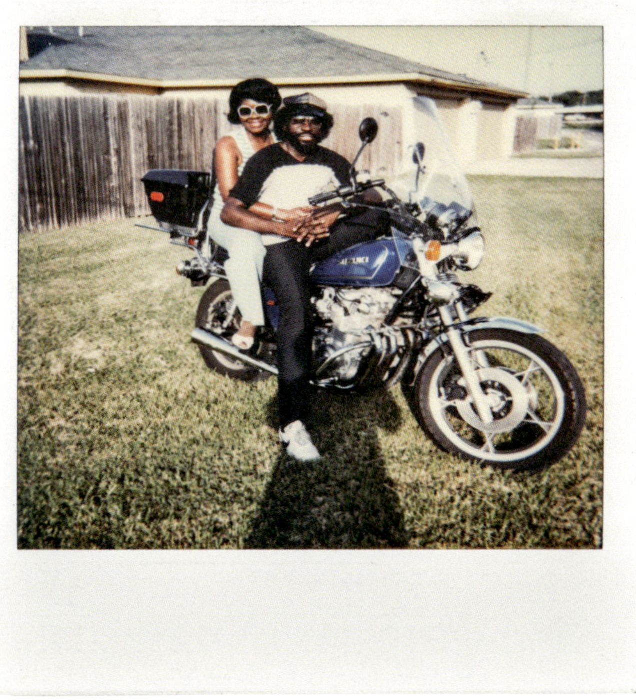

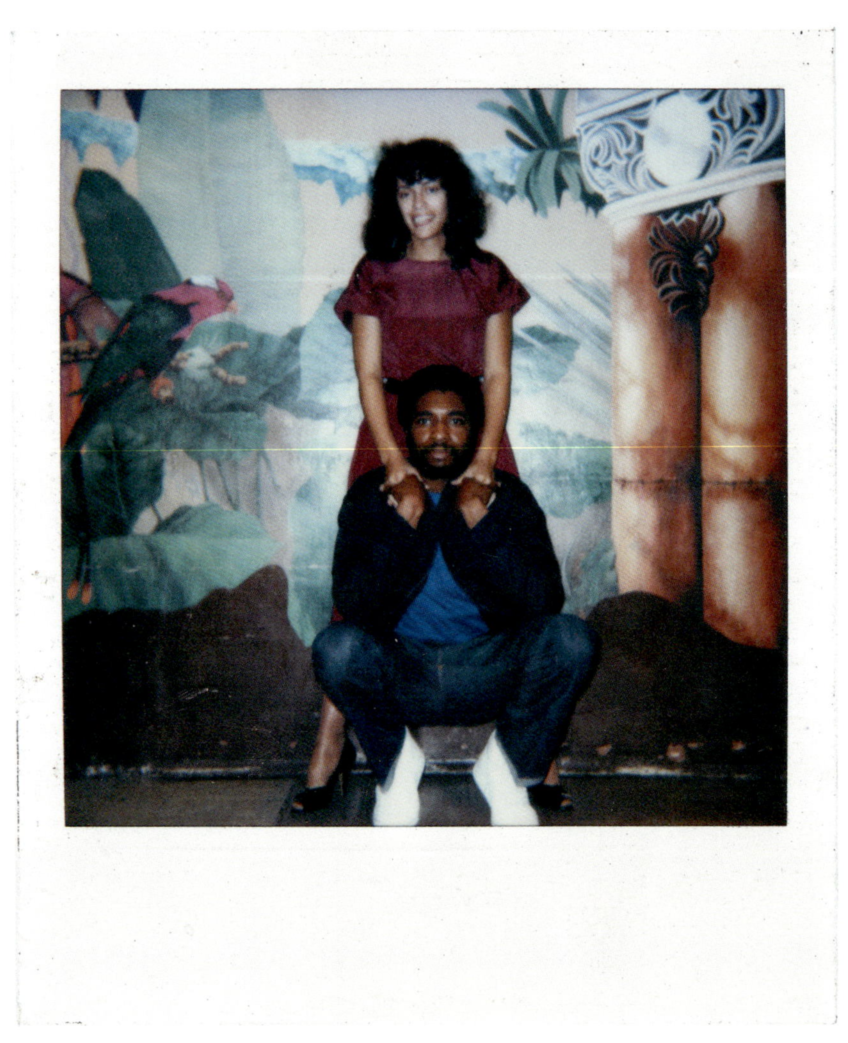

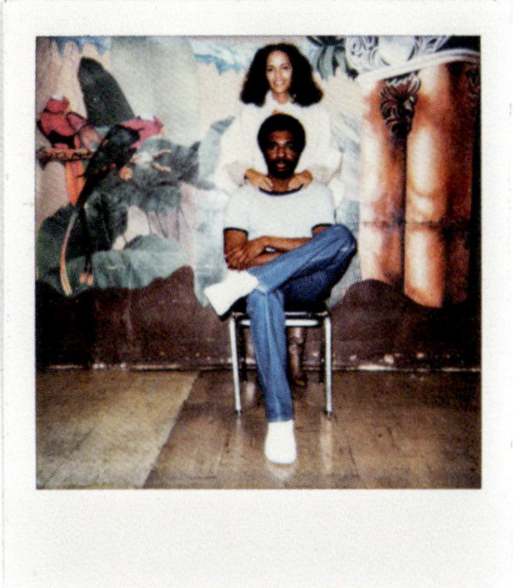
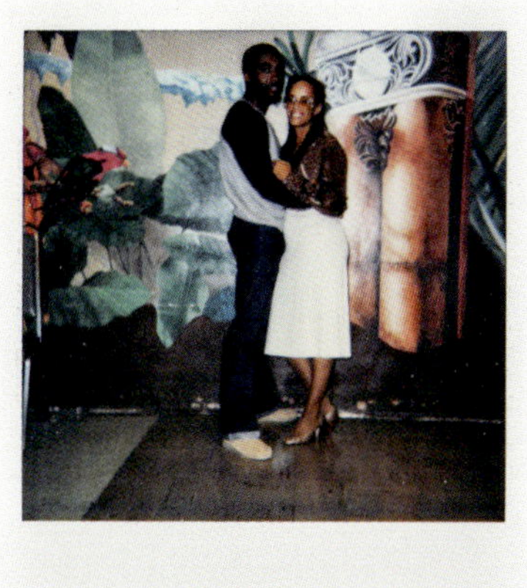
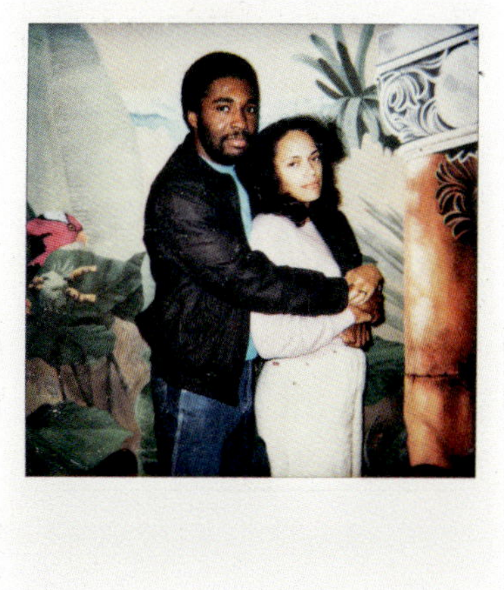
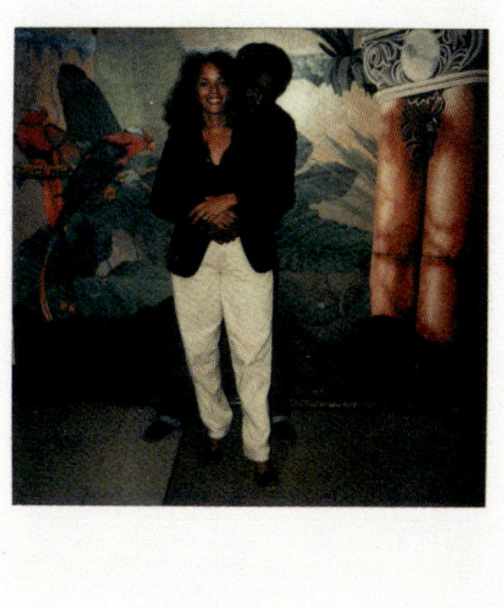

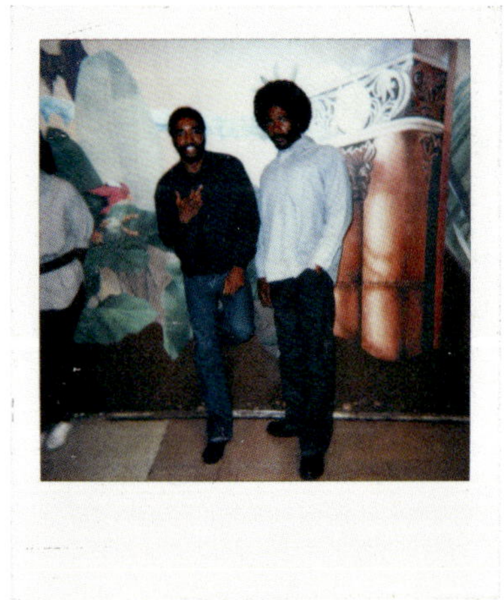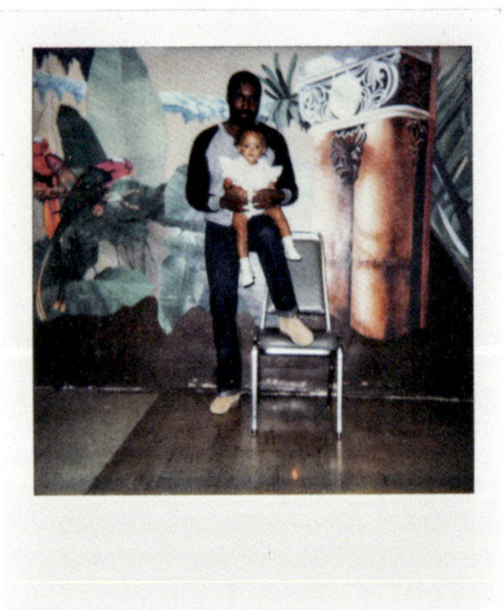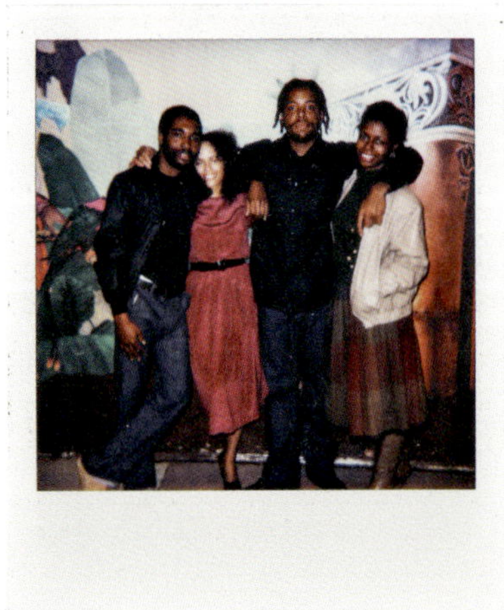

05220124314   POLAROID 1
SAN QUENTIN PRISON
24 December 1982
2018/2282

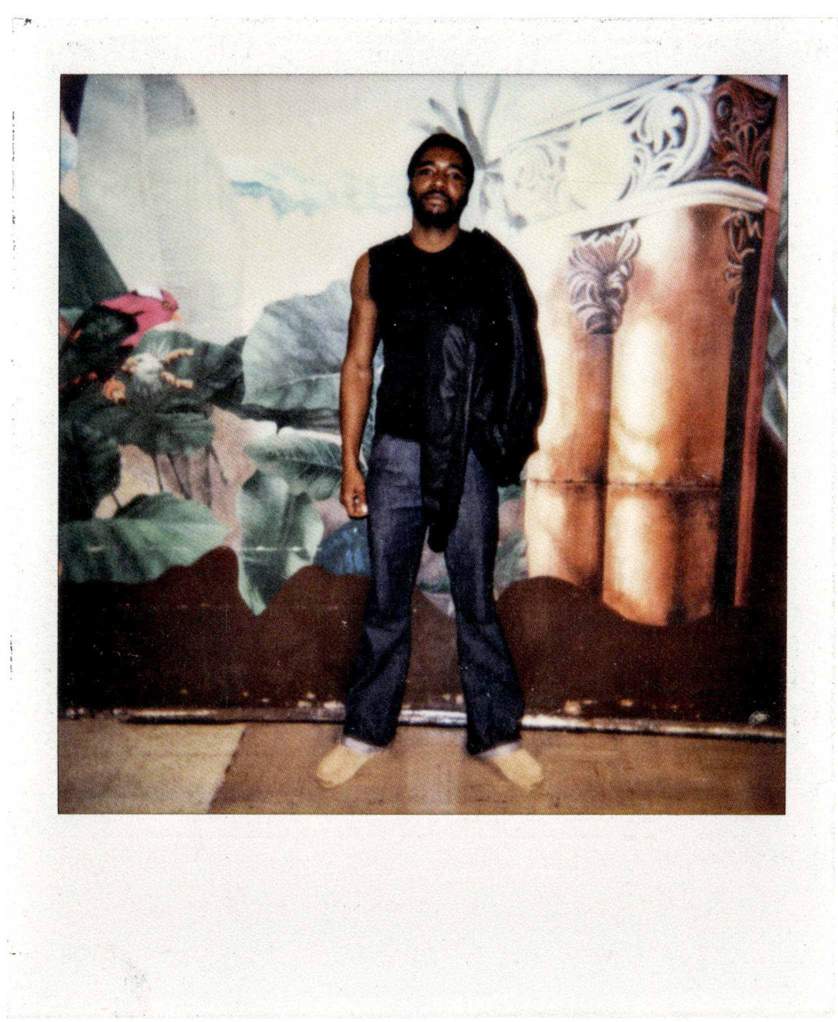

Photographs of Black Life

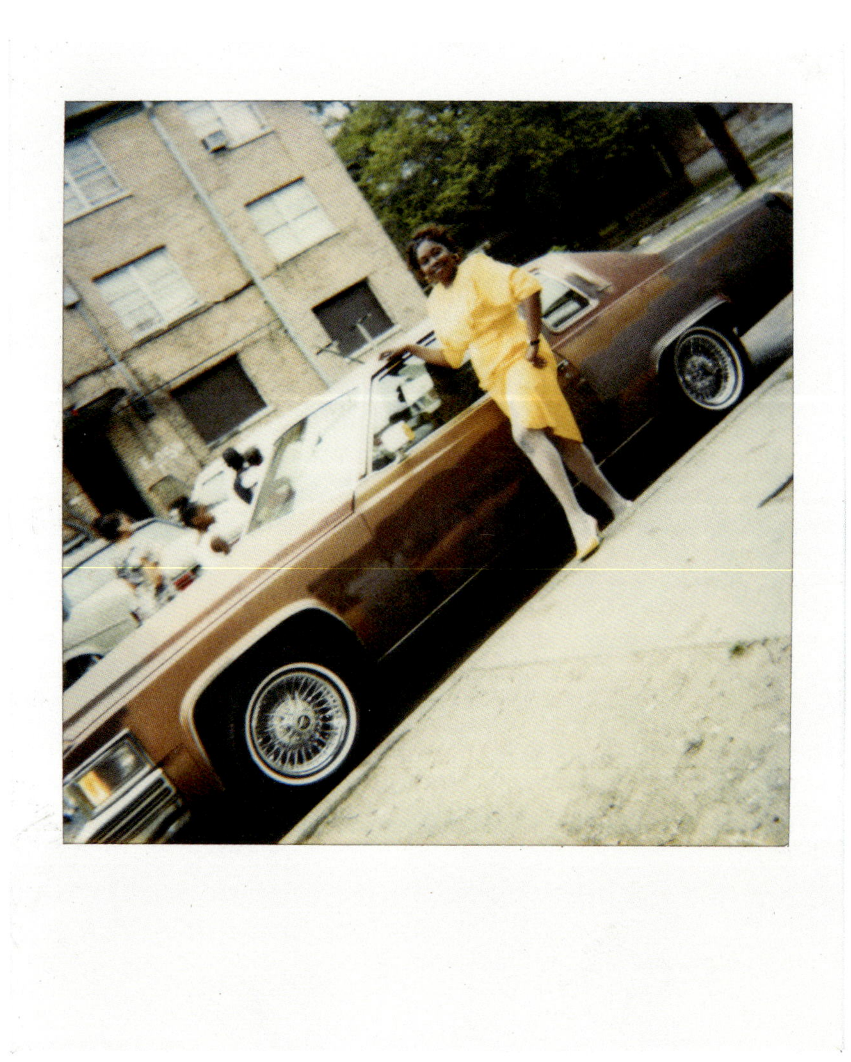

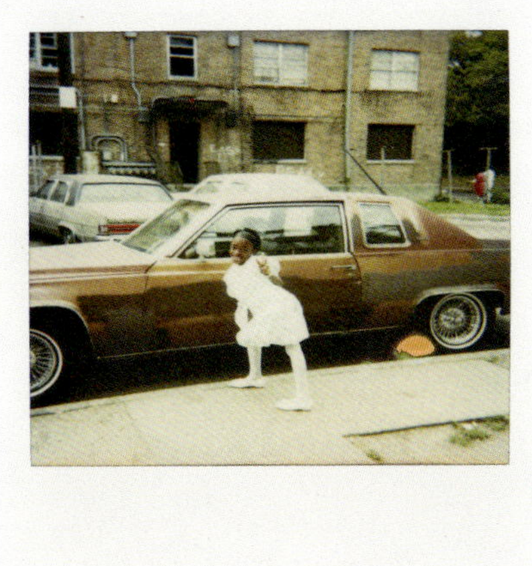

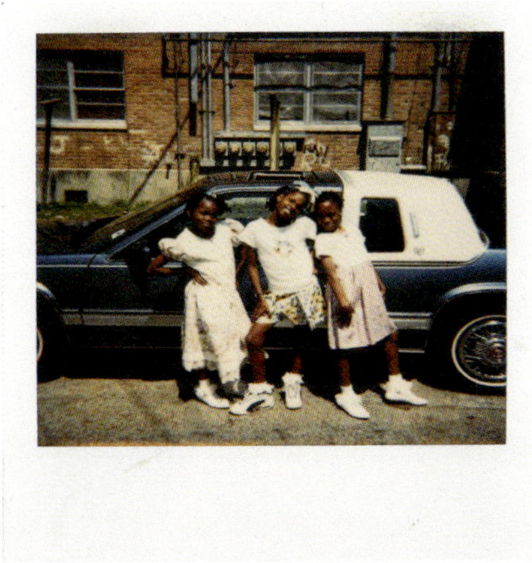

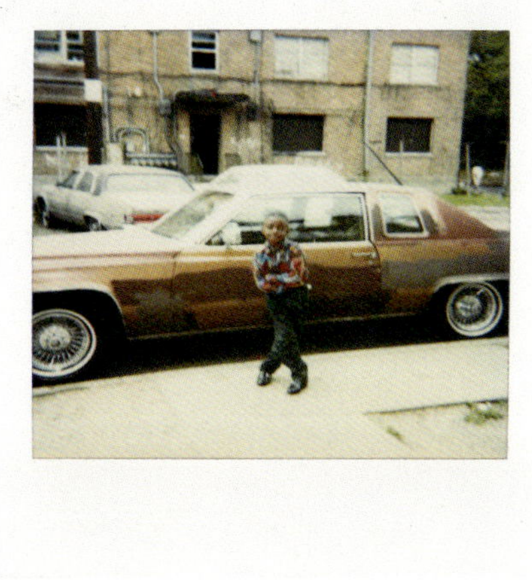

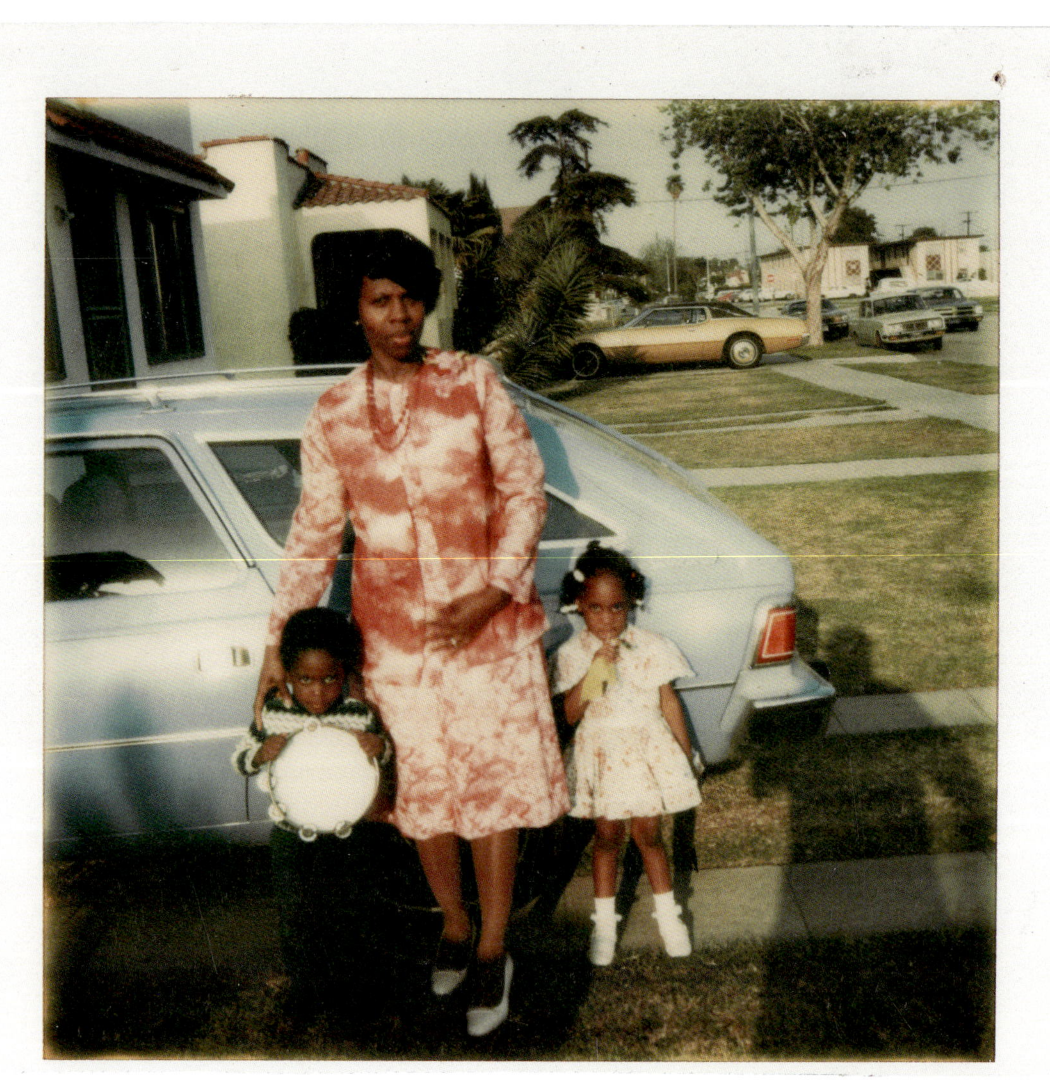

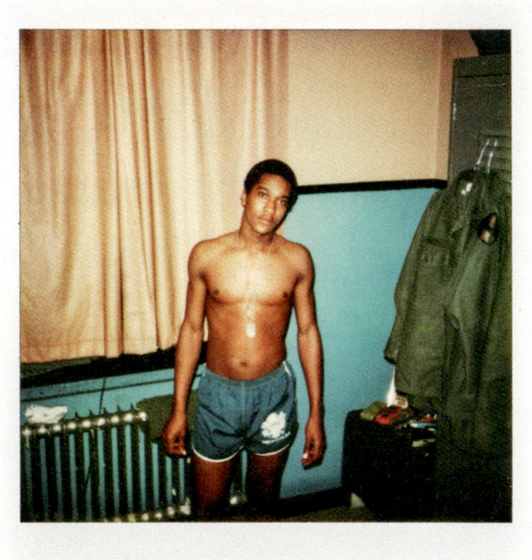

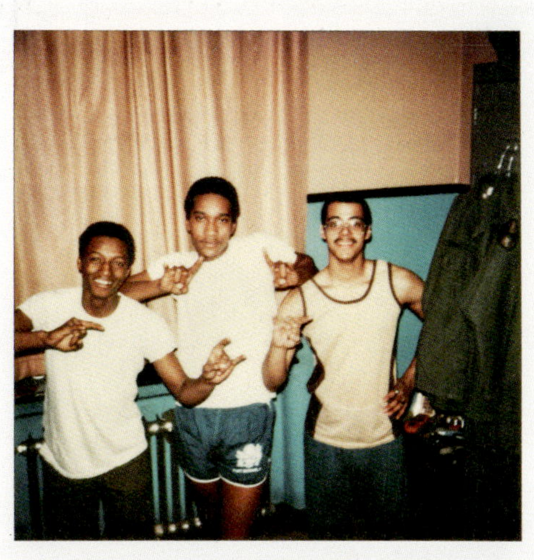

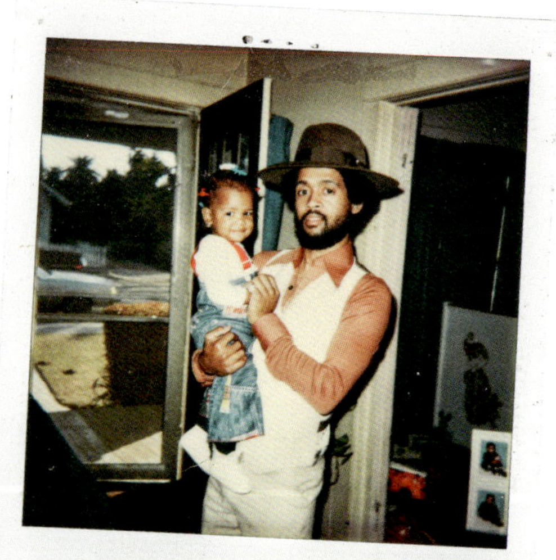

11-18-78 Nuttie & Daddy

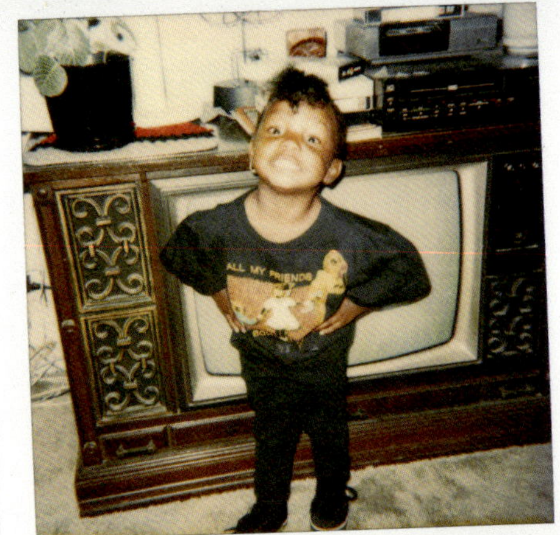

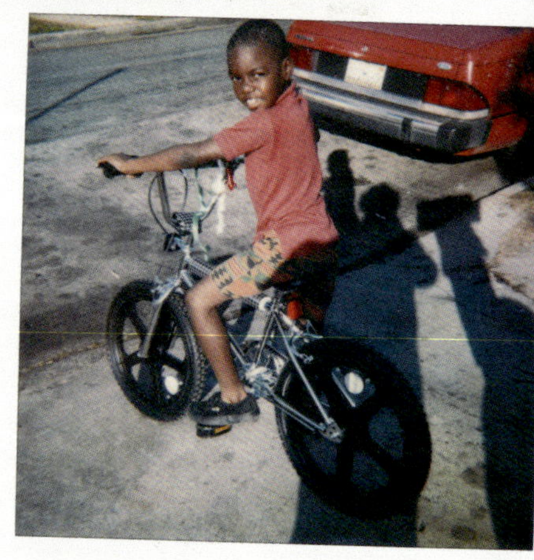

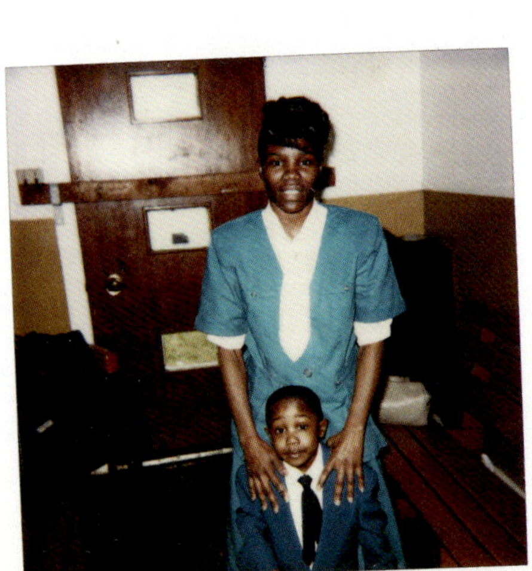

Church Day   2/26/94
Stephen and Mom

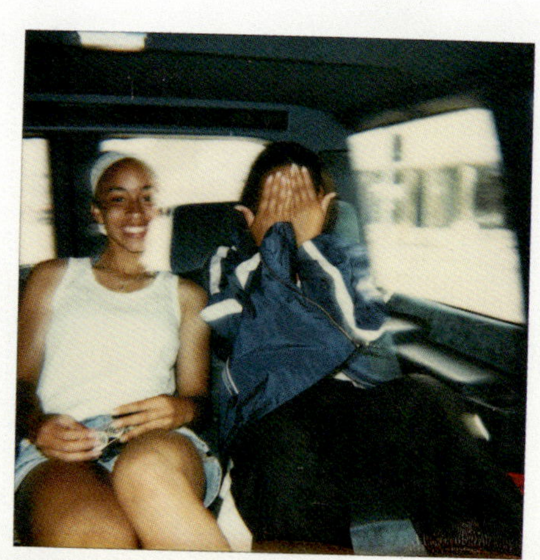

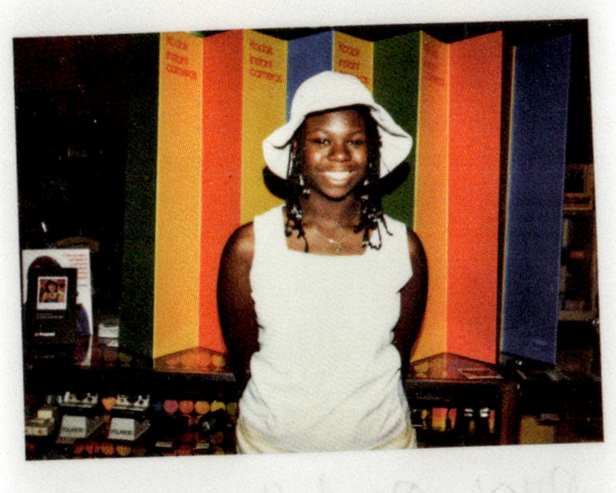

July 8, 1999

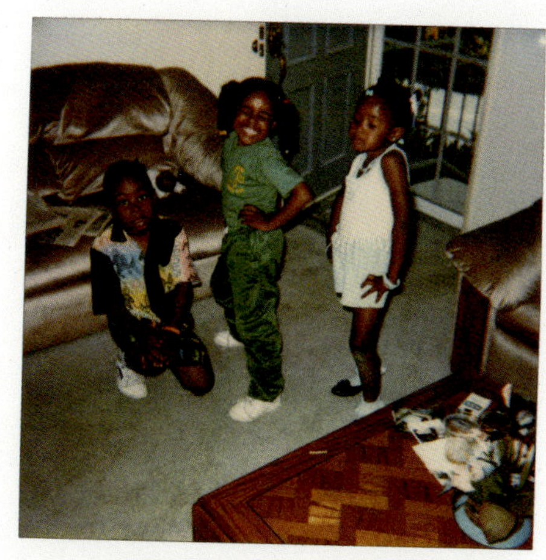

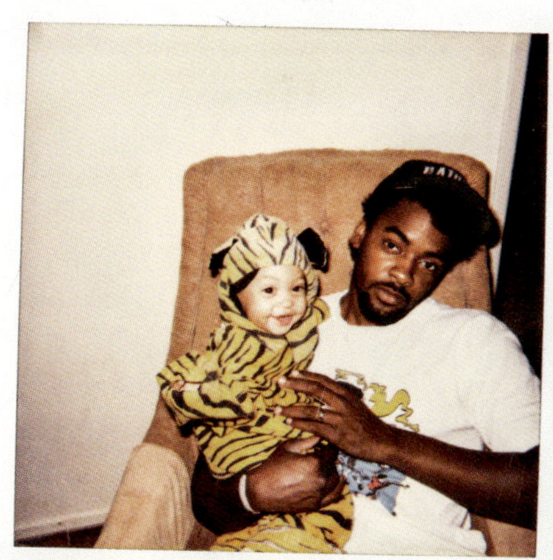

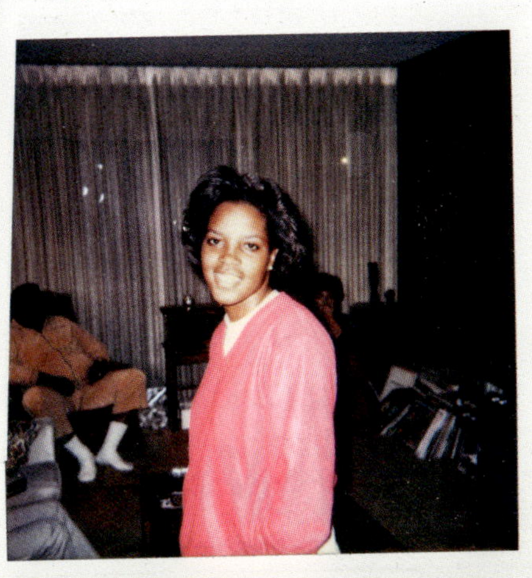

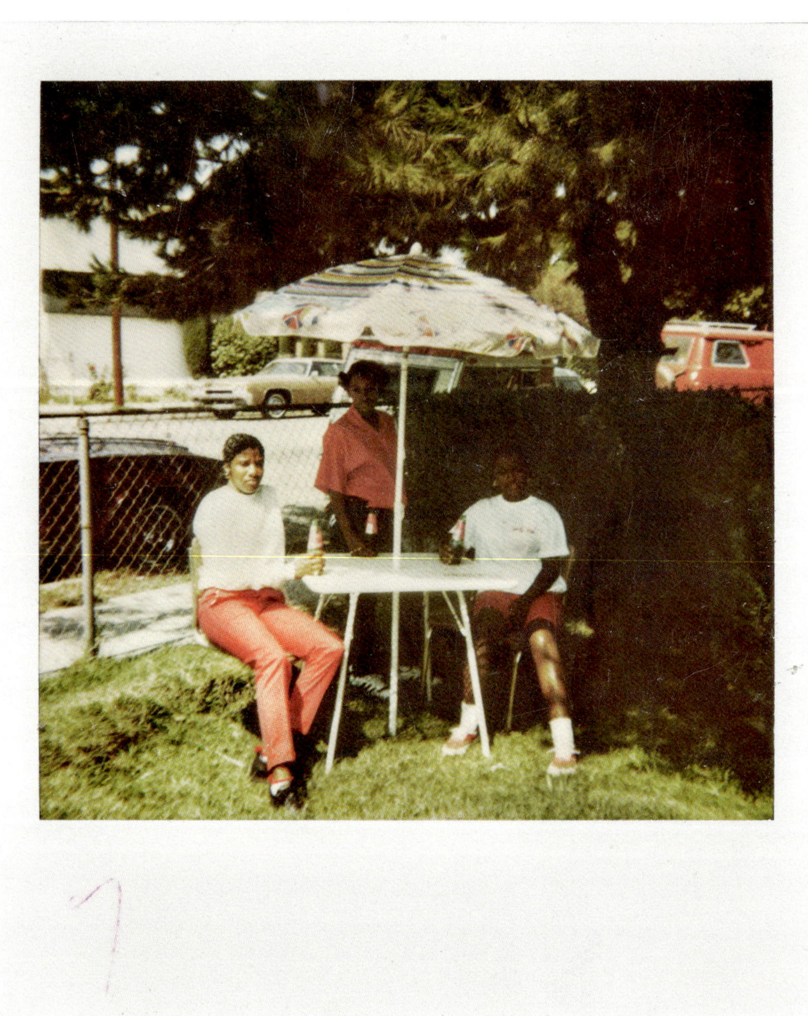

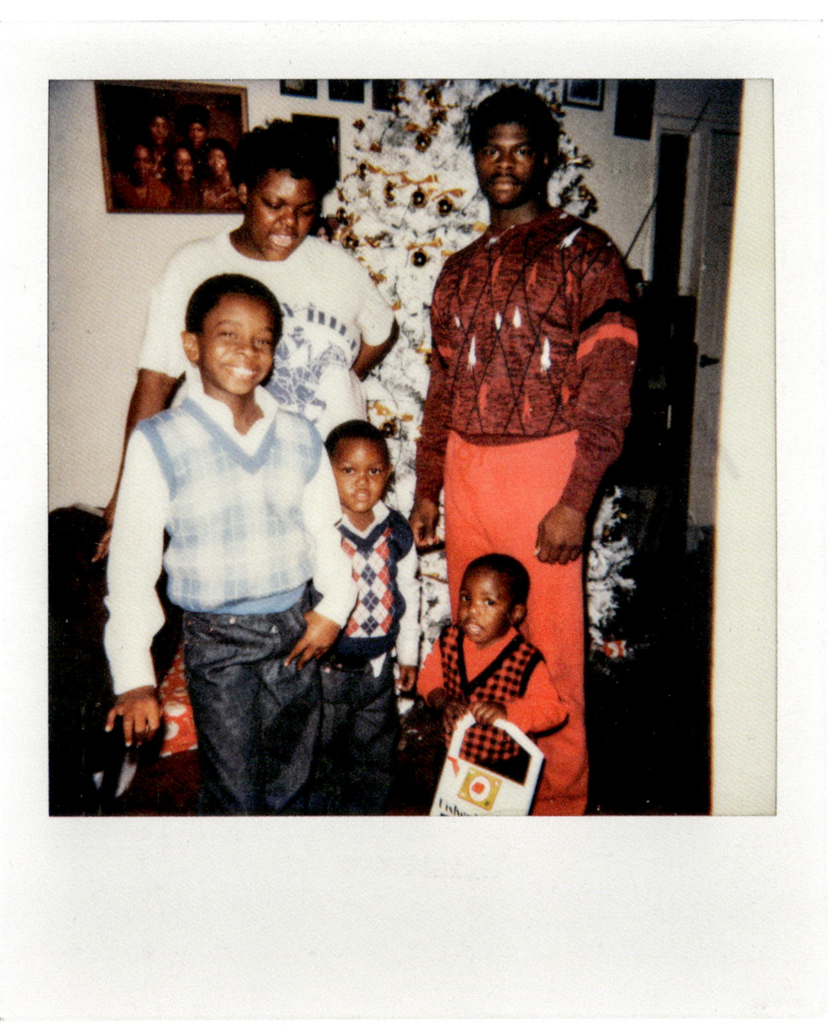

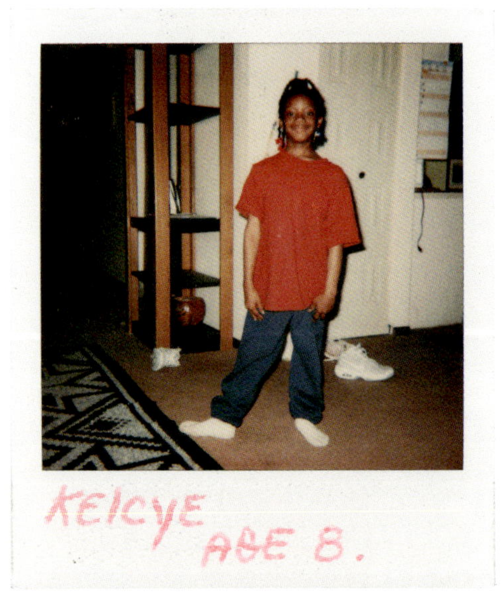

KELCYE
AGE 8.

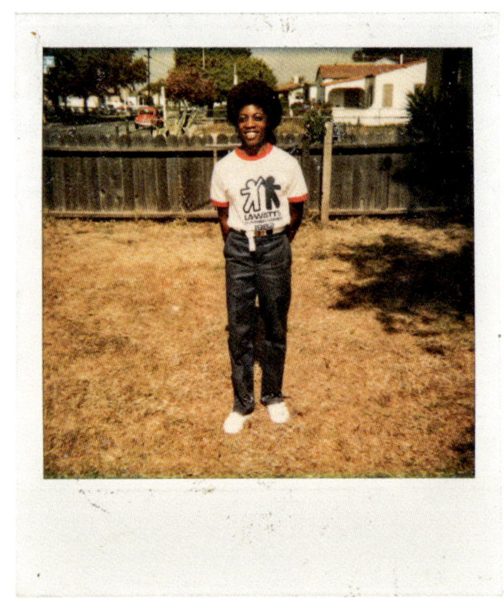

Mama's straight lean held by snow sky, knee deep in invisible whiteness. *The Black cockatoo has the most power*. Me and nem, nem and me, Jay eating meat sticks, ain't that something? The coming-into-being with company under magnolia tree. Sing with me: distinctive sensation of one's own vernacular background. Say, no need for the word "freedom" to account for what this is. Say, "nest," say my anchor, my glory, my sister's arm draped around me. Worlds in that drape.

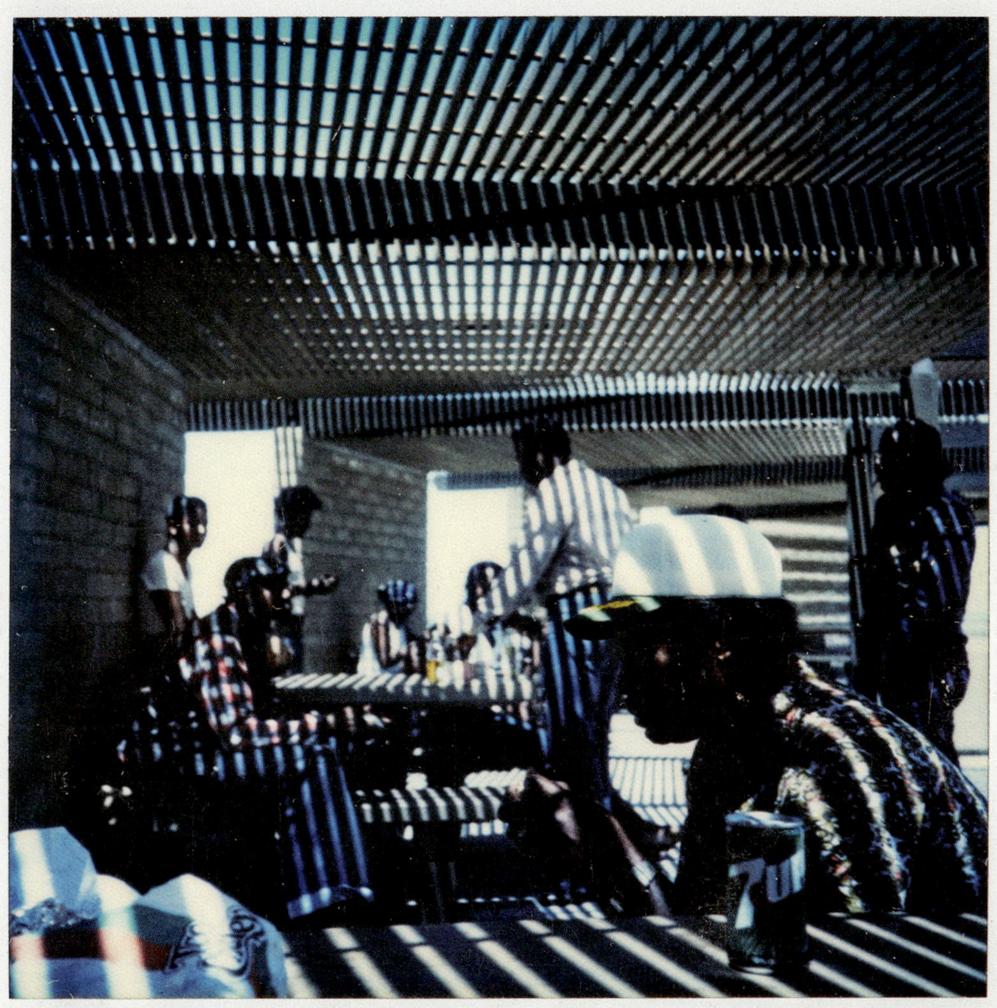

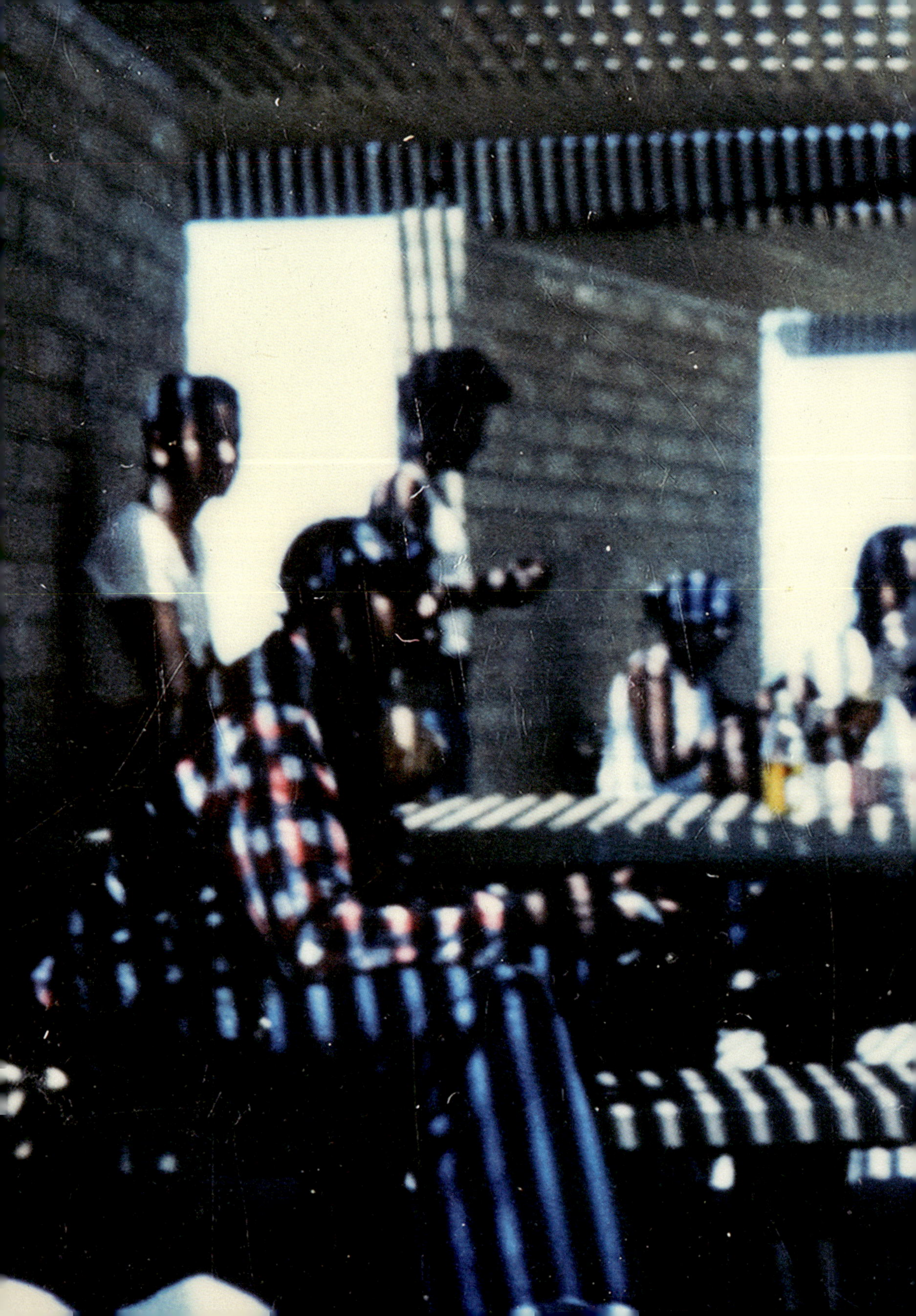

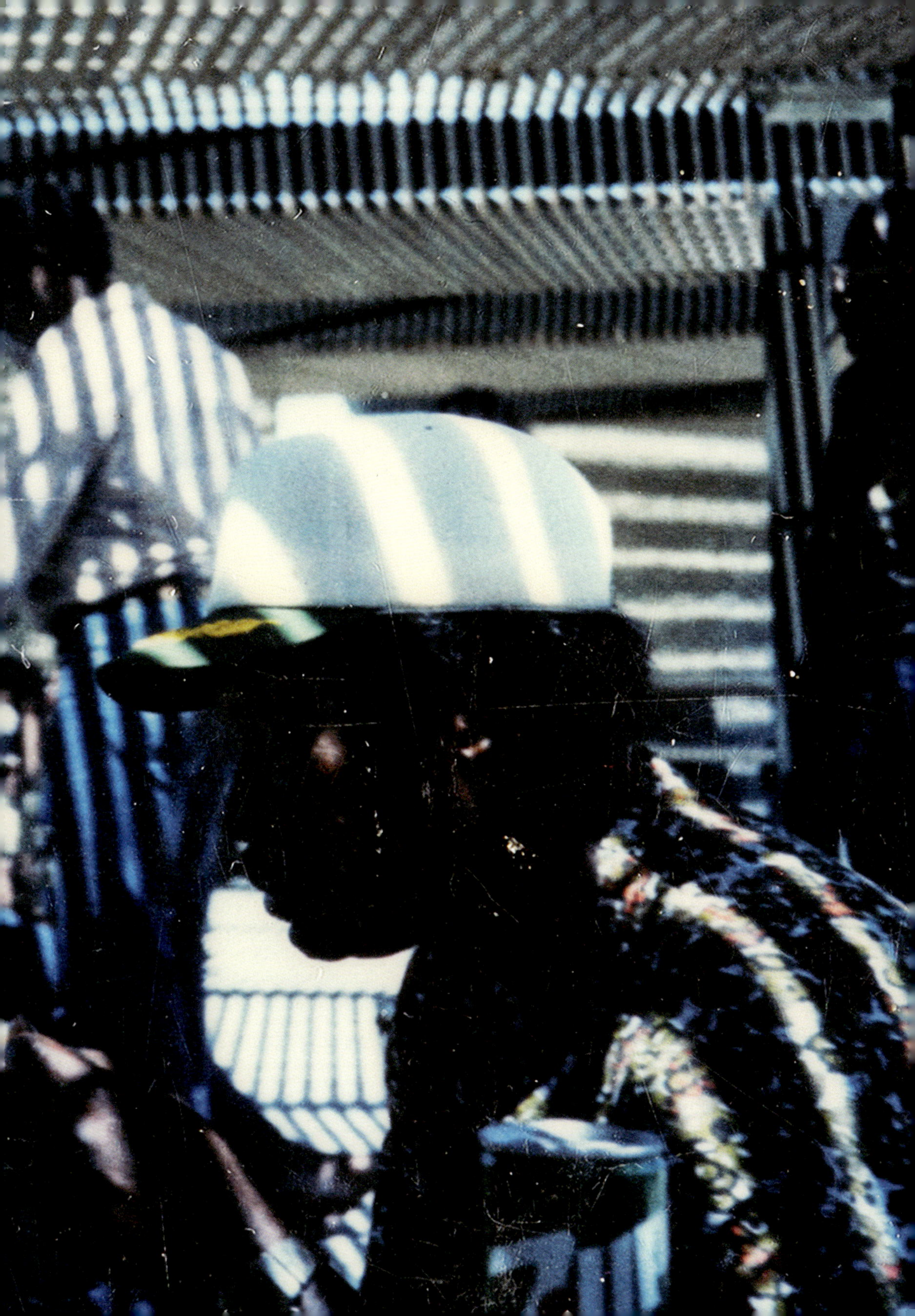

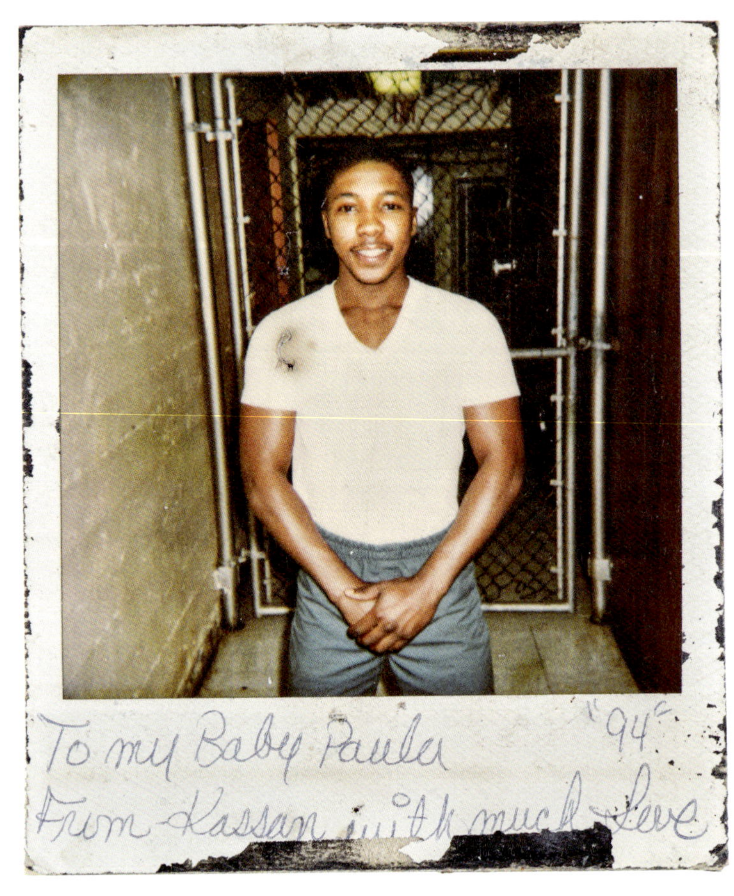

"94"
To my Baby Paula
From Kassan with much Love

was takeN - August 23 - 91
2018/2838

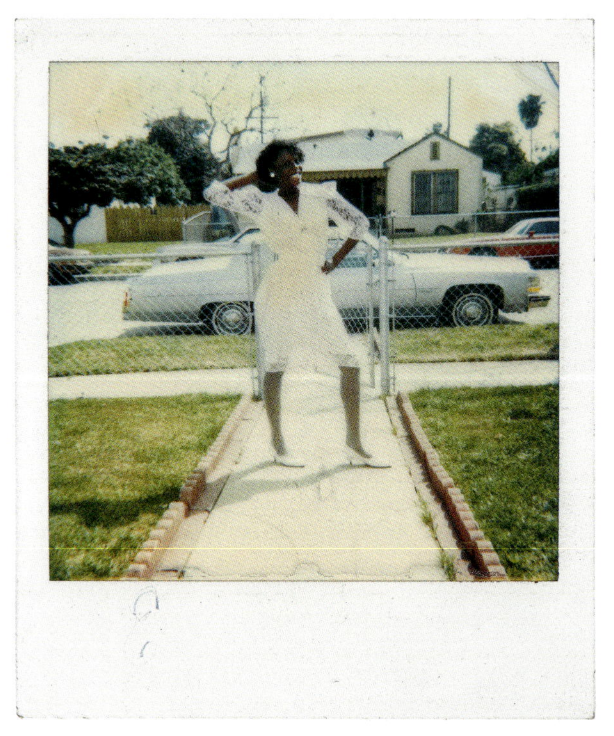

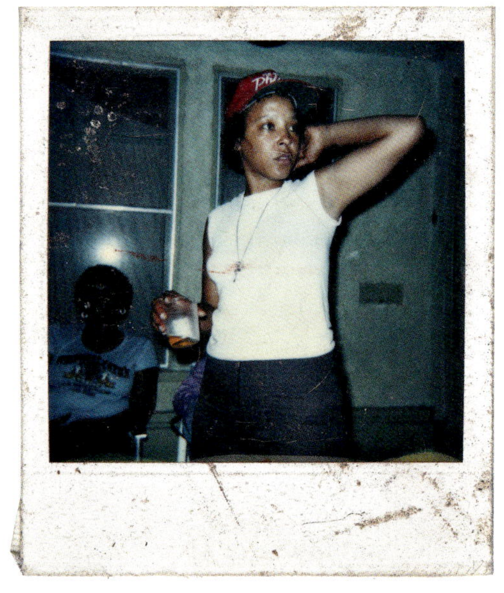

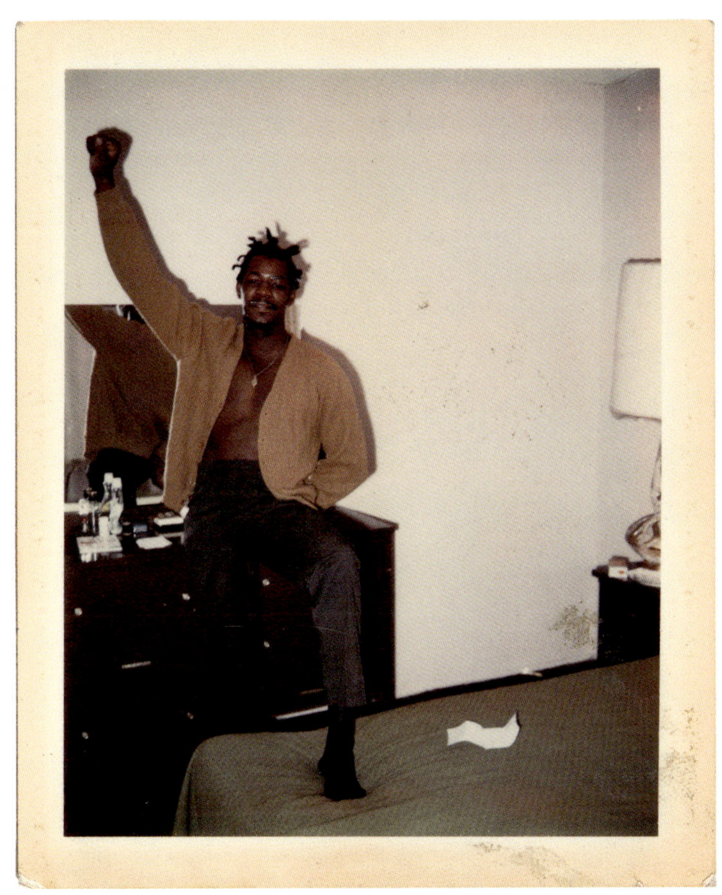

Photographs of Black Life

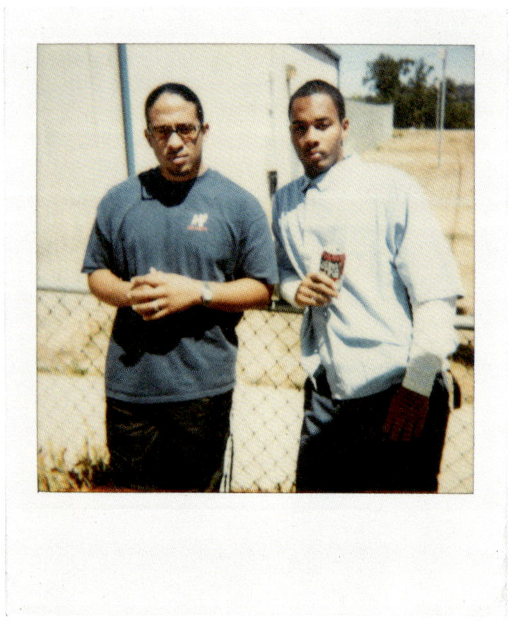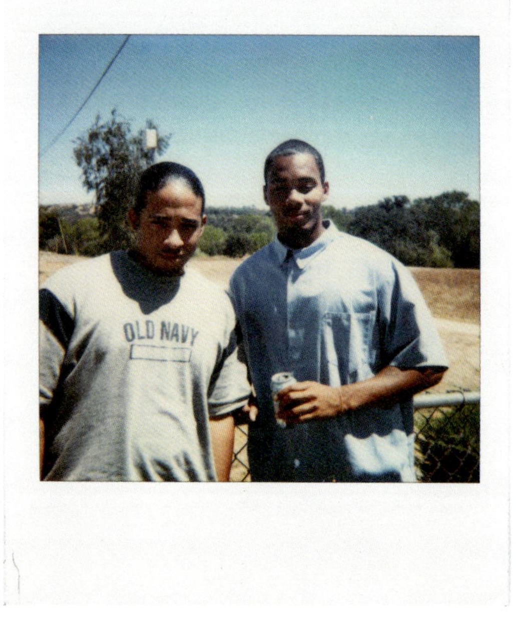

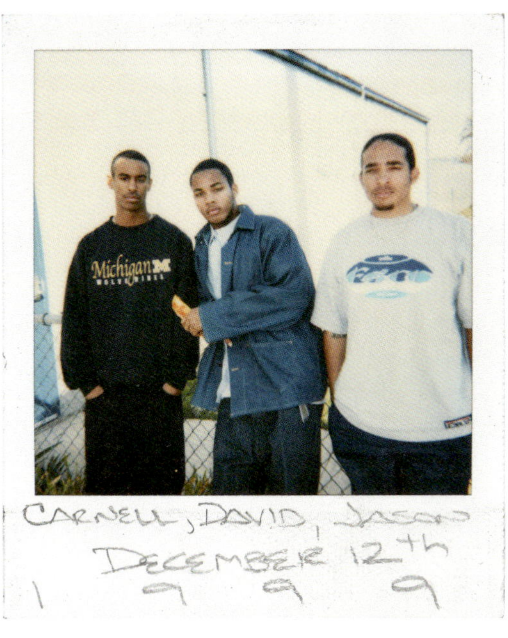

CARNELL, DAVID, JASON
DECEMBER 12th
9   9   9

07933024312   POLAROID 32
12-12-99
2018/2338

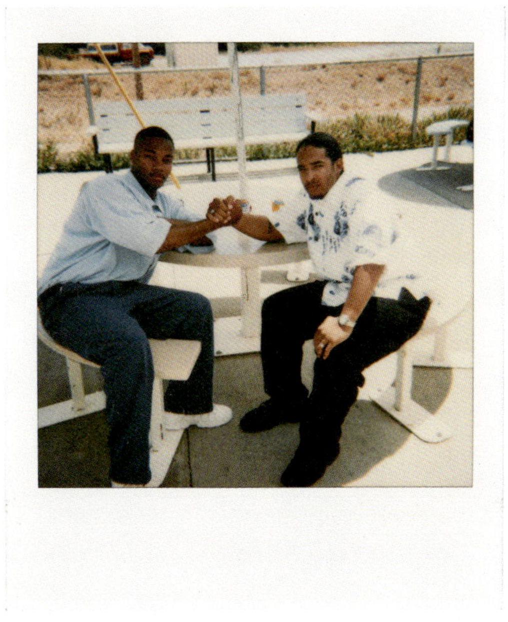

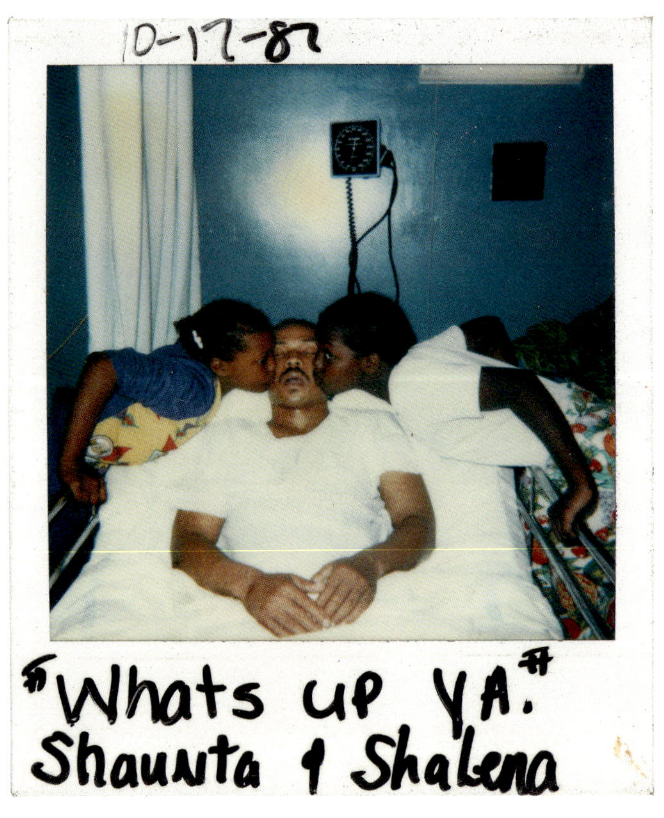
10-17-87
"Whats up YA."
Shaunta & Shalena

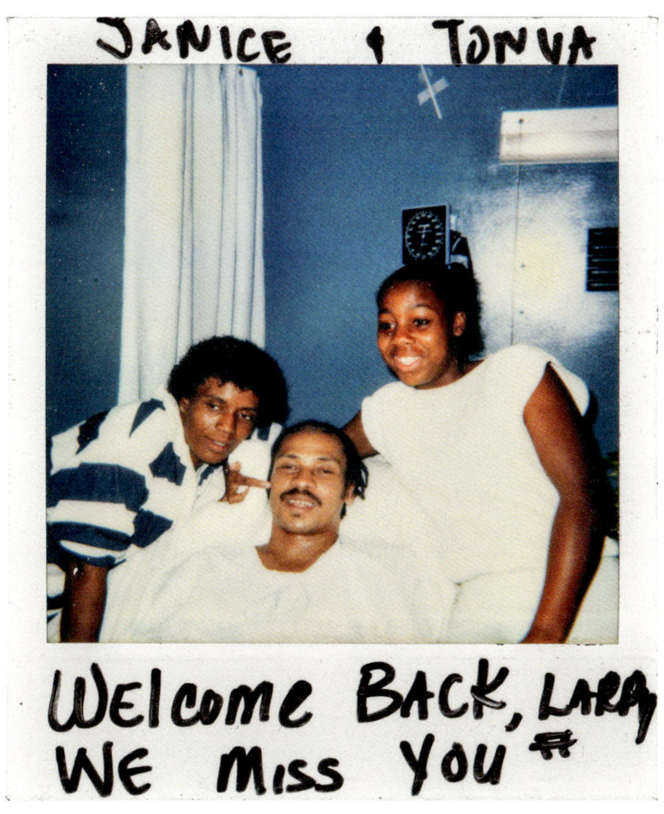
JANICE & TONYA
Welcome BACK, LARRY
WE MISS YOU

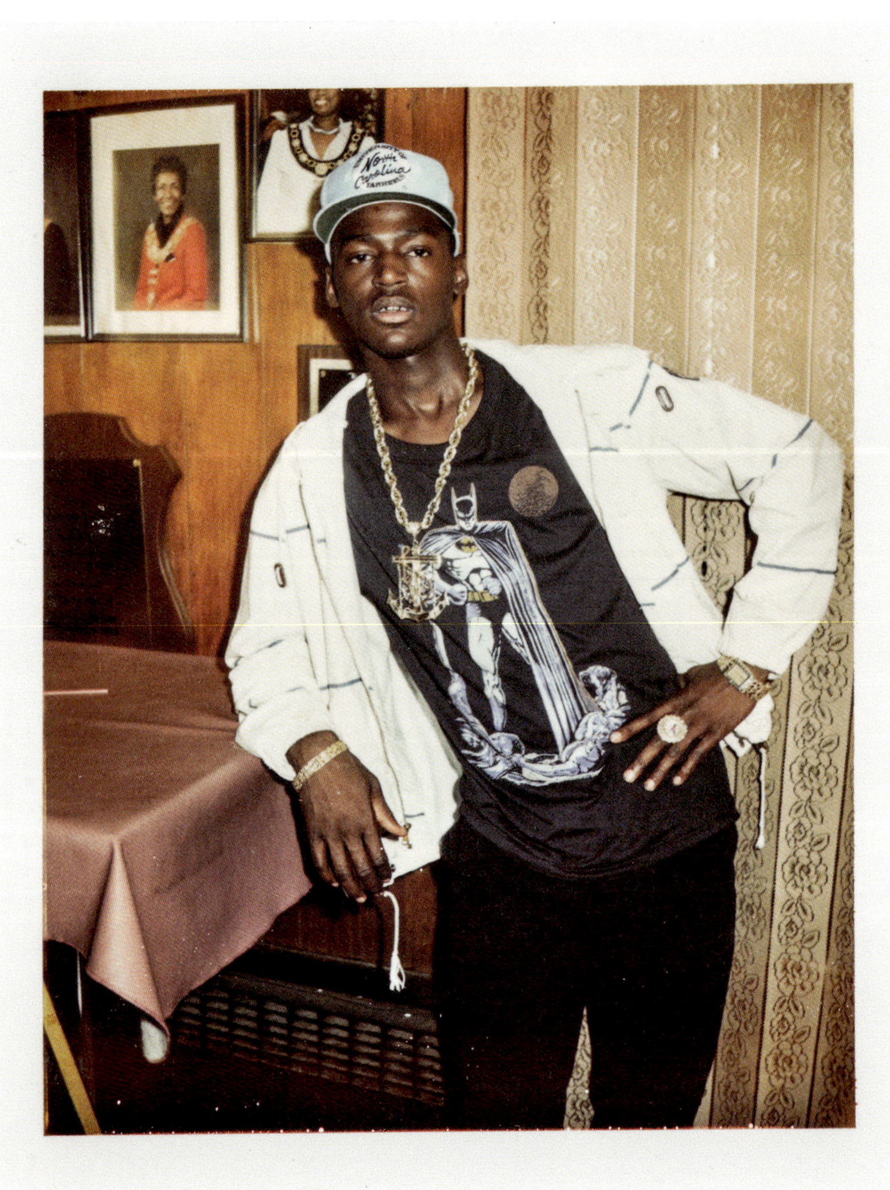

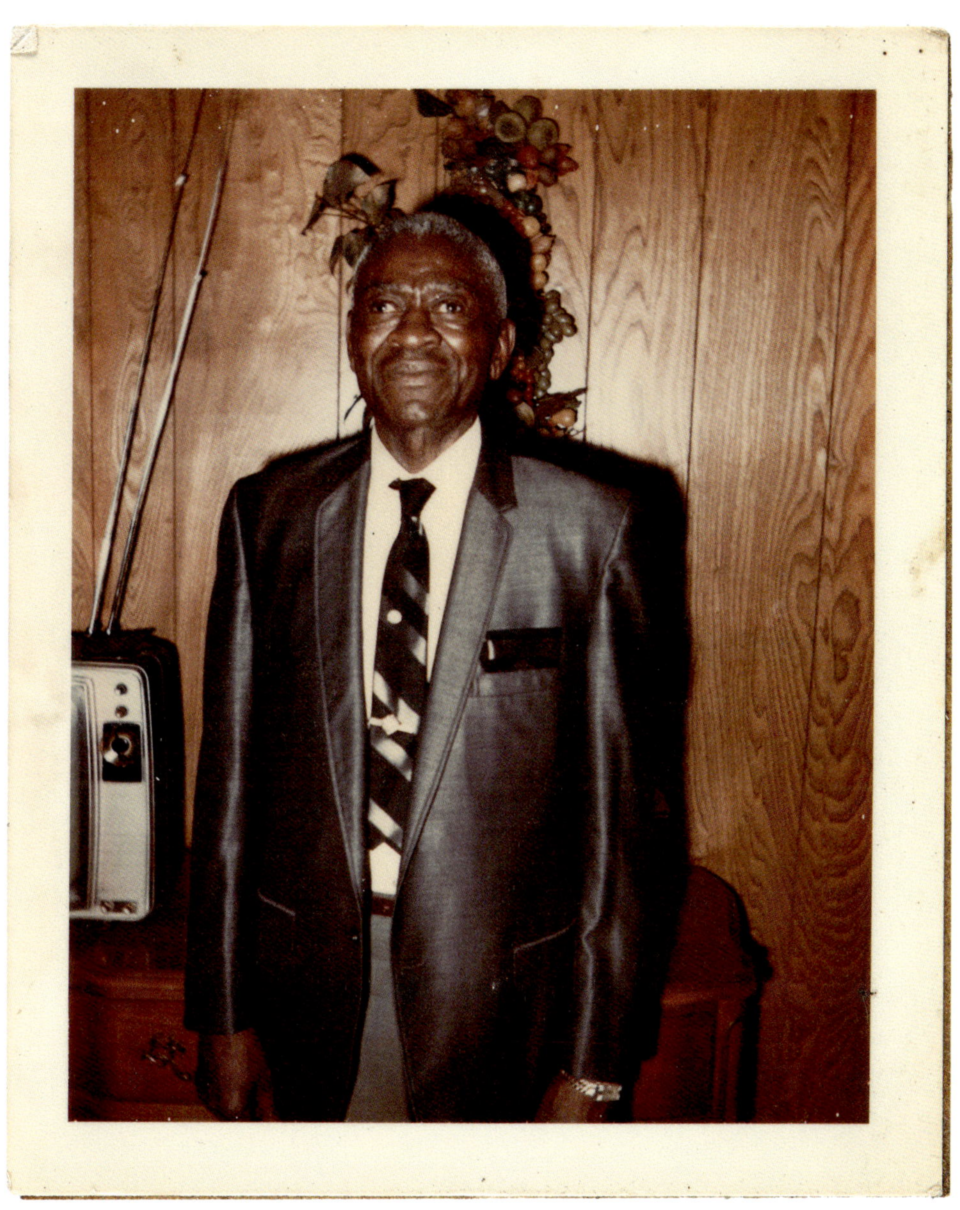

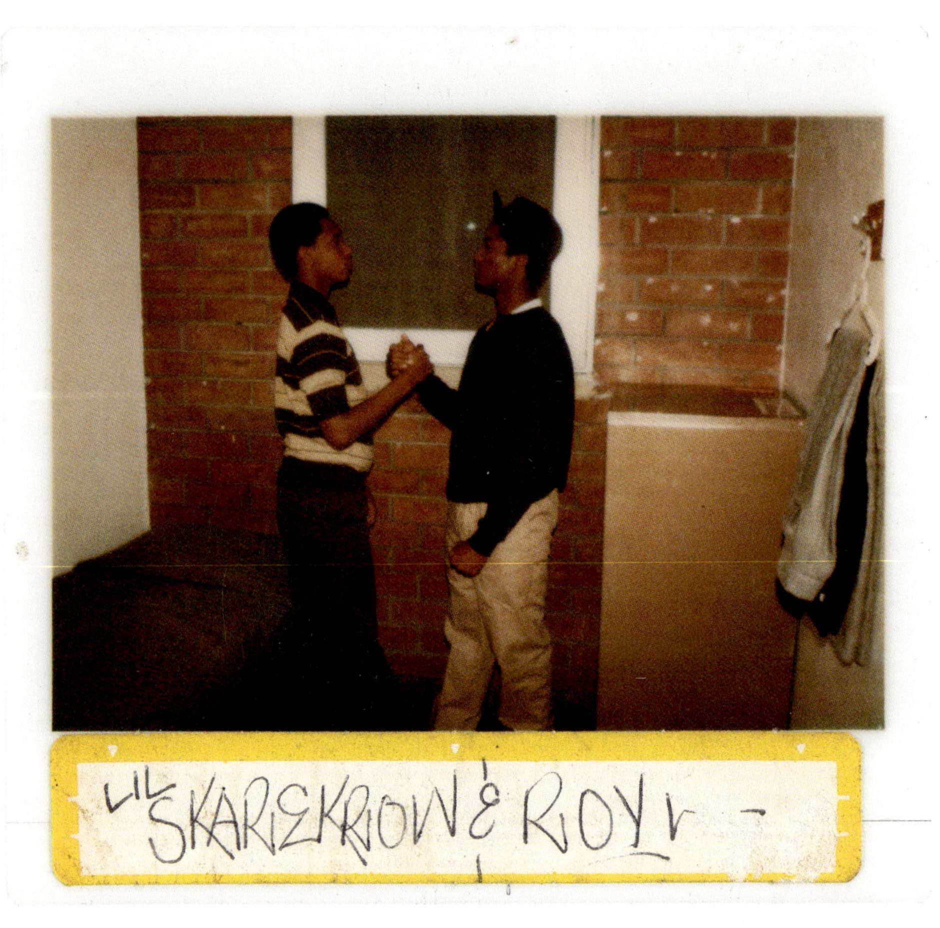

LIL SKARIEKROW & ROY

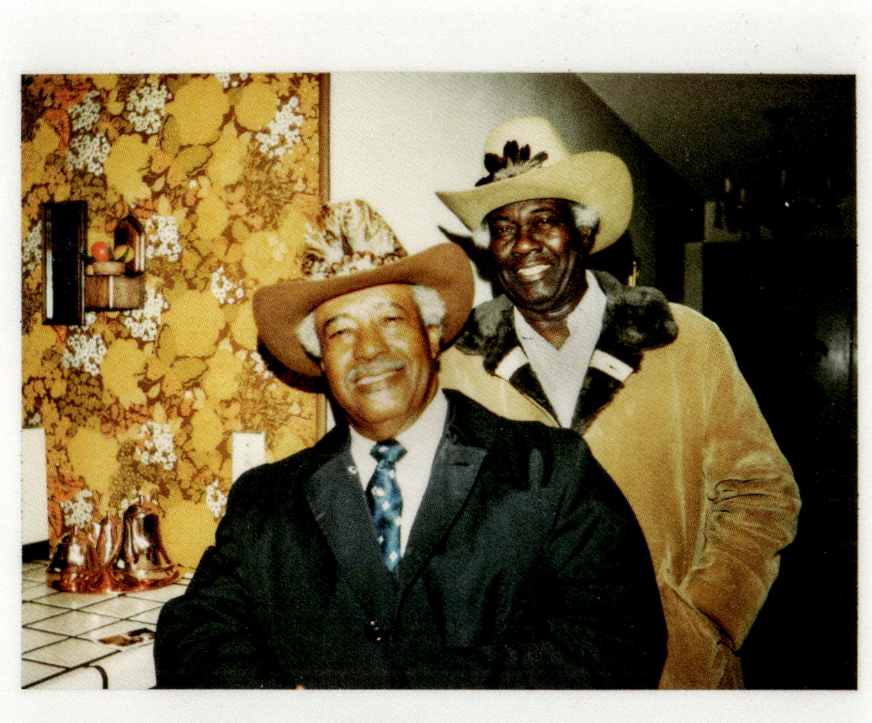

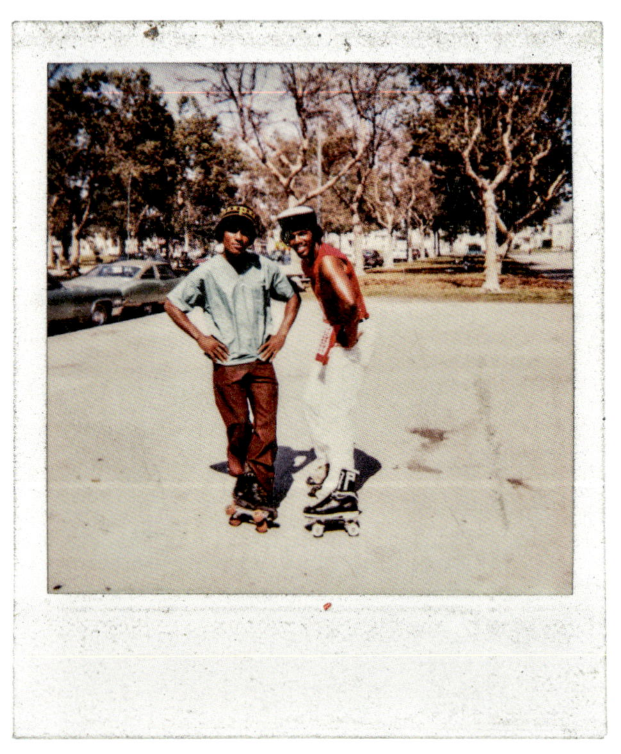

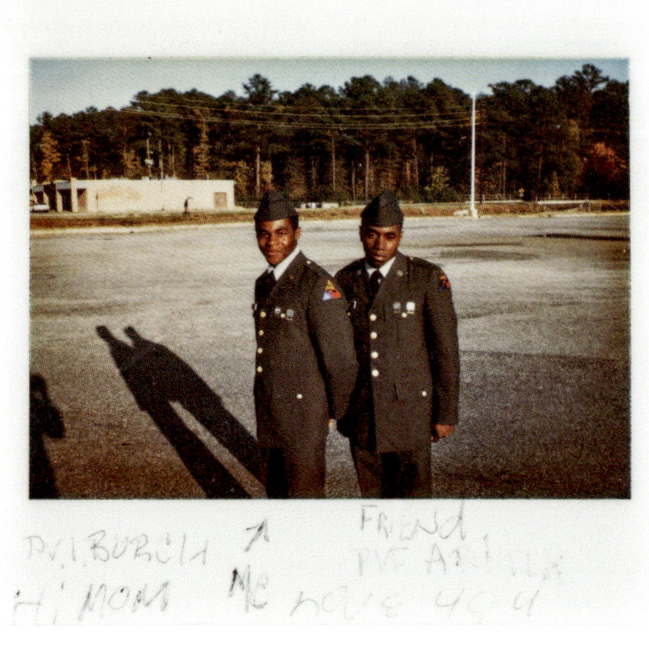

PVT BURCH A FRIEND
PVT A....
HI MOM Me HAVE YOU

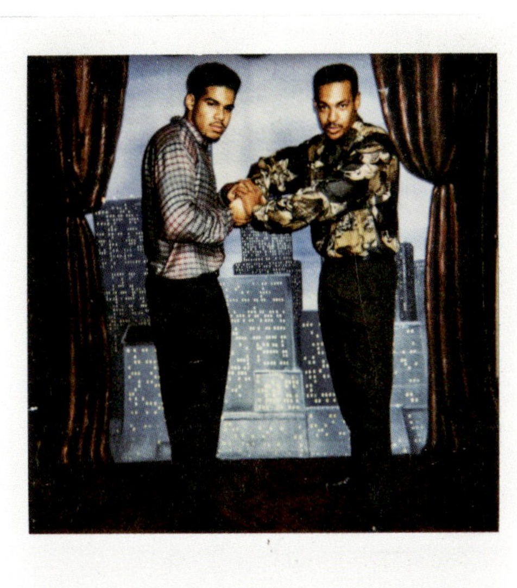

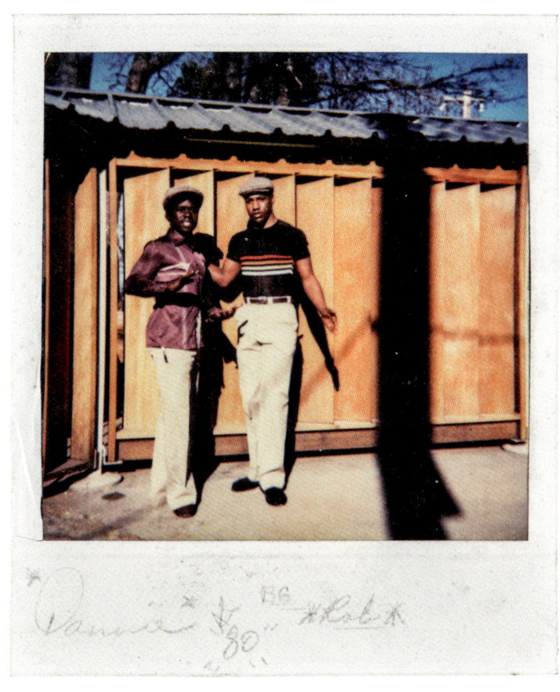

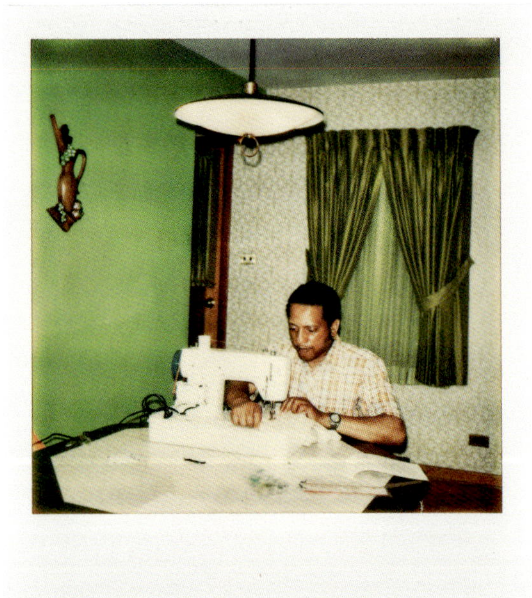

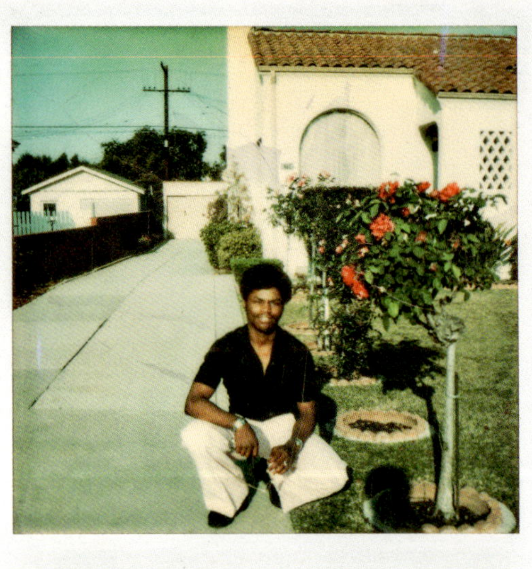

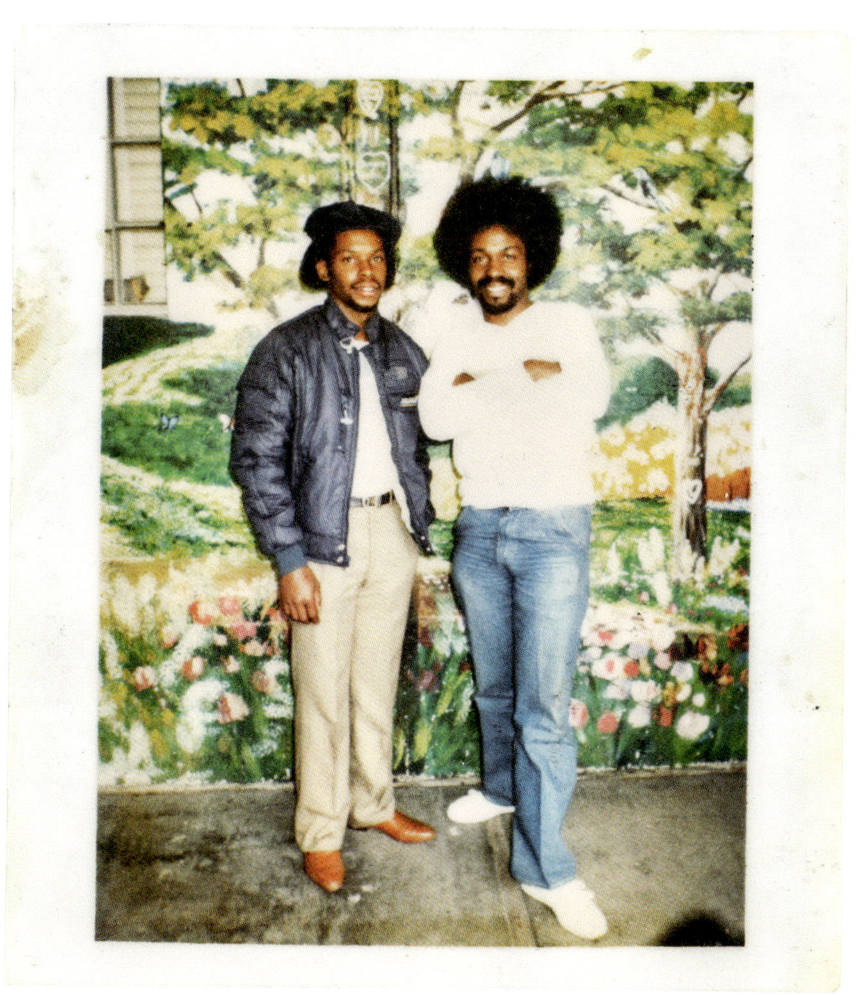

Photographs of Black Life

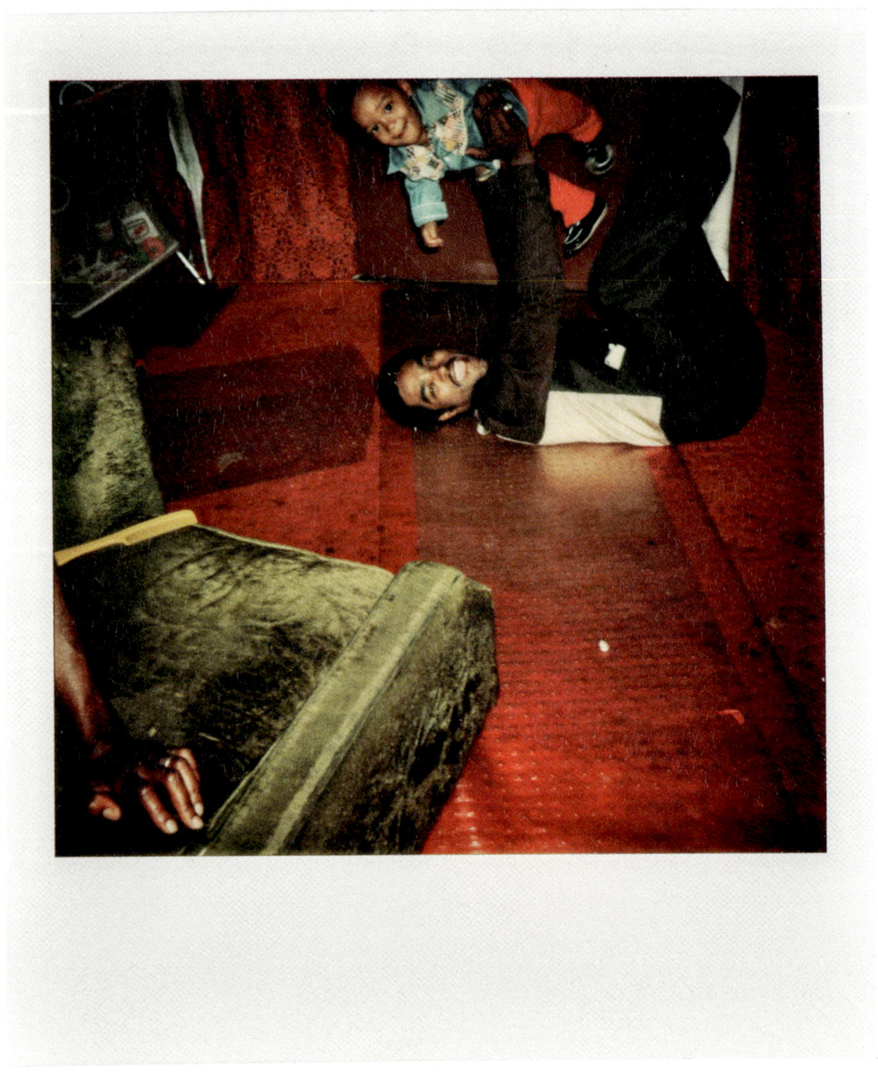

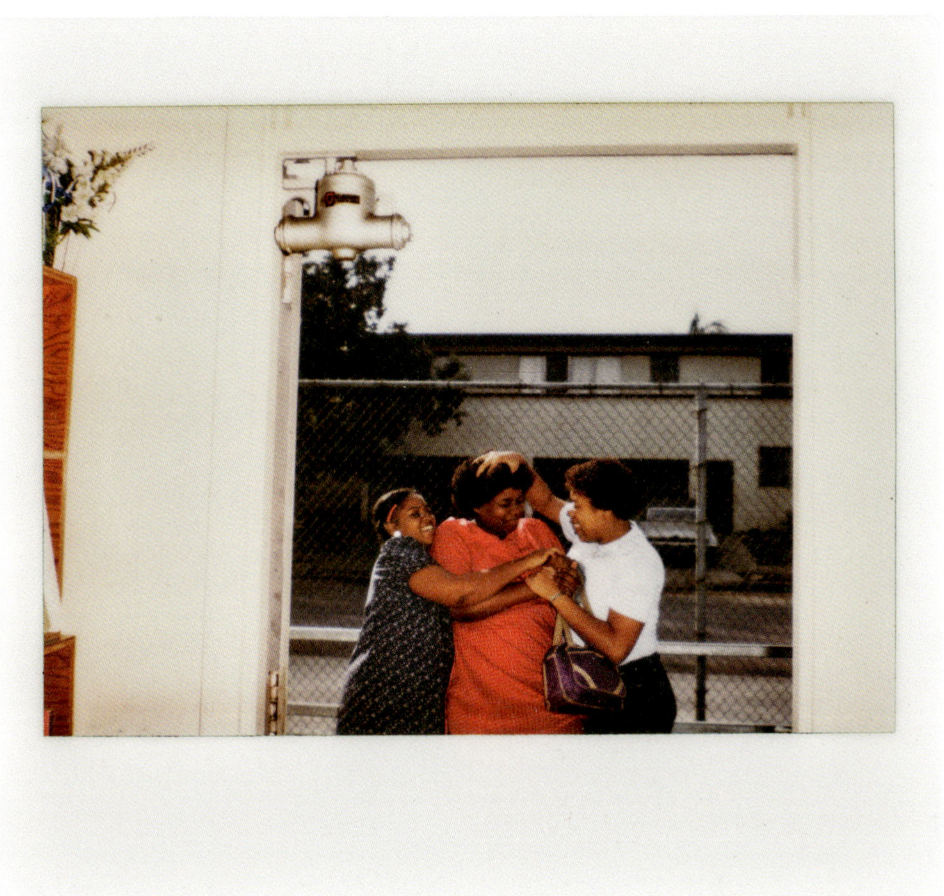

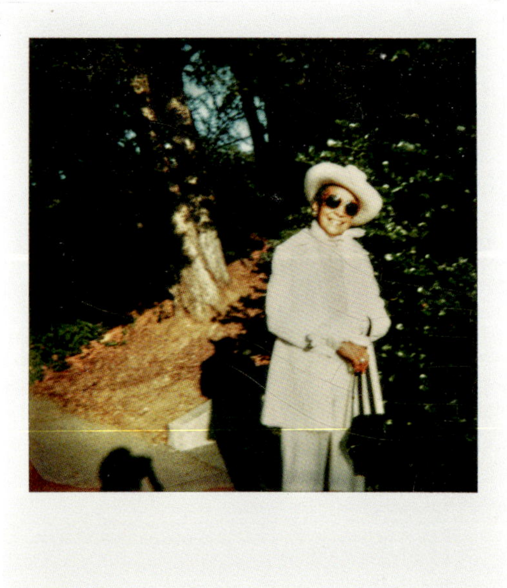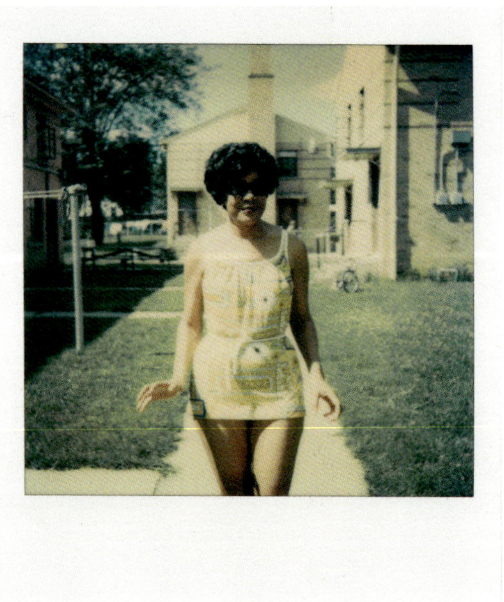

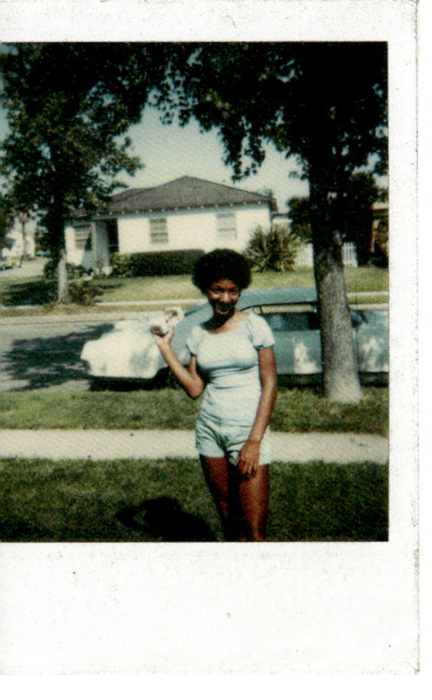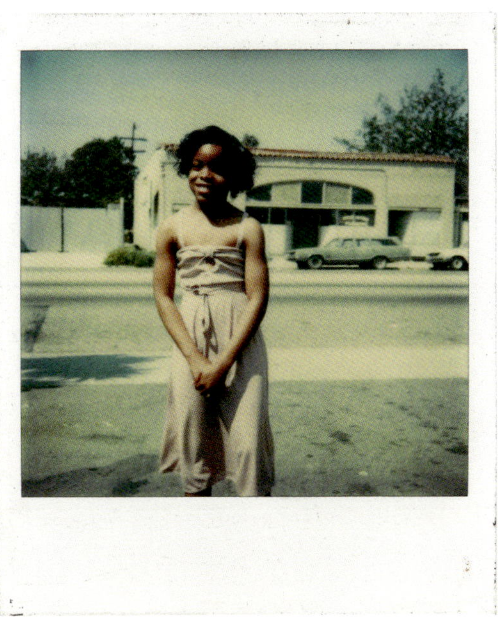

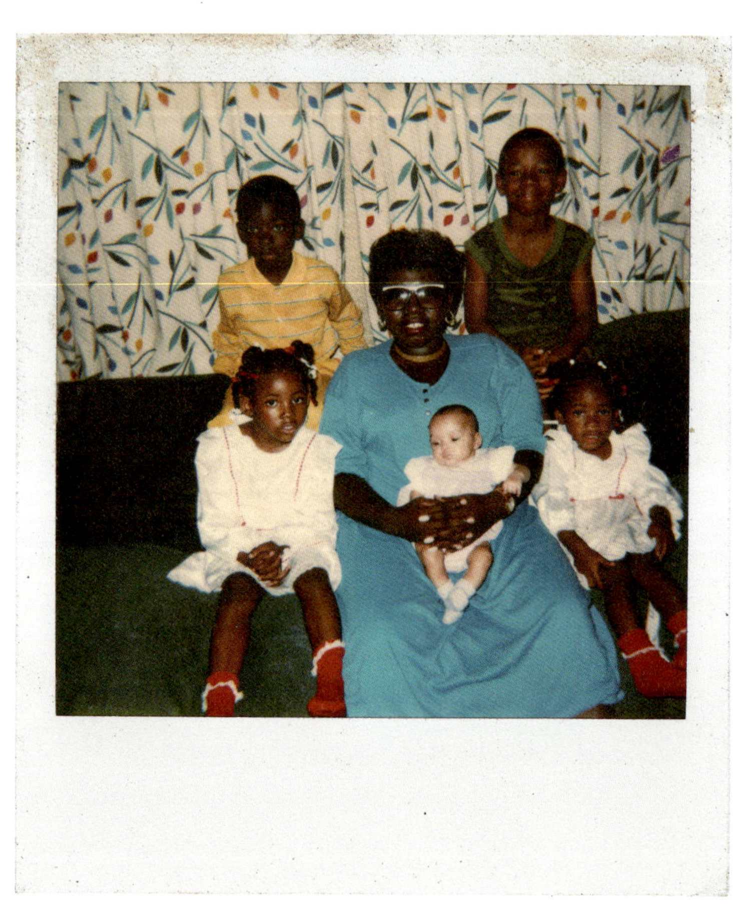

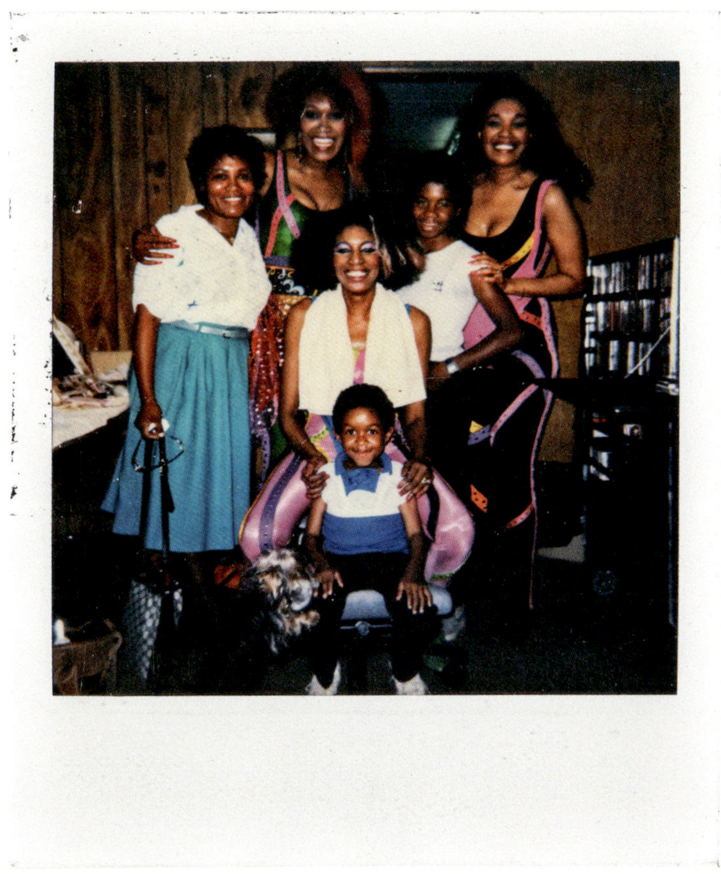

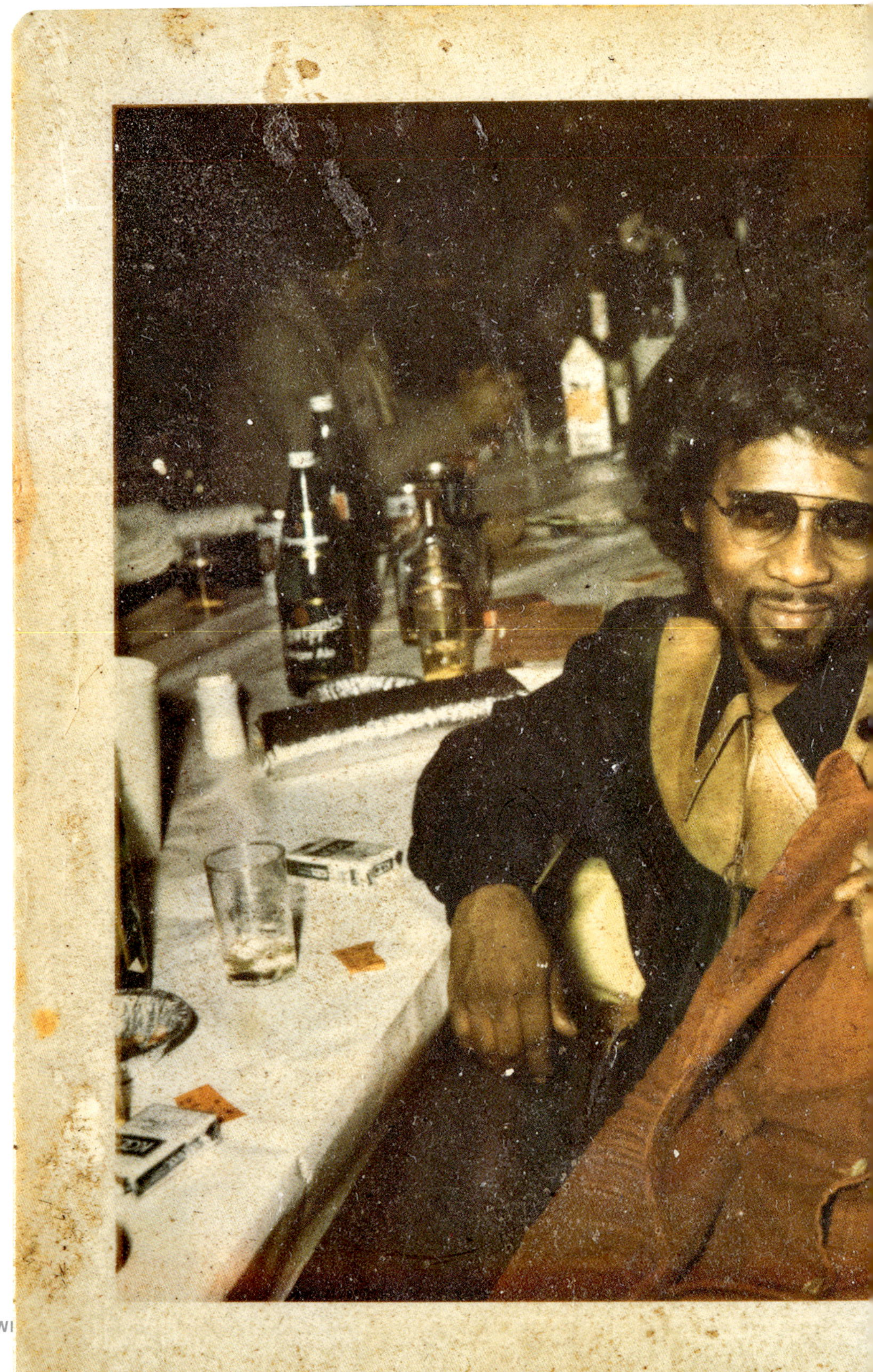

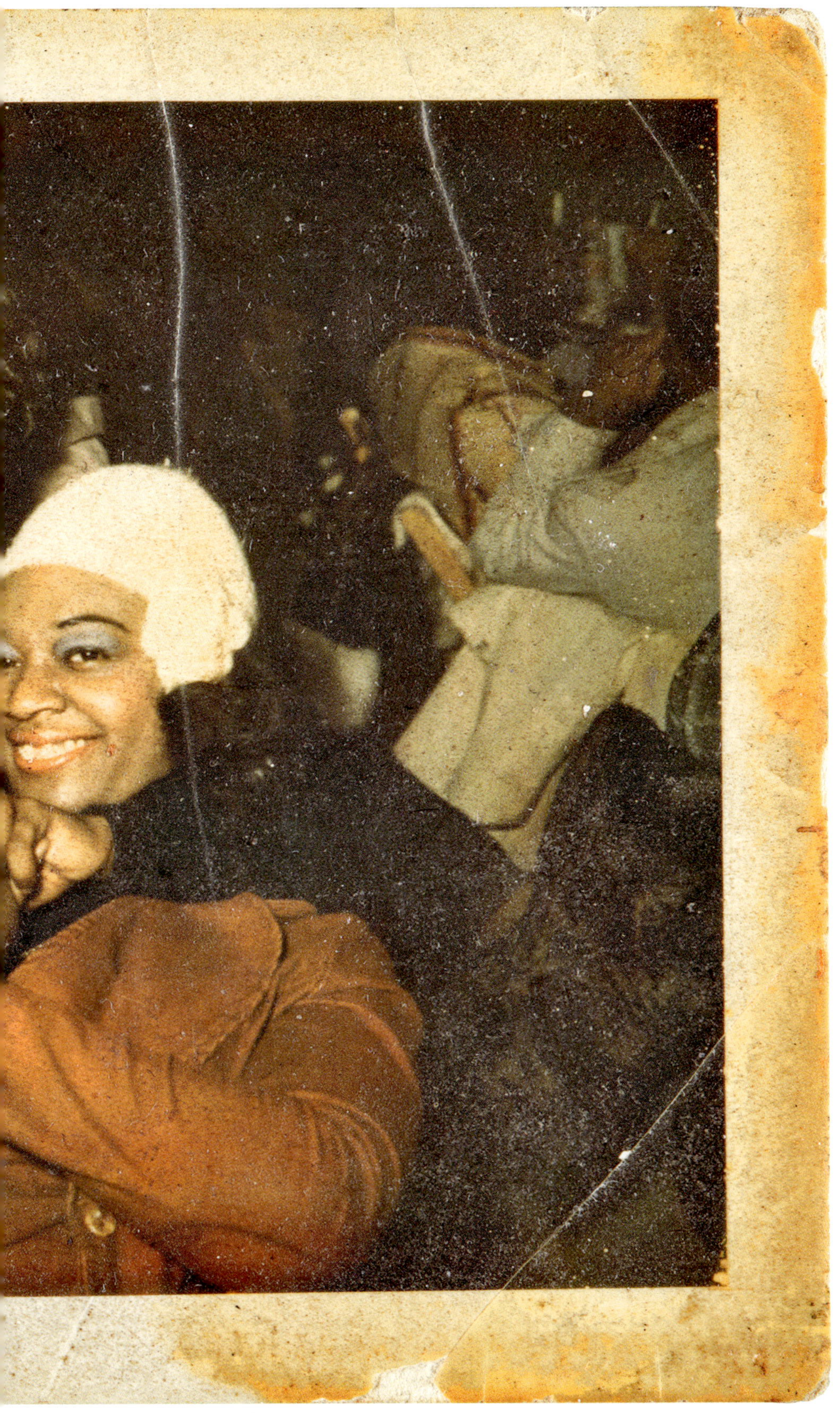

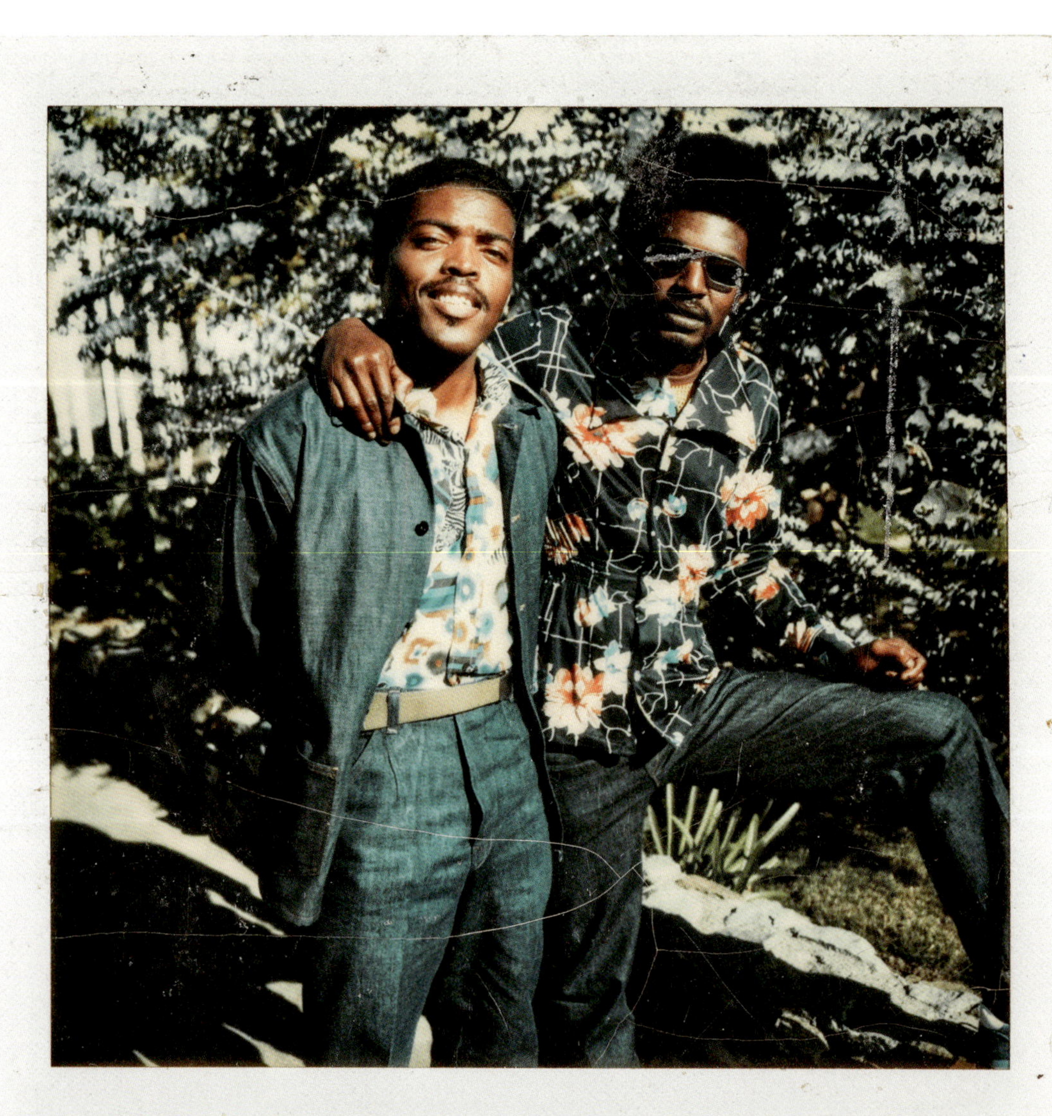

the T.V. picture used
of Clarence for News Media

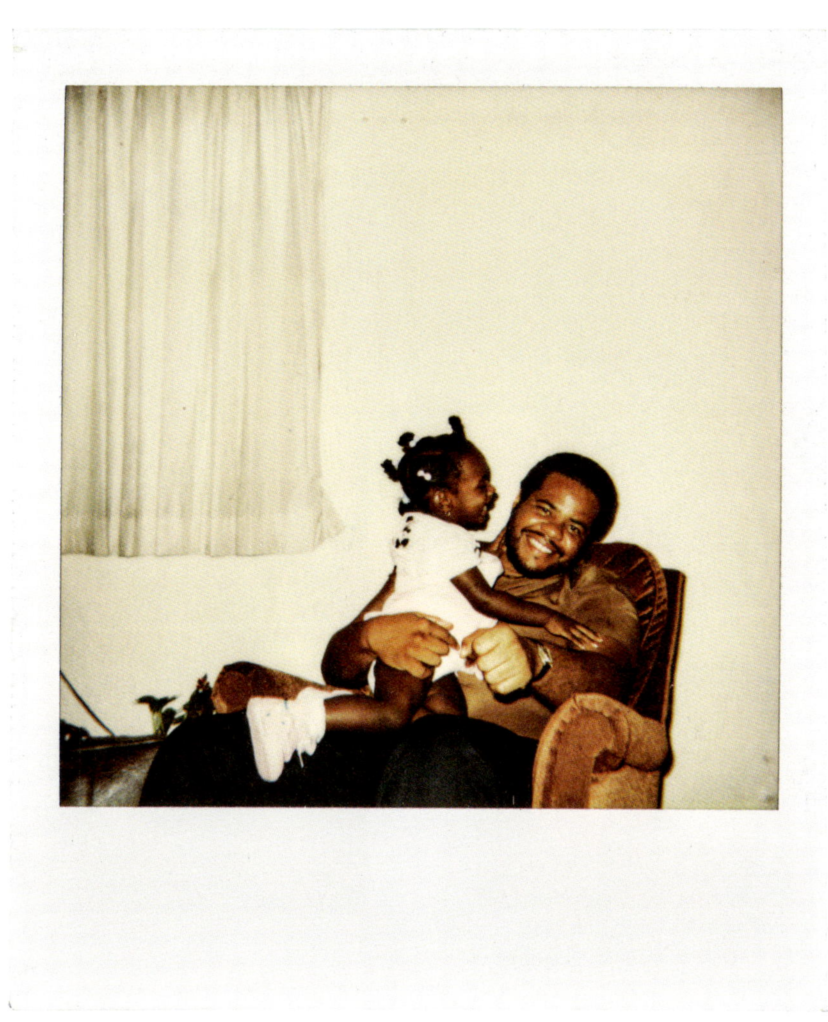

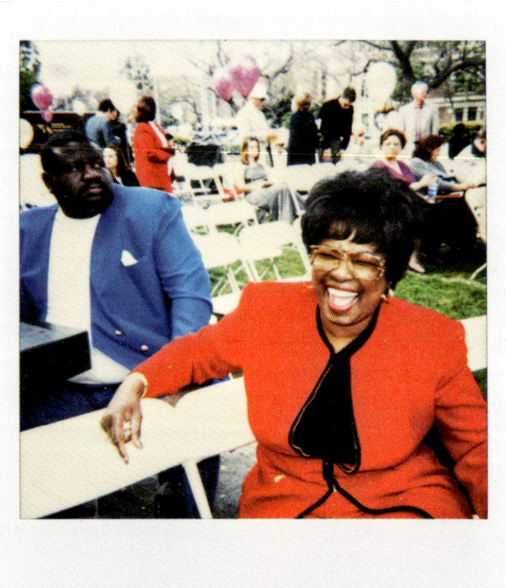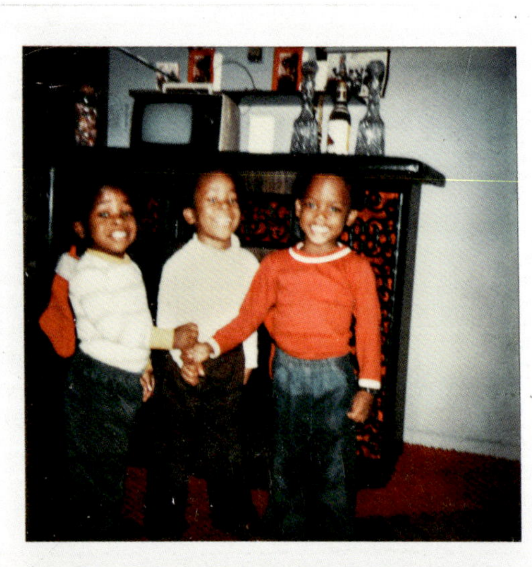

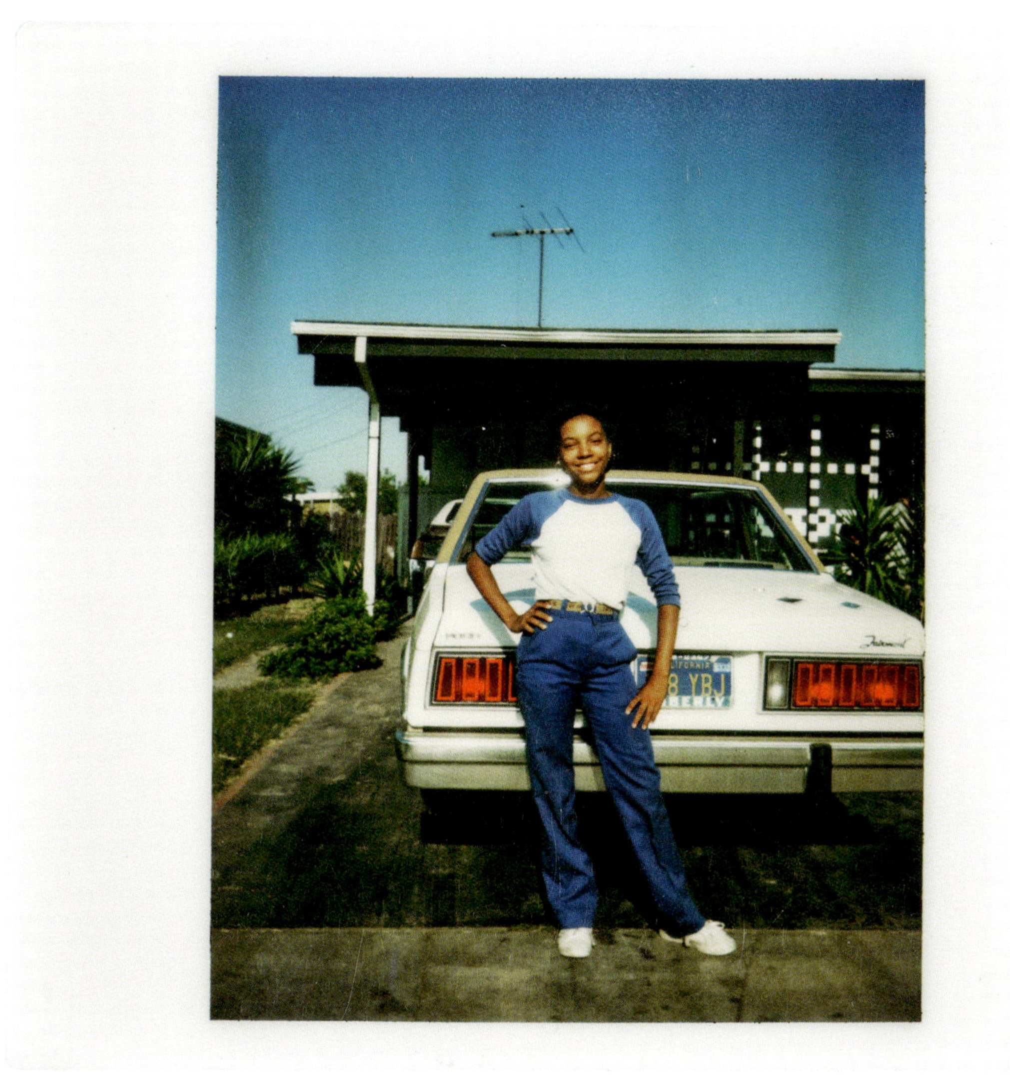

All myths dislodged and down your
throat they go. Go on, row a boat. Kick
some rocks in that pungent yearn for
access. Roots of your tongues hangry
in the juggernaut, in periphery. There
are times for radical privacy. There are
times when the night is wet, when the
moon shows up like an apparition in
reflective glare. Only they/we know
that's Uncle So-and-So, bright as what
would be touch.

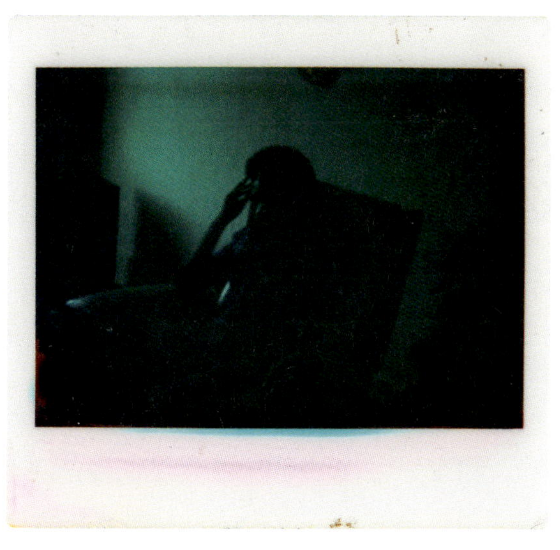

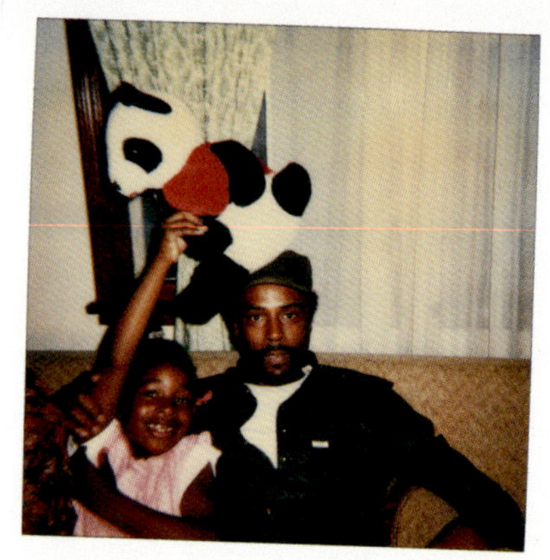

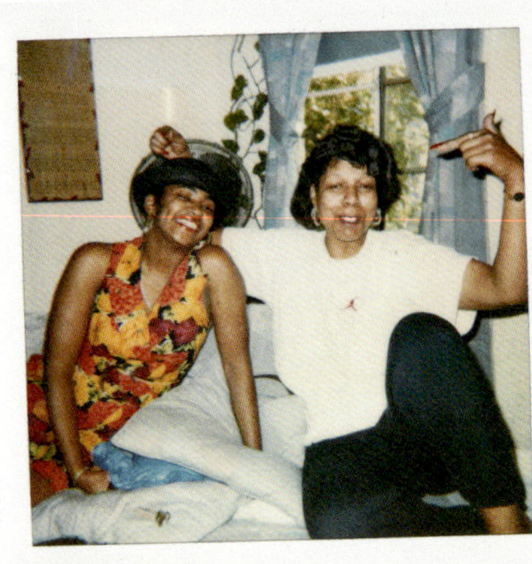

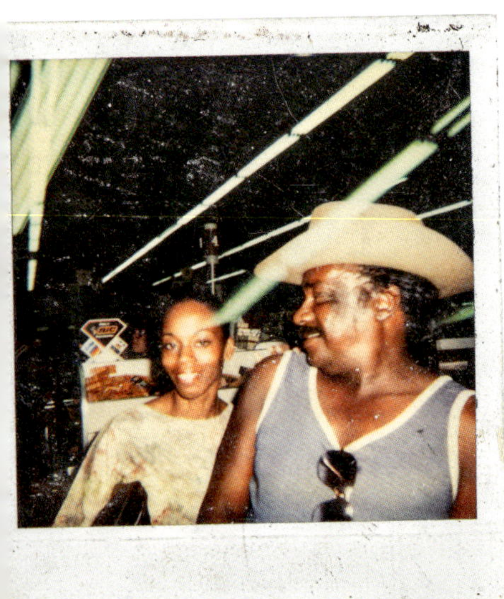

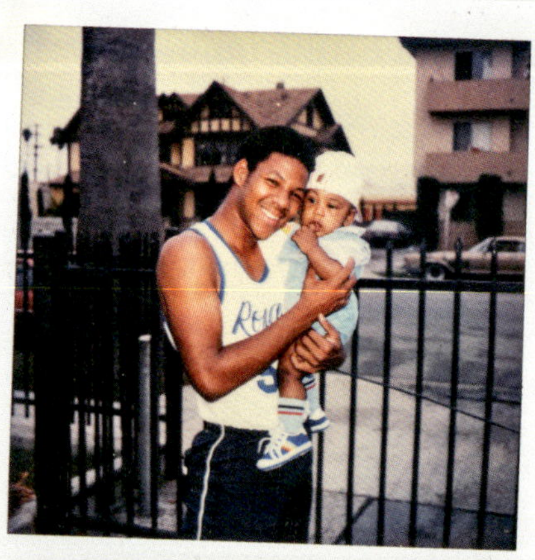

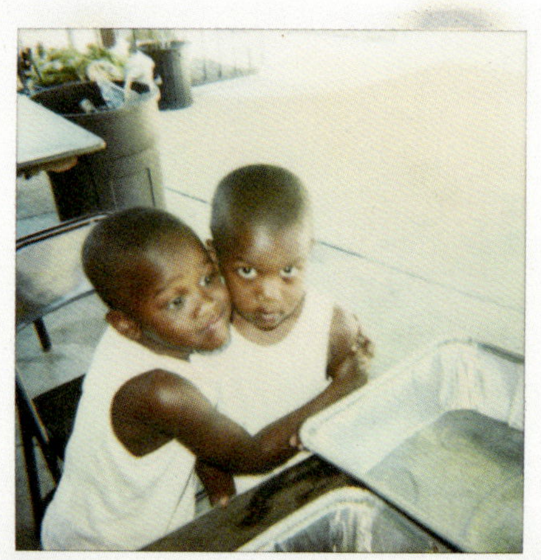

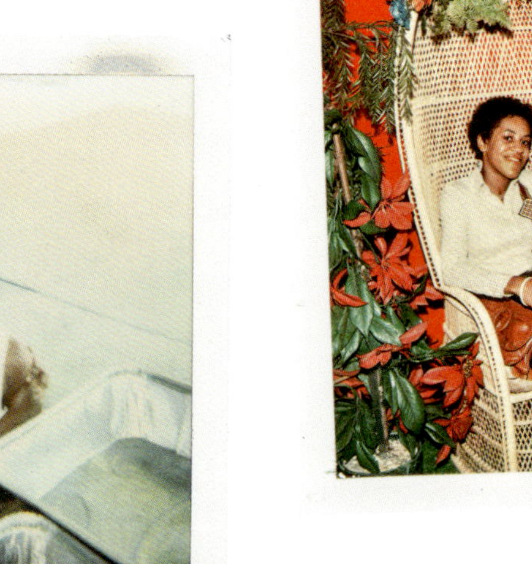

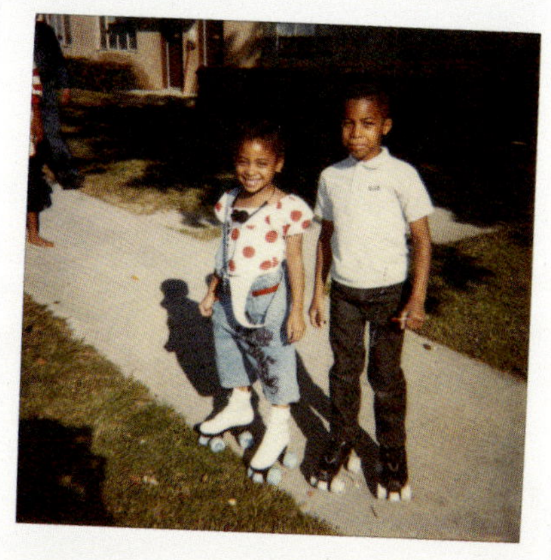

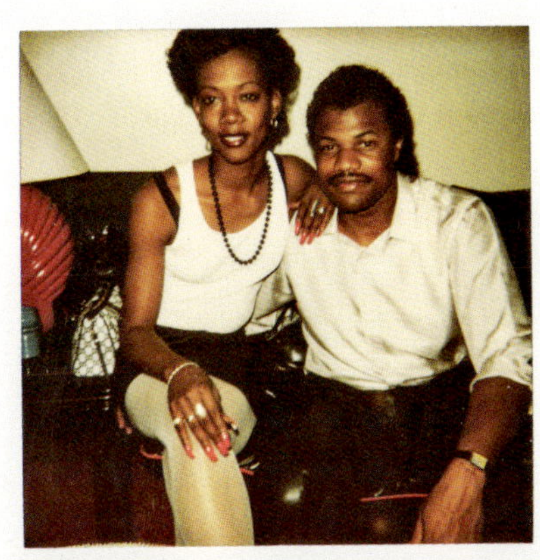

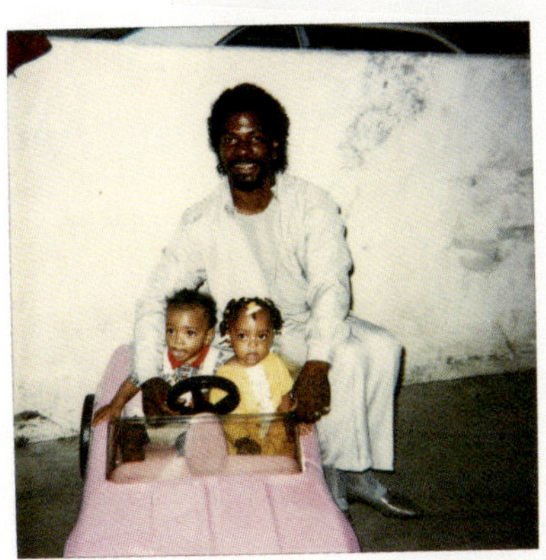

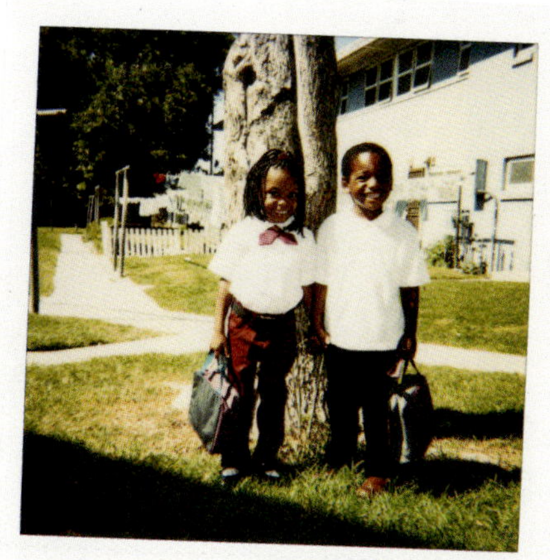

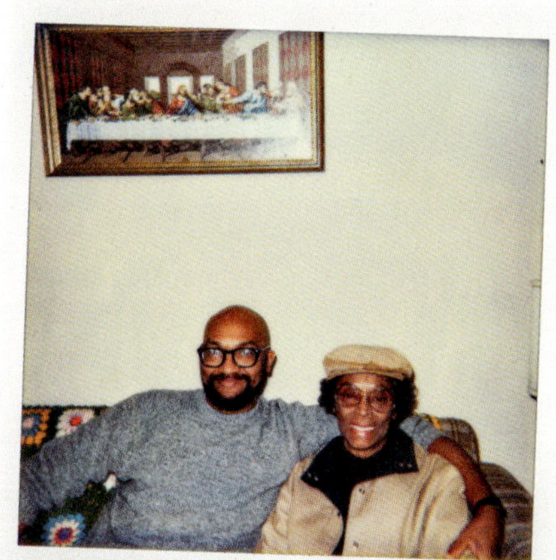

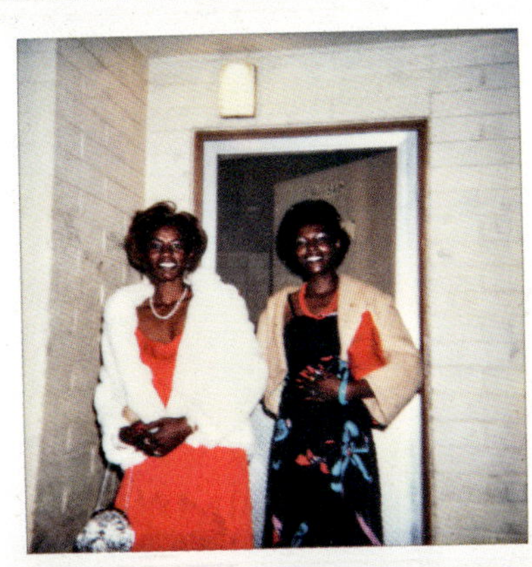

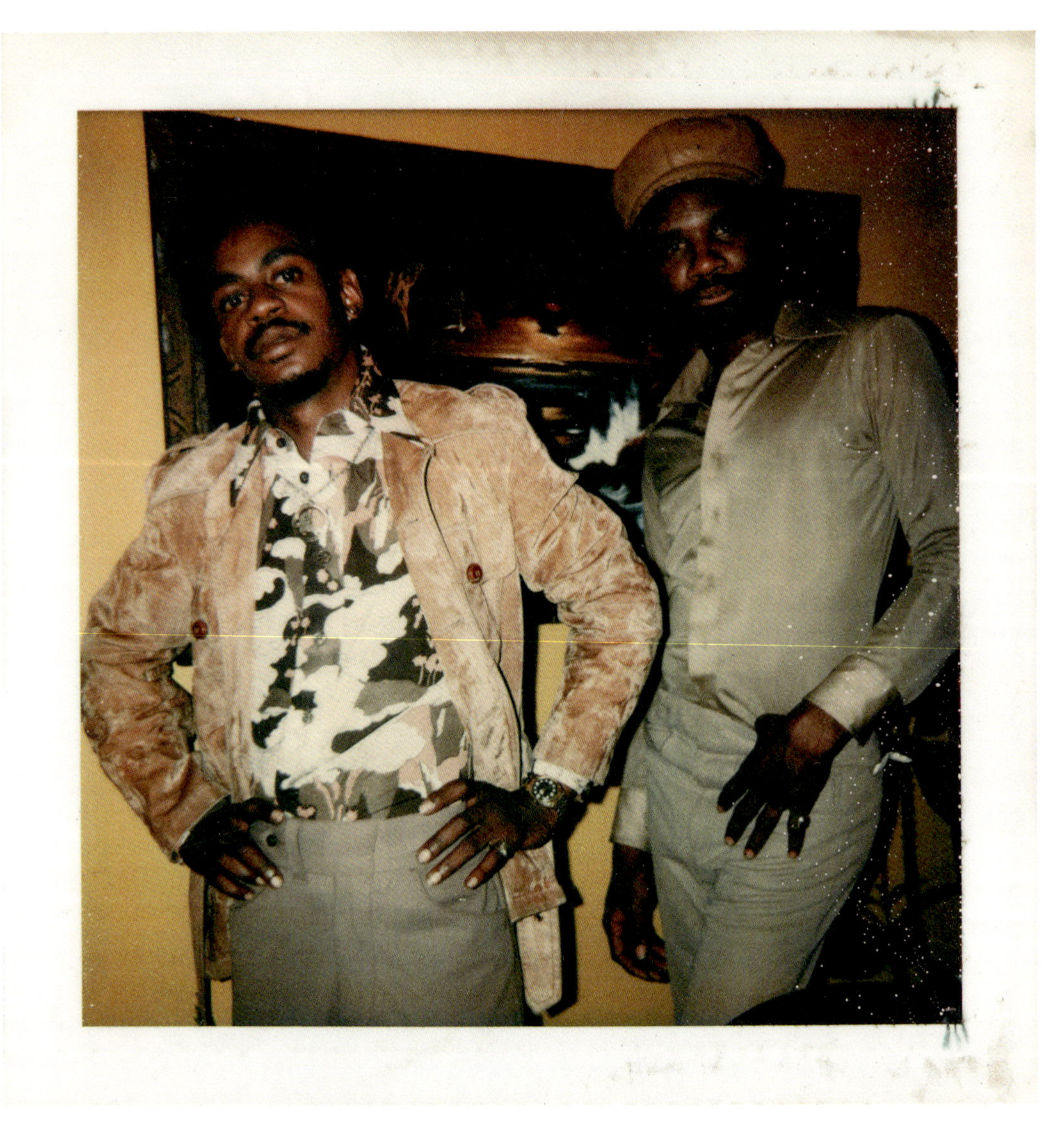

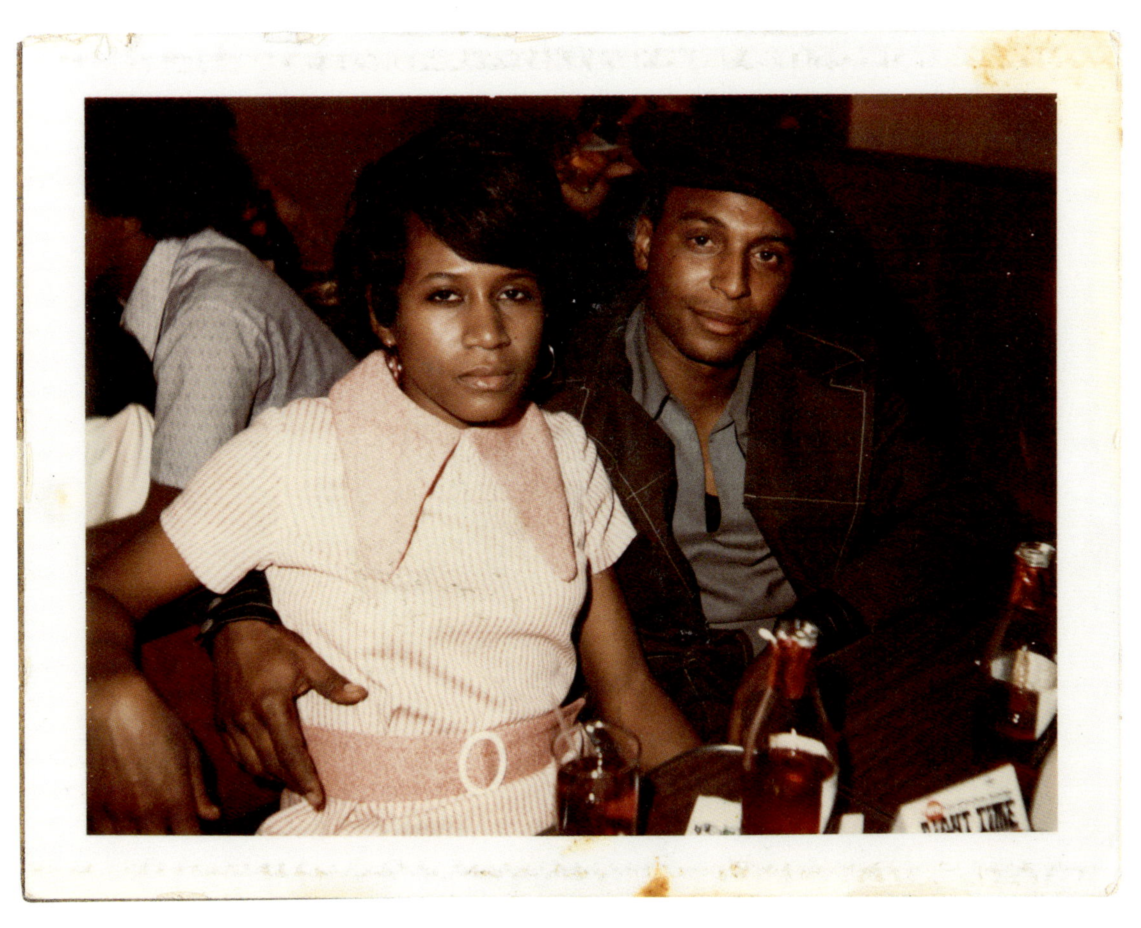

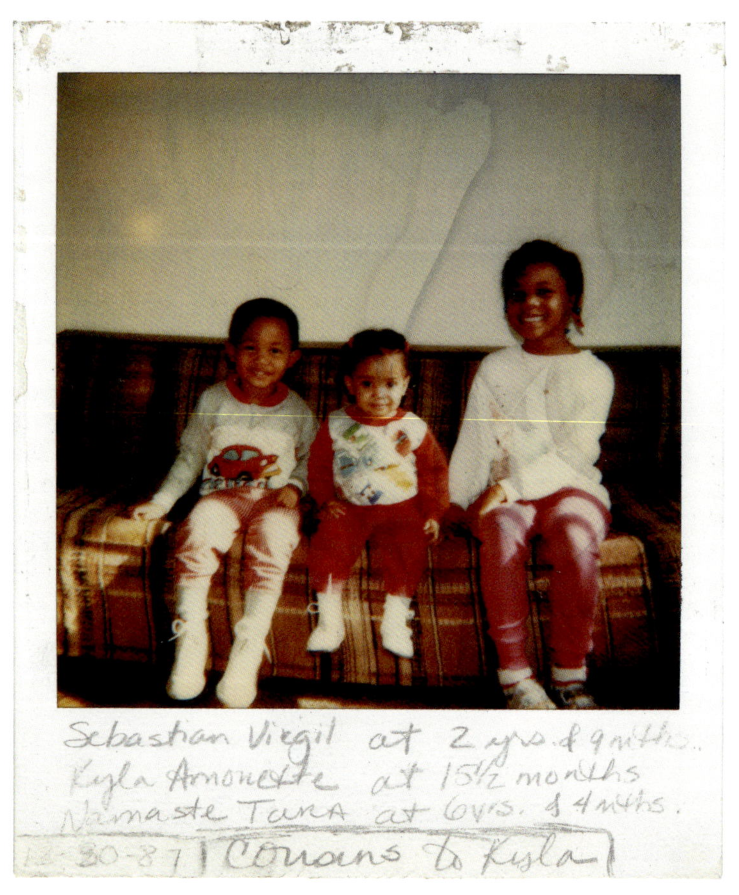

Sebastian Viegil at 2 yrs. & 9 mths.
Kyla Amonette at 15½ months
Namaste Tara at 6 yrs. & 4 mths.
12-30-87 | Cousins to Kyla |

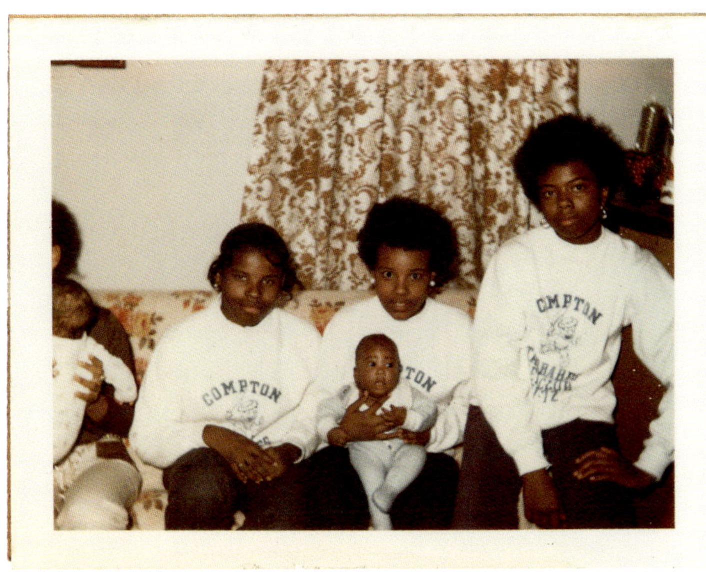

AN ORIGINAL POLAROID® LAND PHOTOGRAPH

SUBJECT_________________________________ DATE 10-15-71

NAME____

ADDRESS____

____

REGULAR SIZE COPIES	
WALLET SIZE COPIES	
5 x 7 ENLARGEMENTS	
8 x 10 ENLARGEMENTS	
35mm SLIDES	

For your convenience
when ordering copies,
indicate the number of
copies desired in the
appropriate box for the
size(s) you select.

P558A-1 5/70

Printed in U.S.A.

2018/756

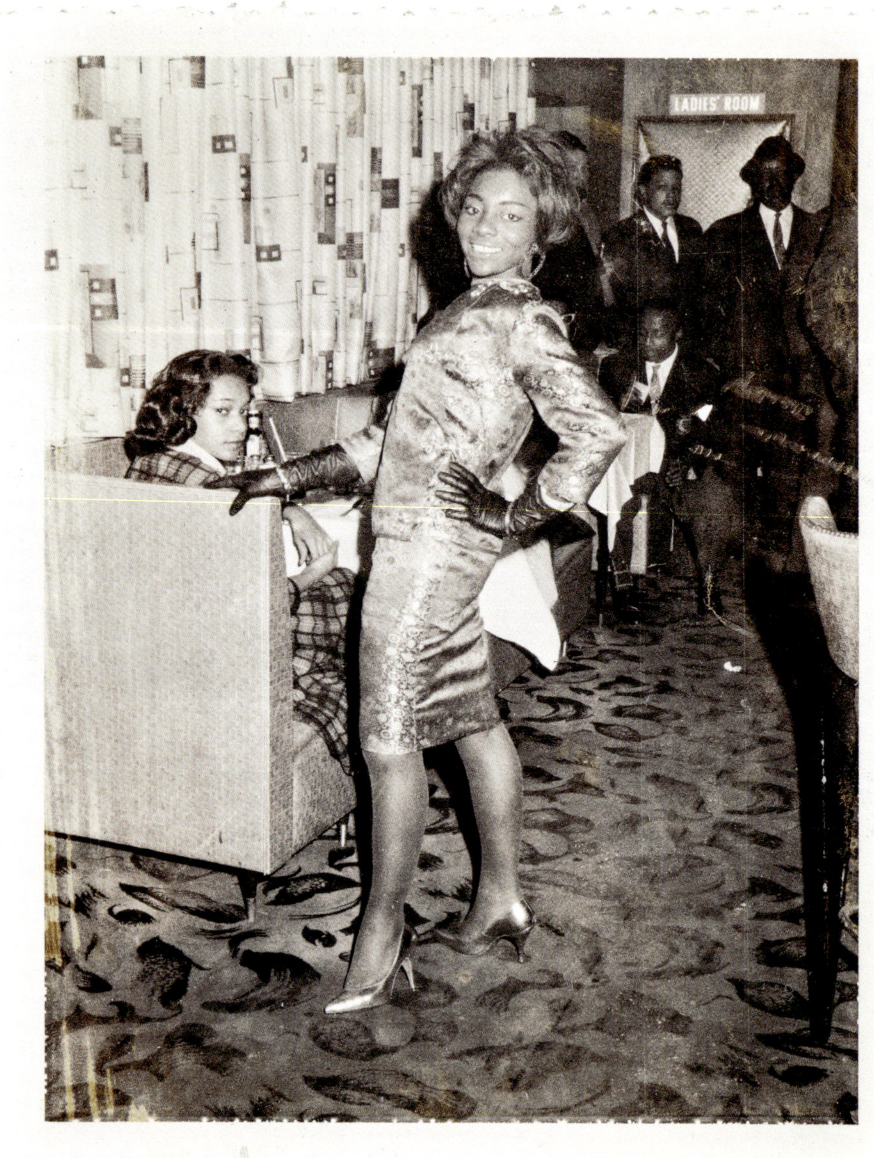
LADIES' ROOM

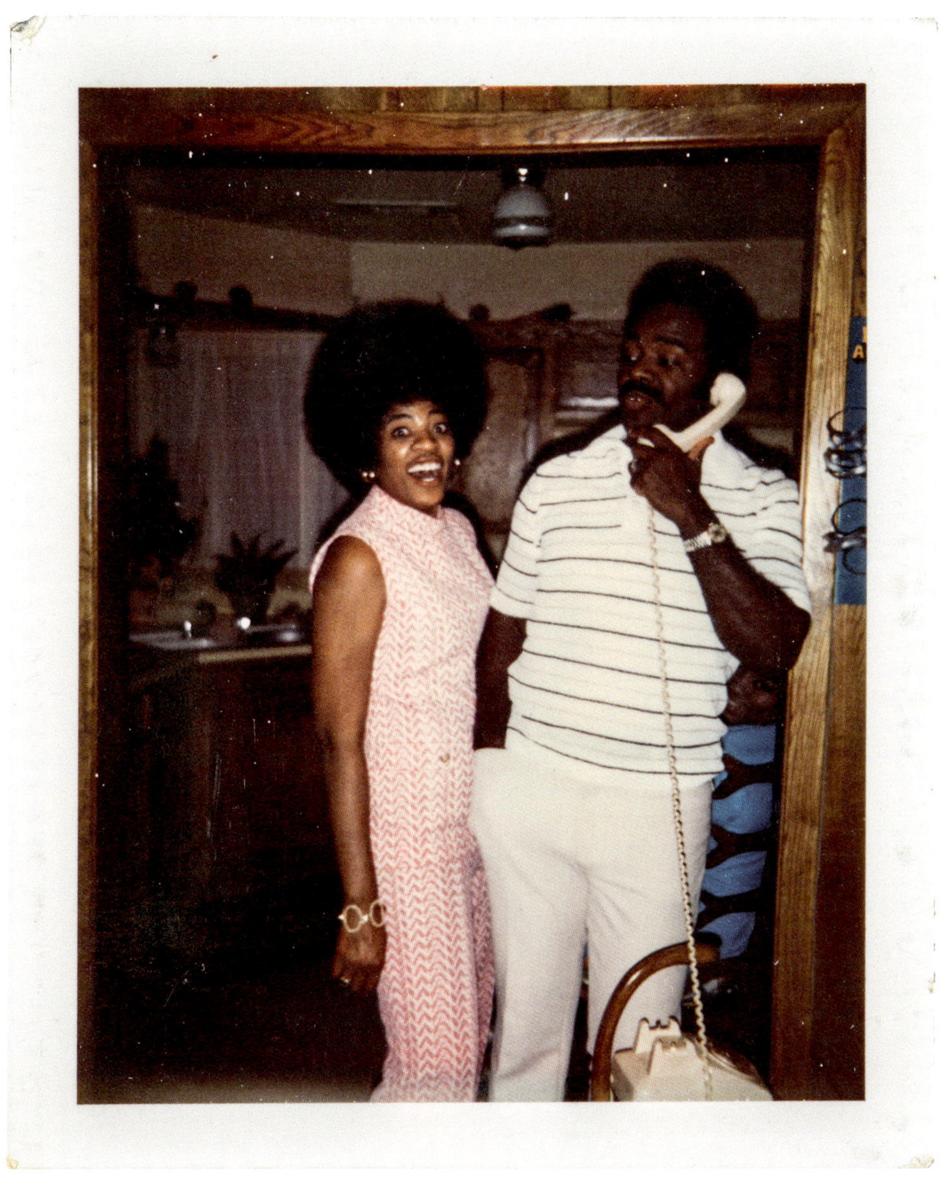

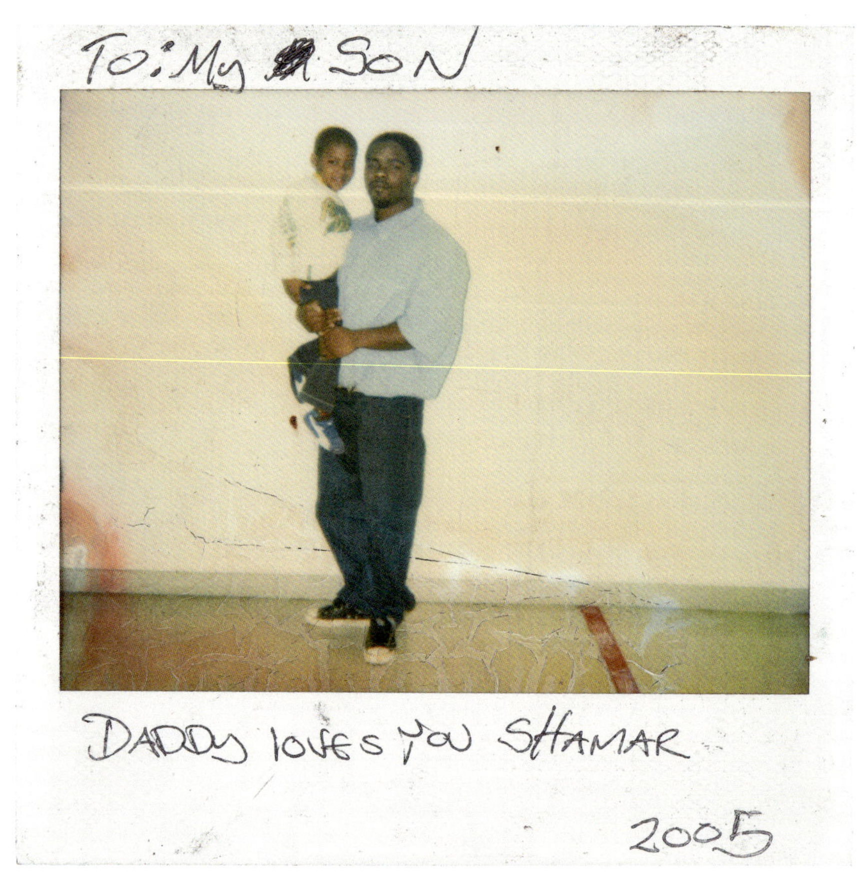

To: My SON
DADDy loves you SHAMAR
2005

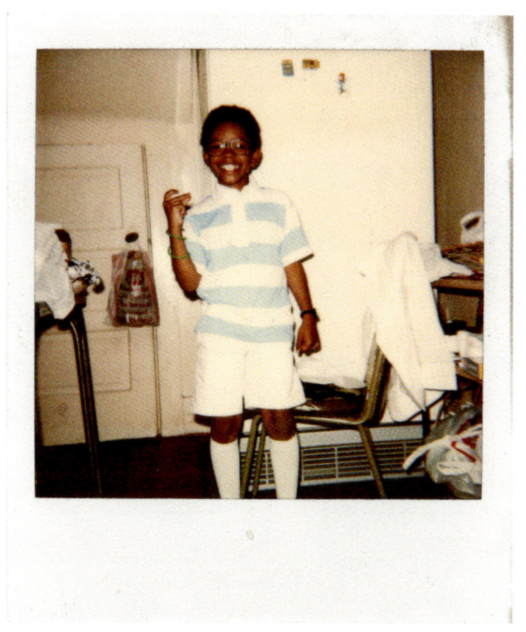

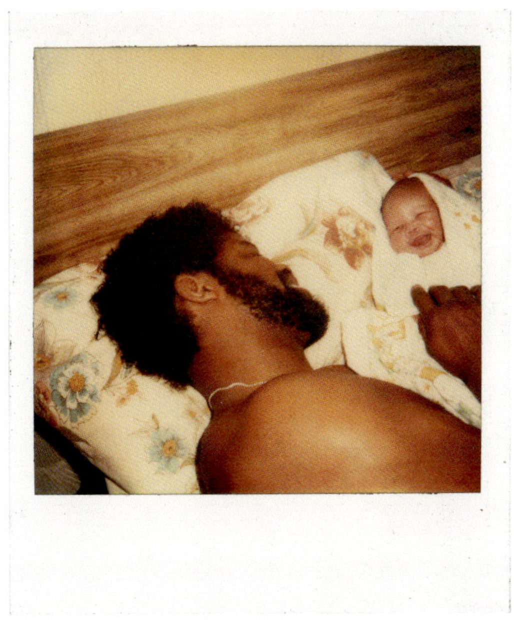

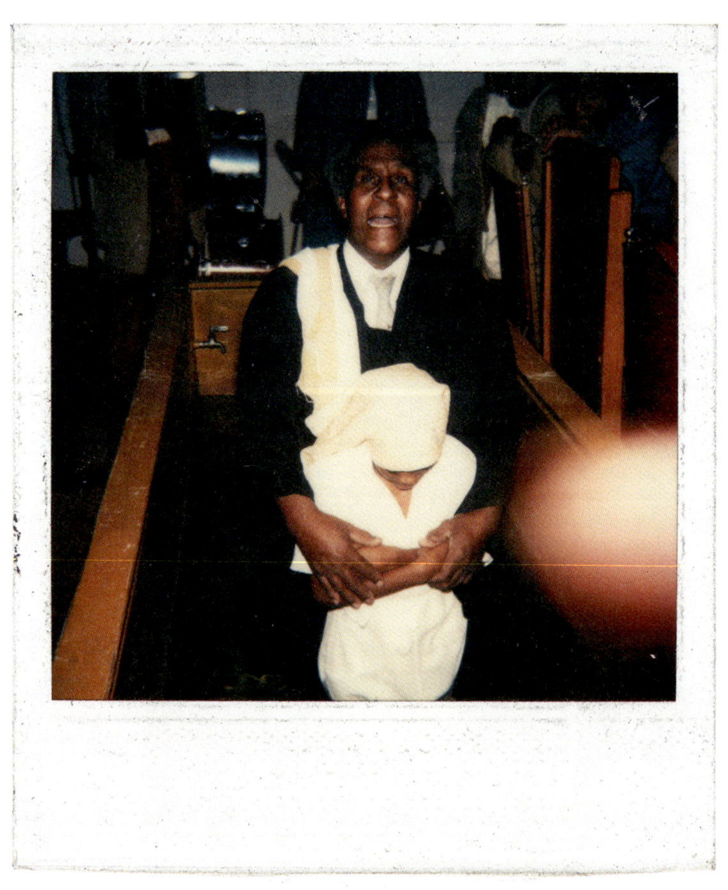

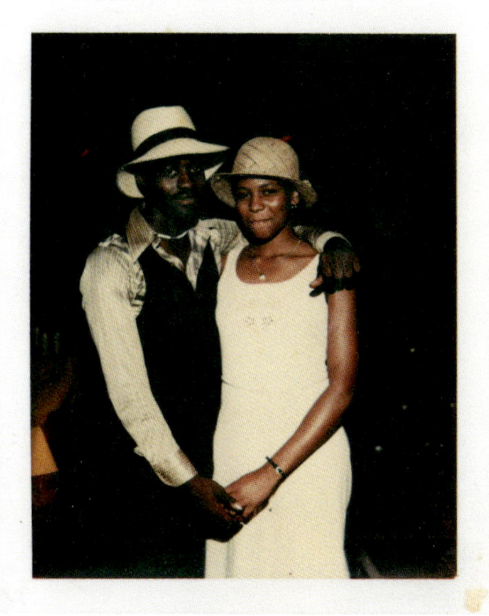

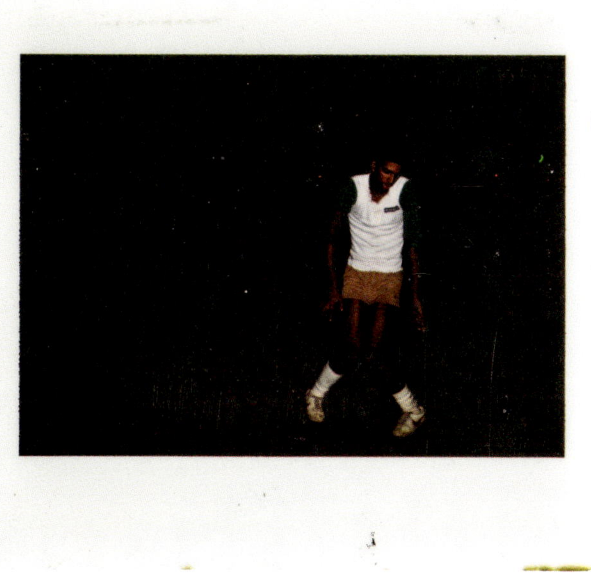

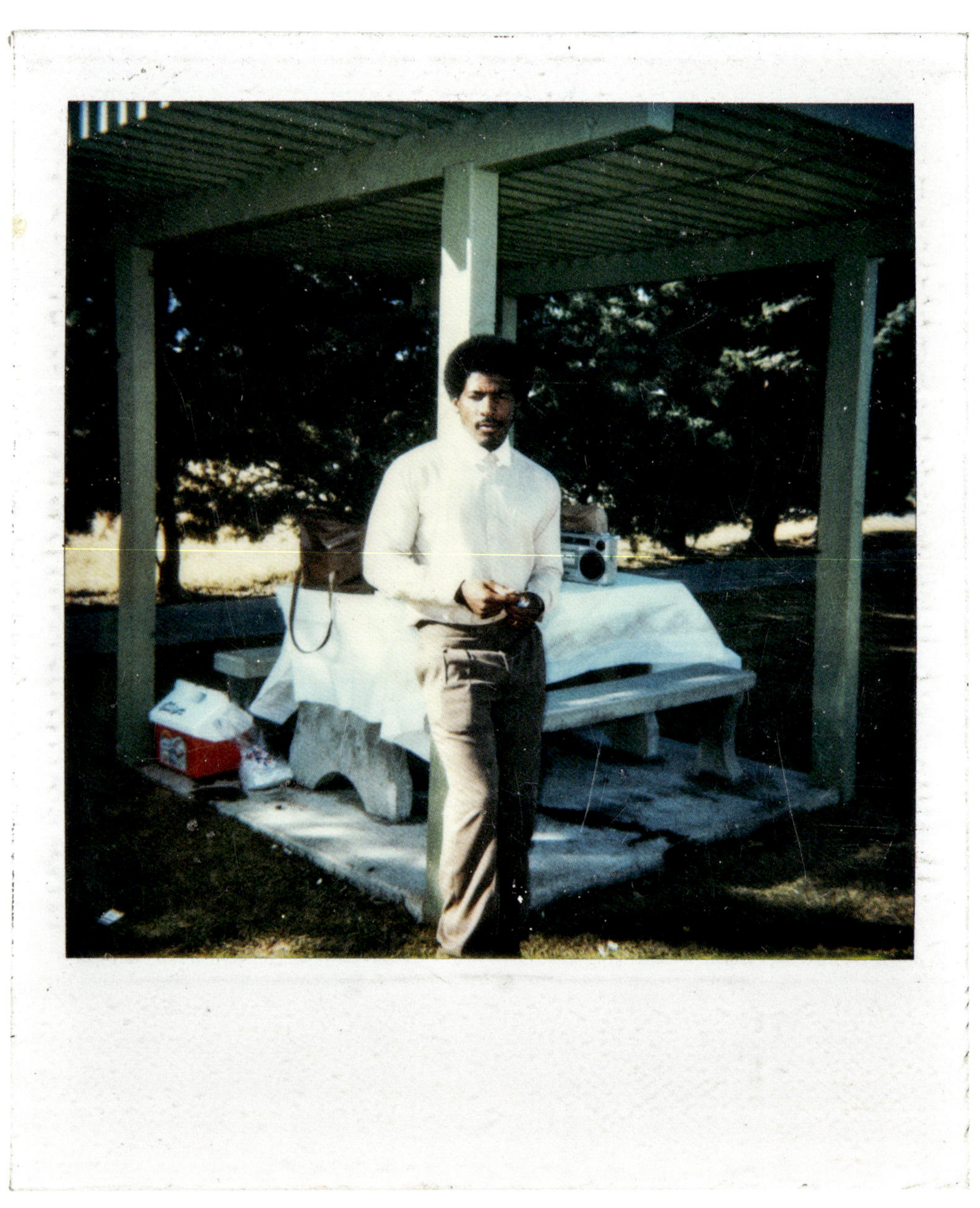

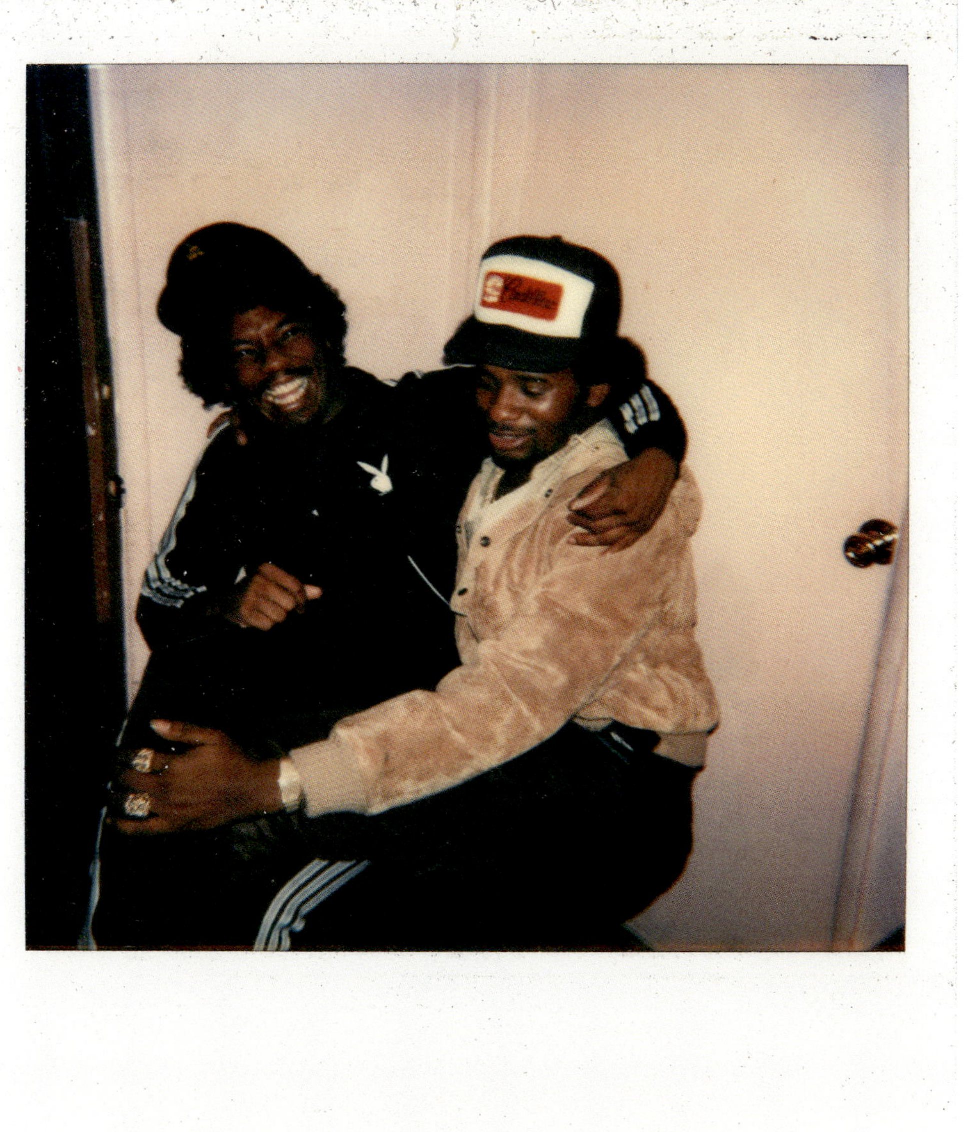

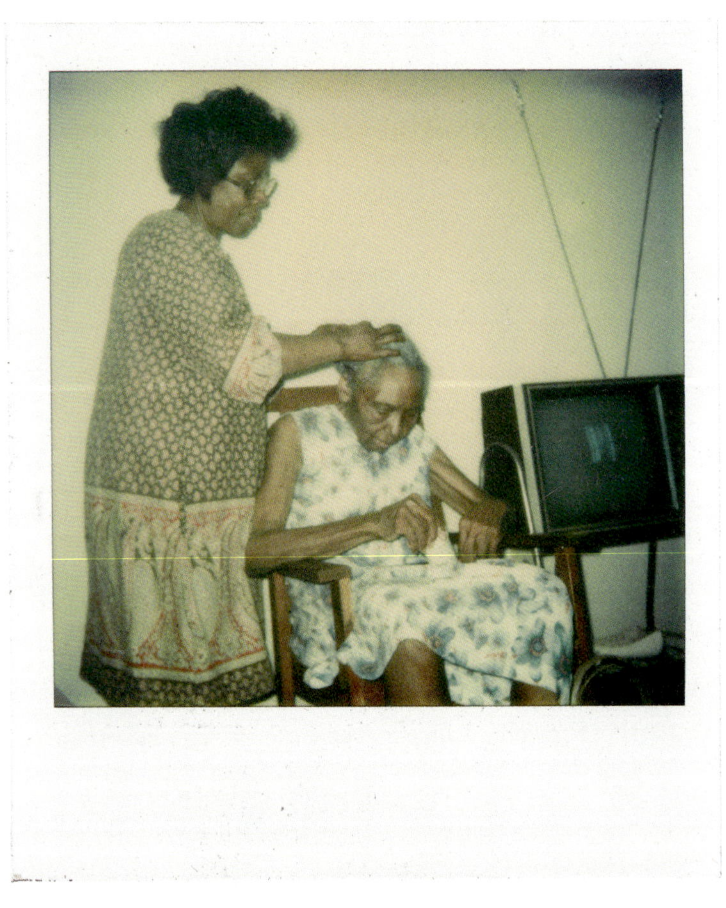

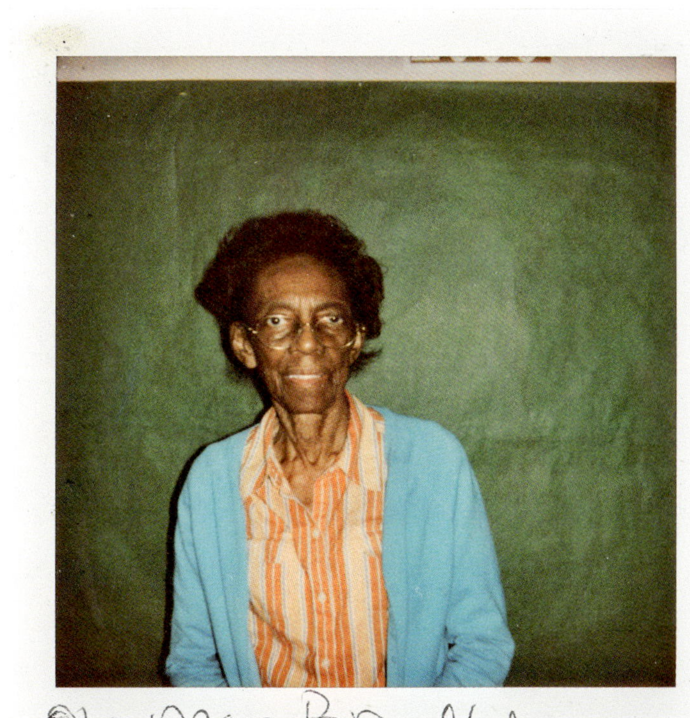

Ola Mae Bradly
"what did you say darling"

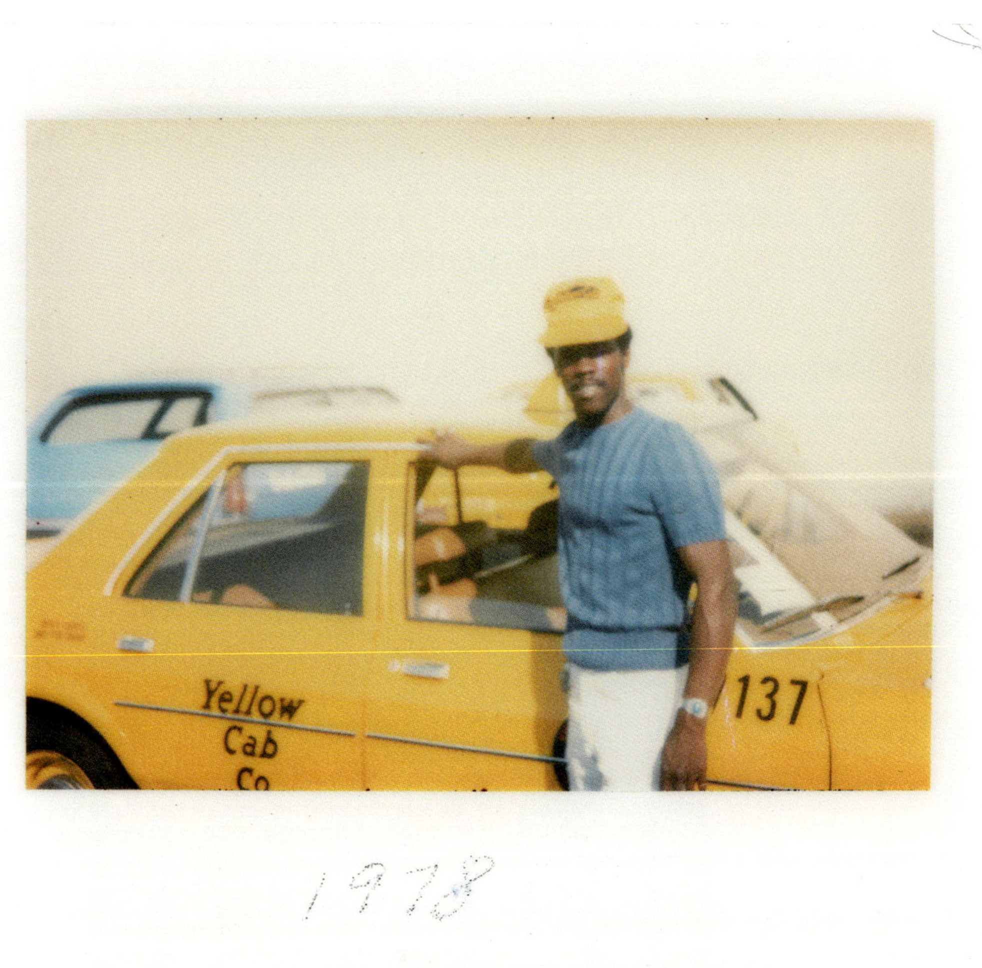

Yellow
Cab
Co
137
1978

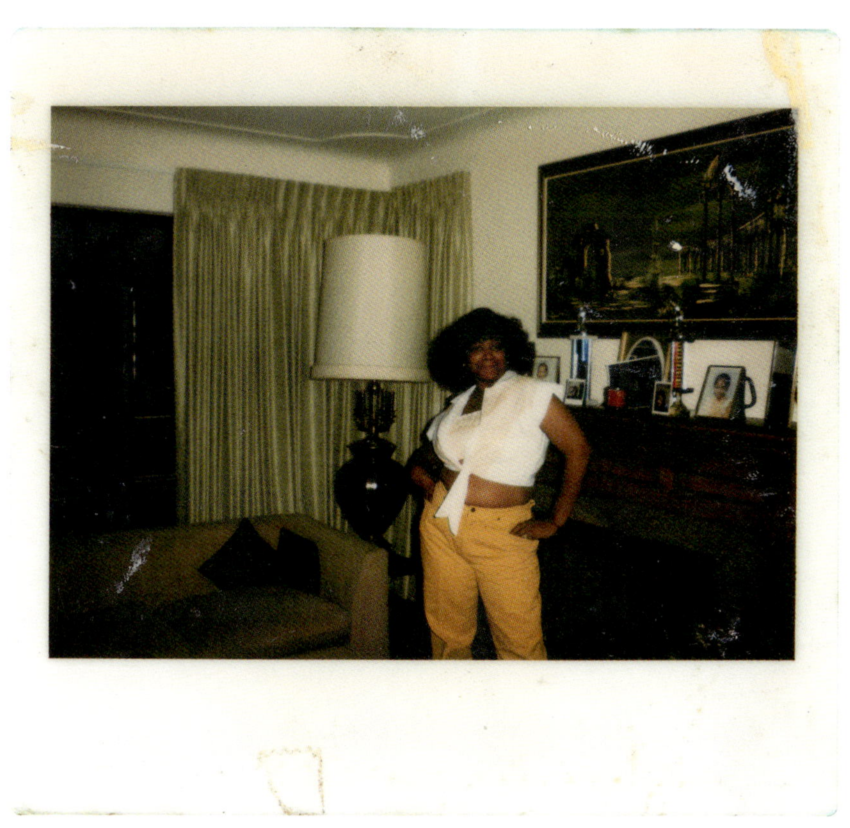

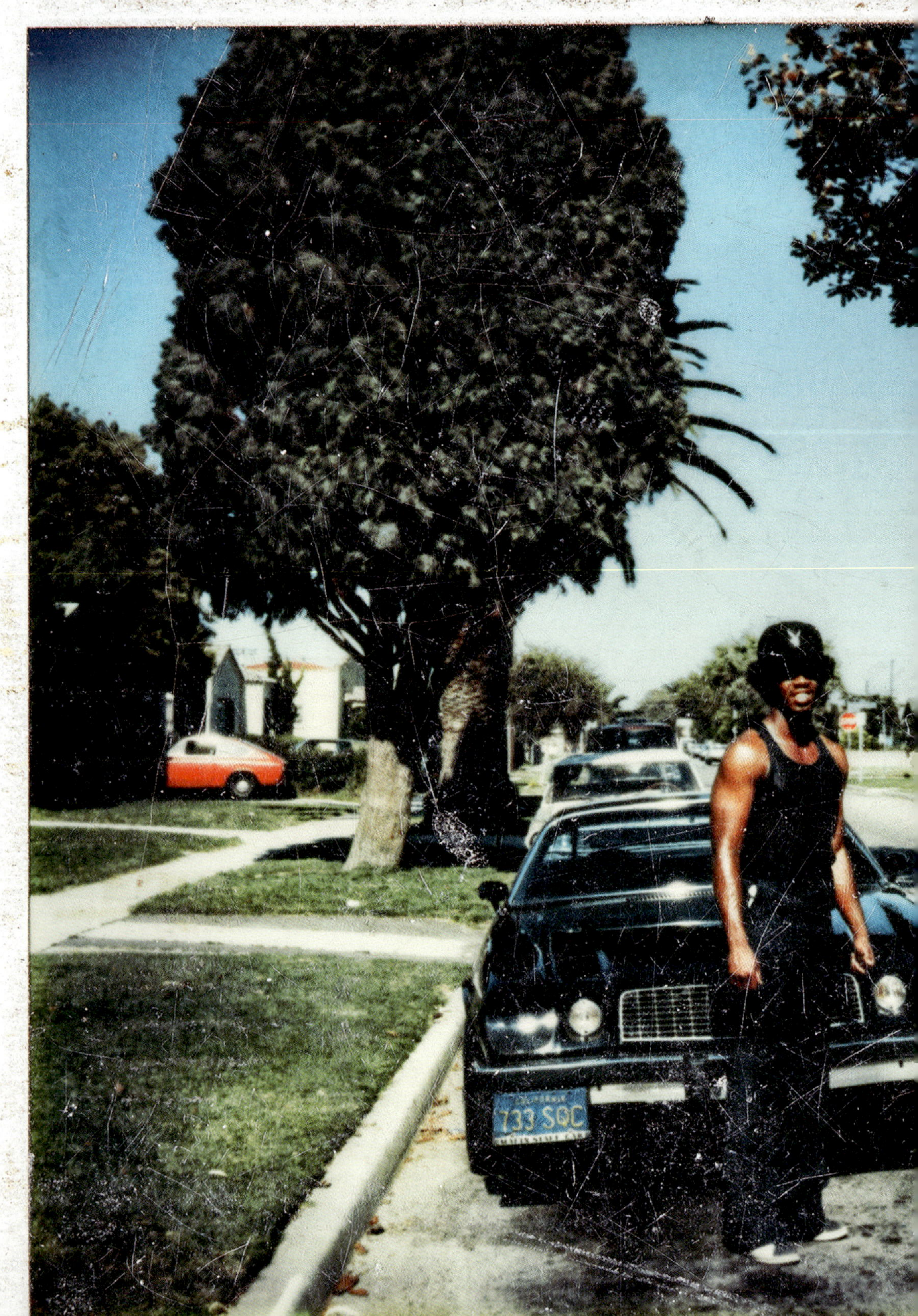

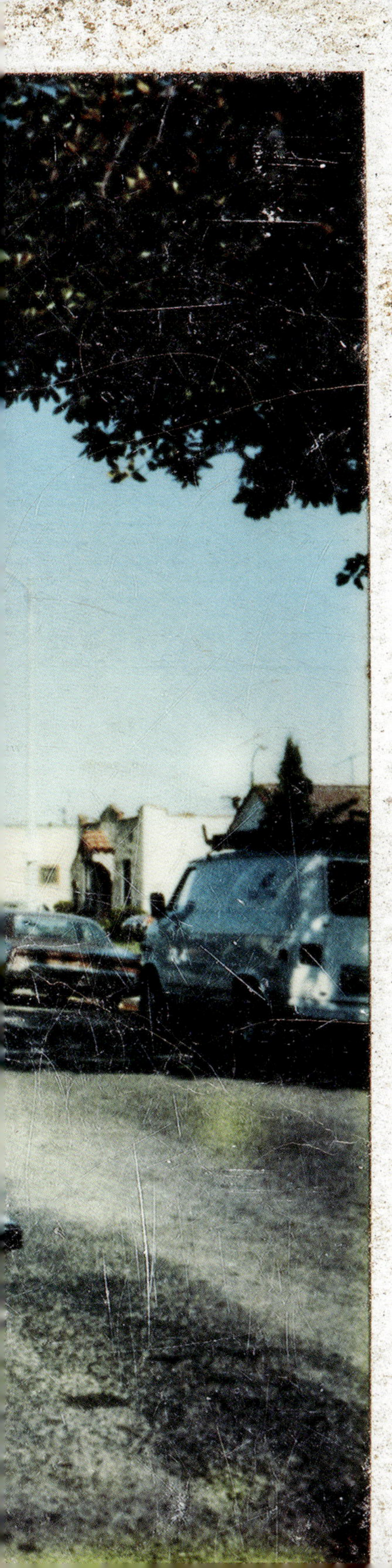

Photographs of Black Life

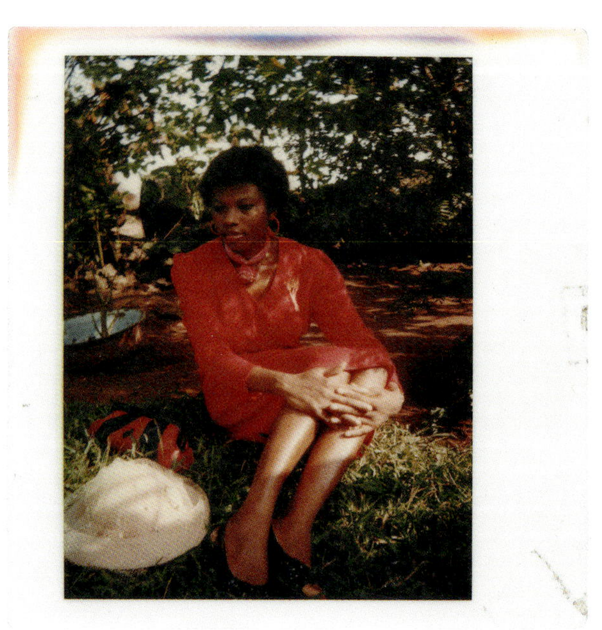

Monique just knowing she is so damn fine against red Beamer. Somebody's momma's purse like a weapon. Little crib babies not caring. Swift in swag. Hats. Those collars. White-walled tires. Penchant for protection, arms woven into cloth, how we do, a sign, a signal singing, no strain at all. If a photo is music, so tenderly it hums. If there is a "freedom" place inside Sylvia Wynter's "near total alienation," feel it now. Hang your hat on your hanging hands. Where the sun don't shine, it obliterates. Supposition: fractal. My hirsute maker, my subjectitude. We are not strangers in this strange land.

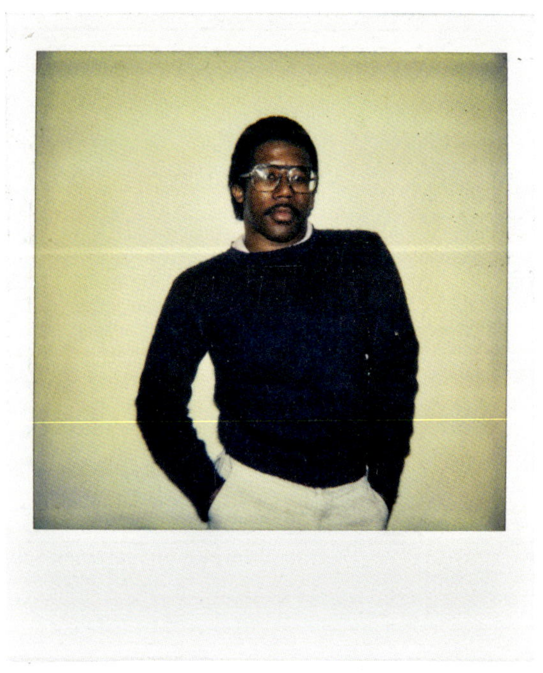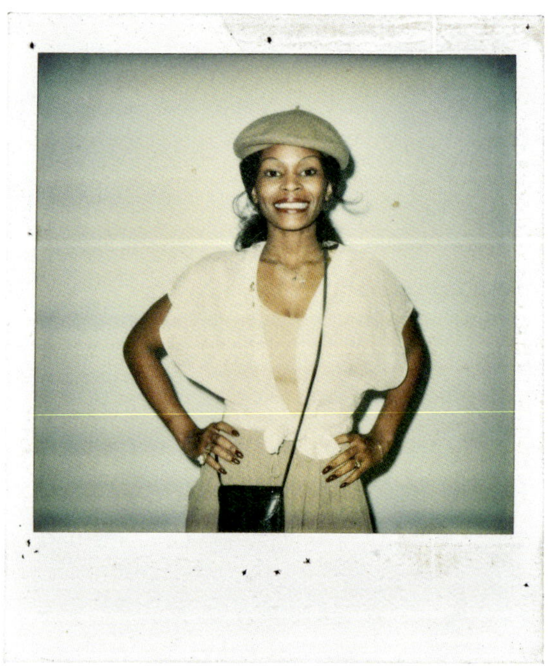

Photographs of Black Life

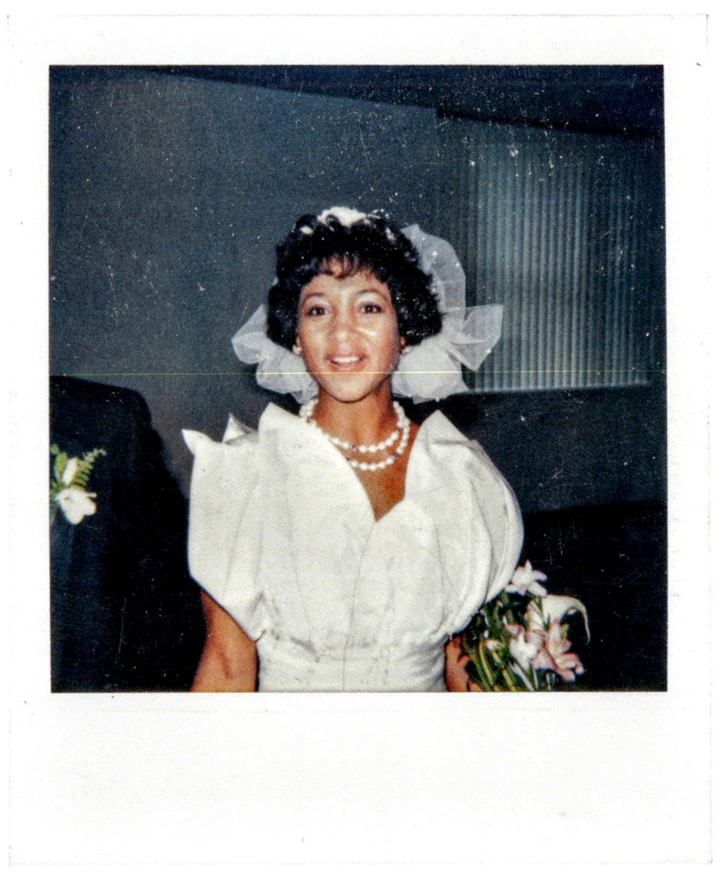

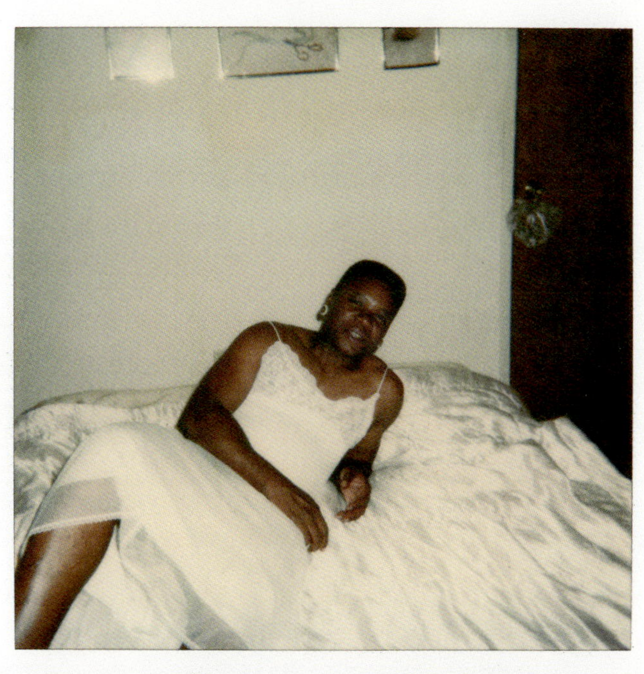

Photographs of Black Life

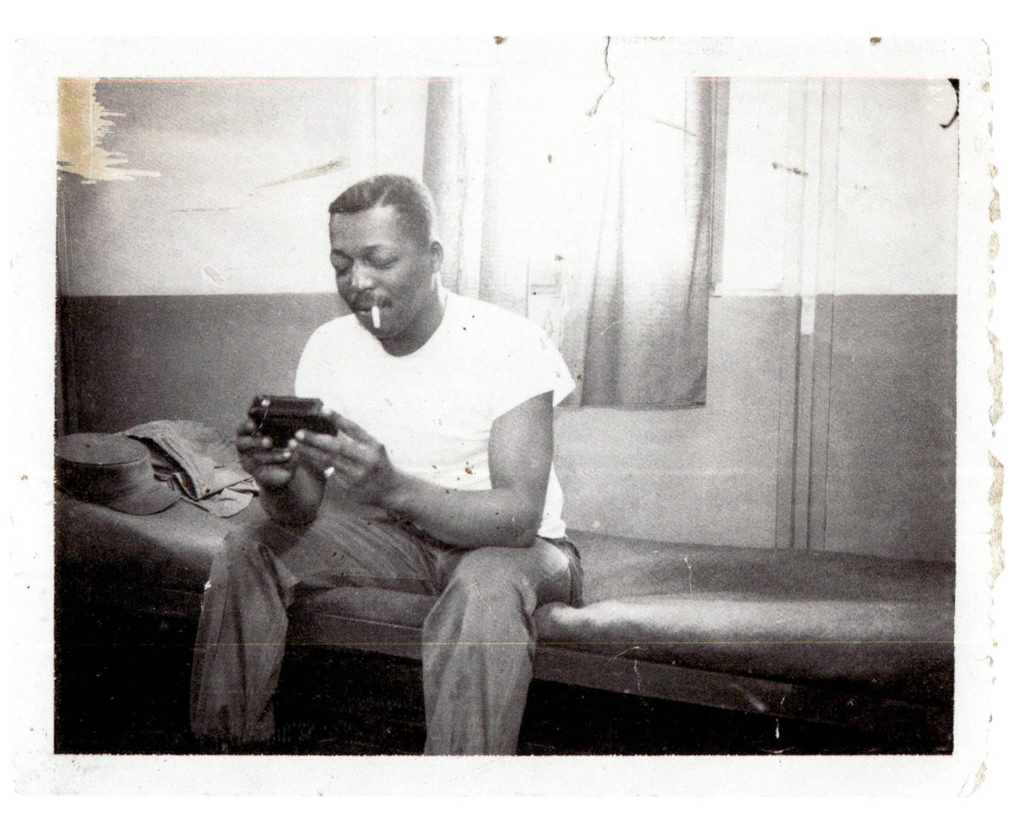

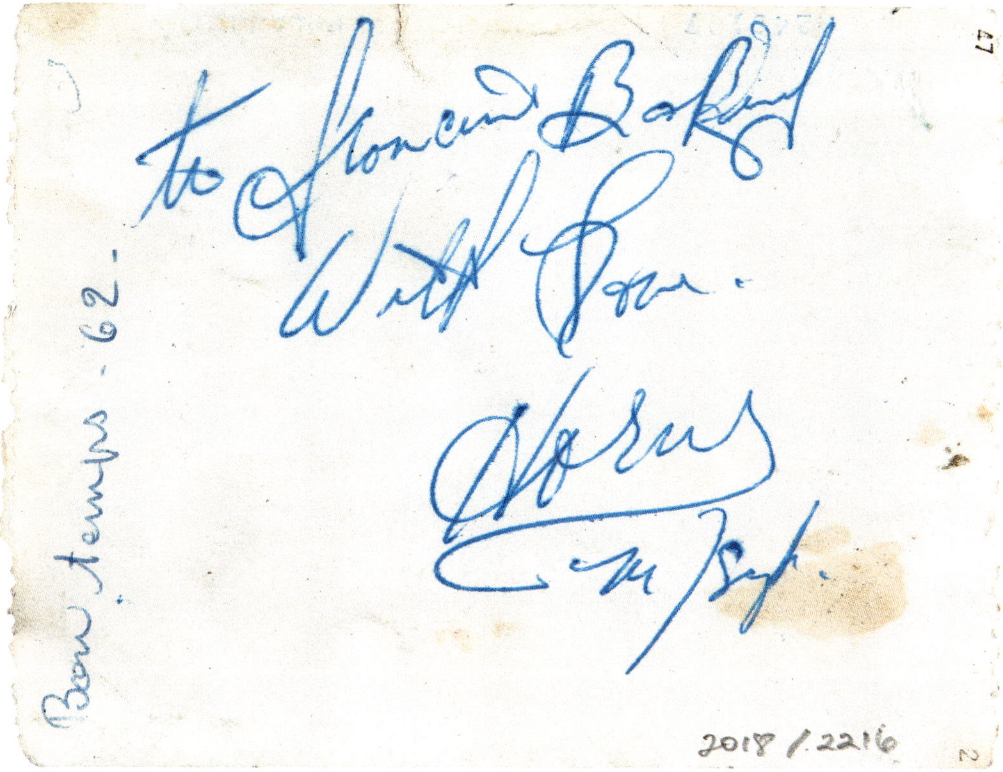

Bon temps - 62 -

To Florence Bakford
With Love -

2018 / 2216

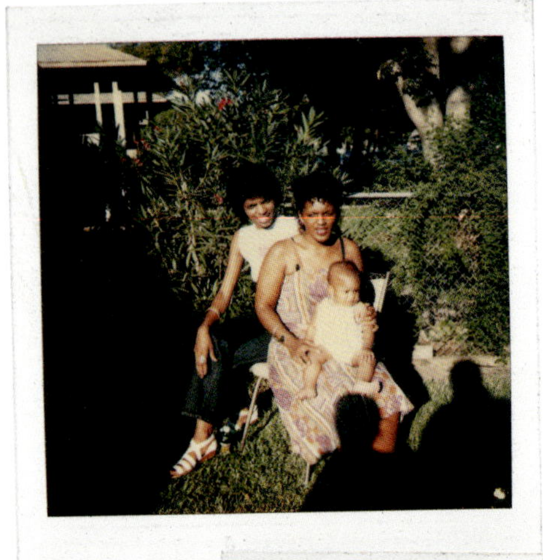

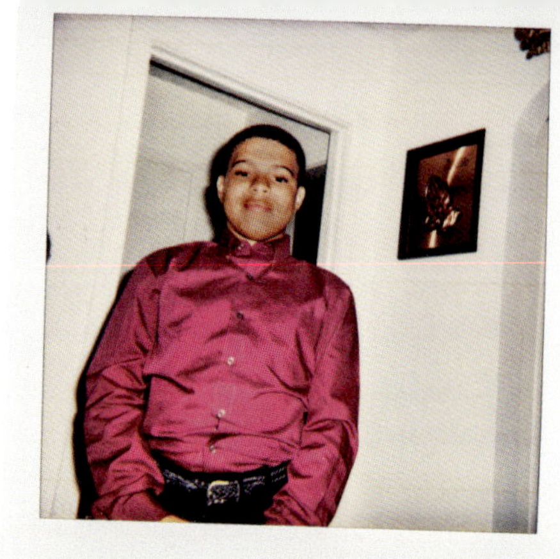

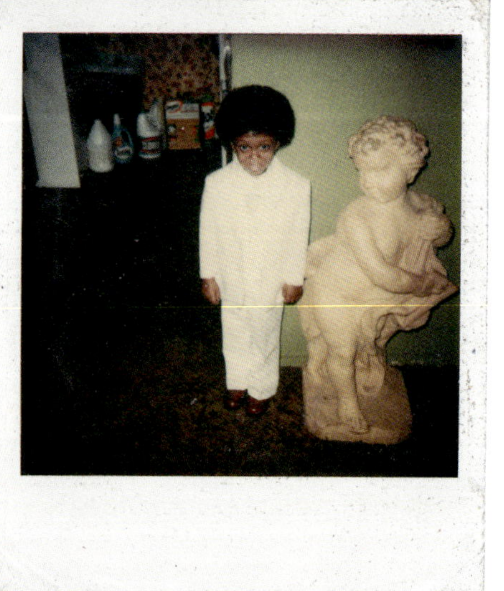

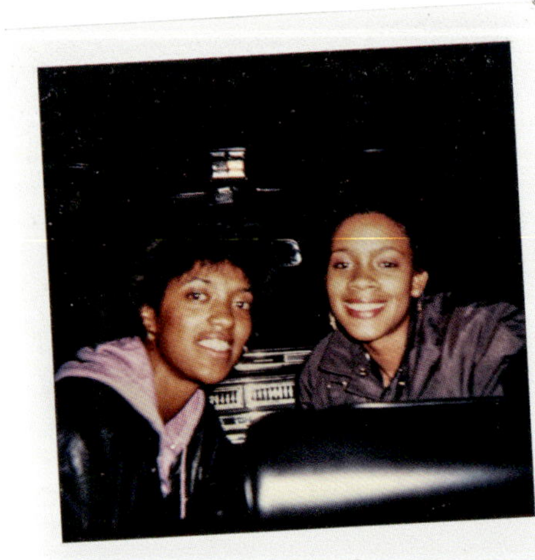

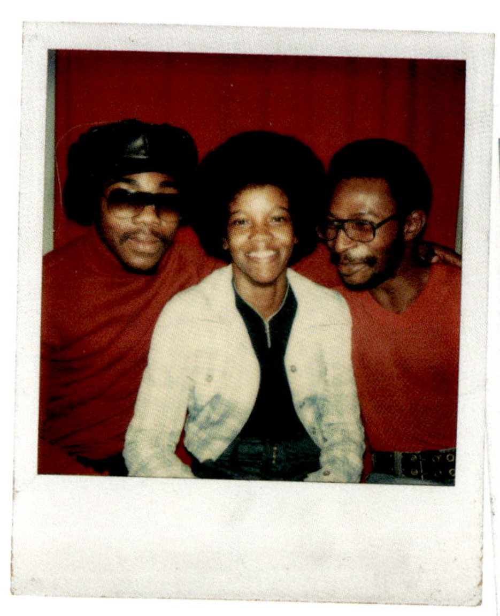

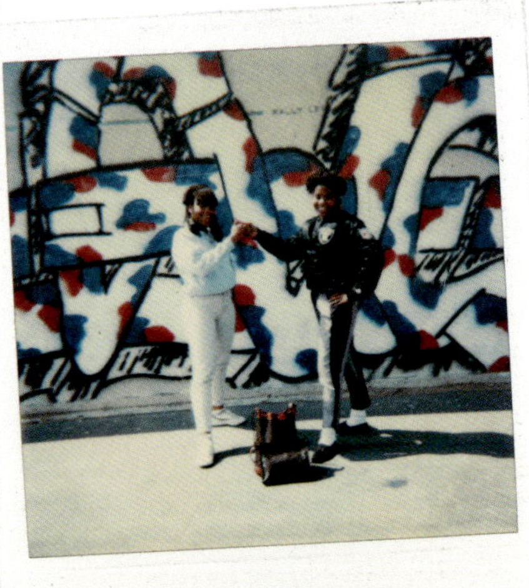

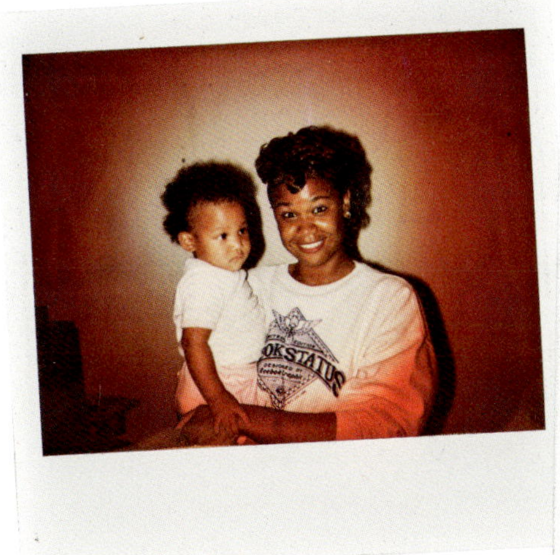
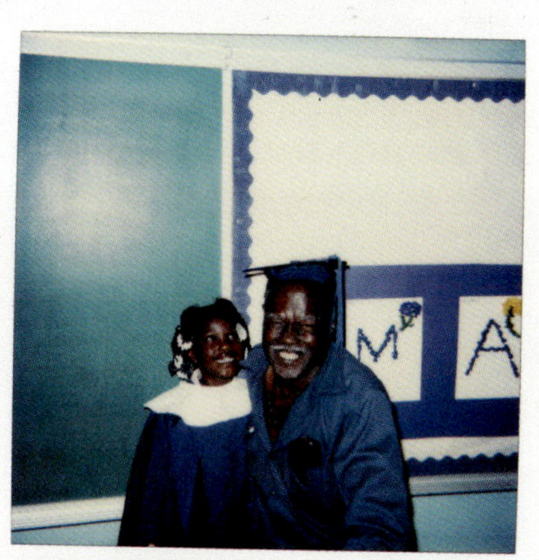
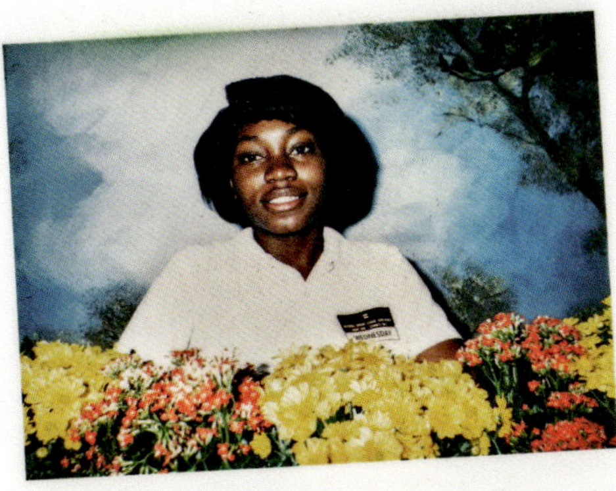
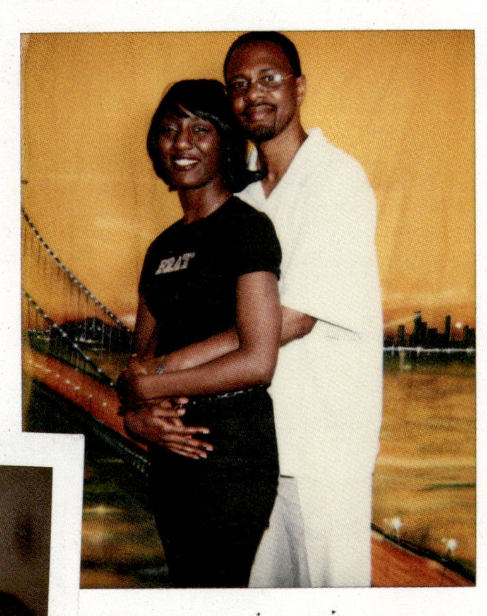

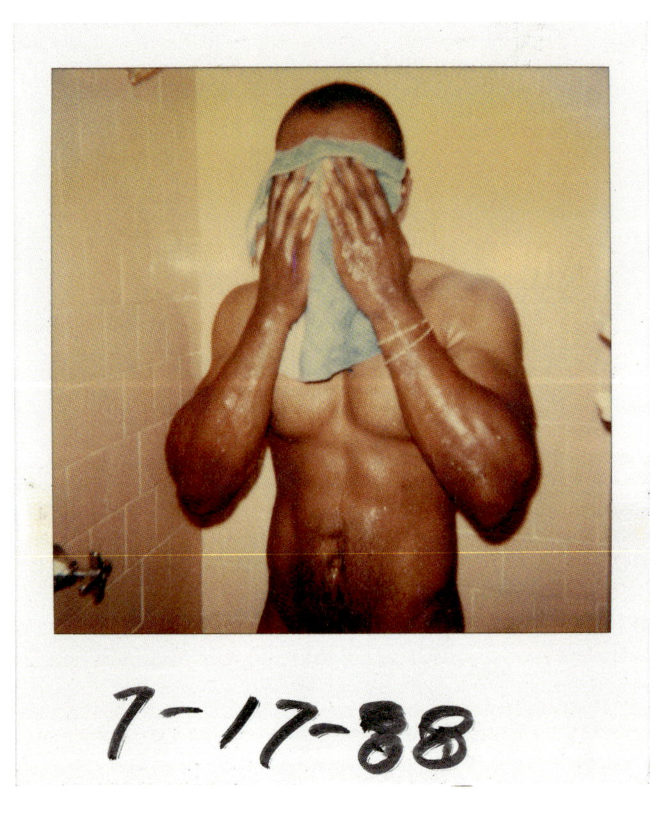

7-17-88

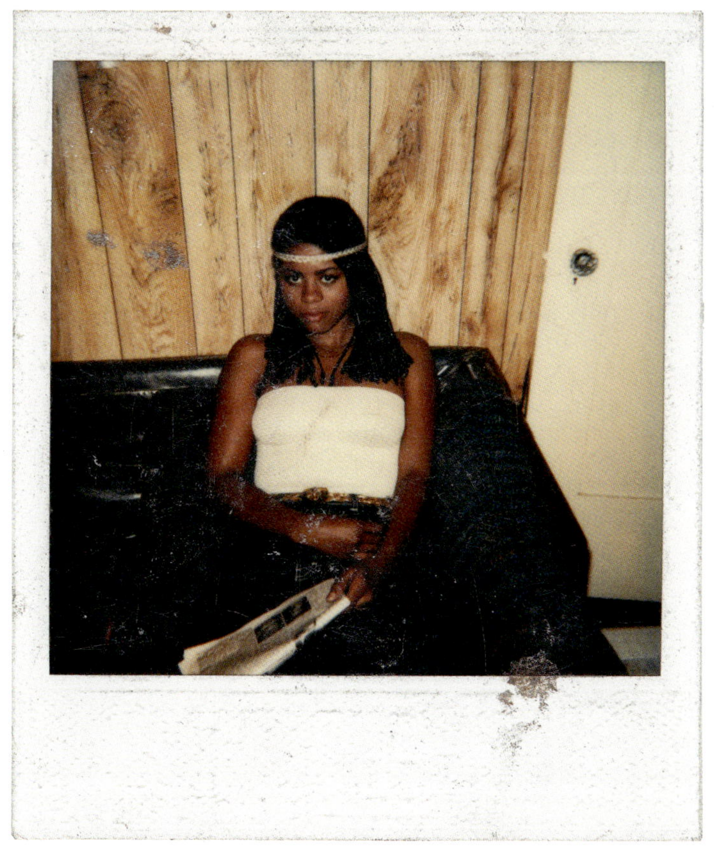

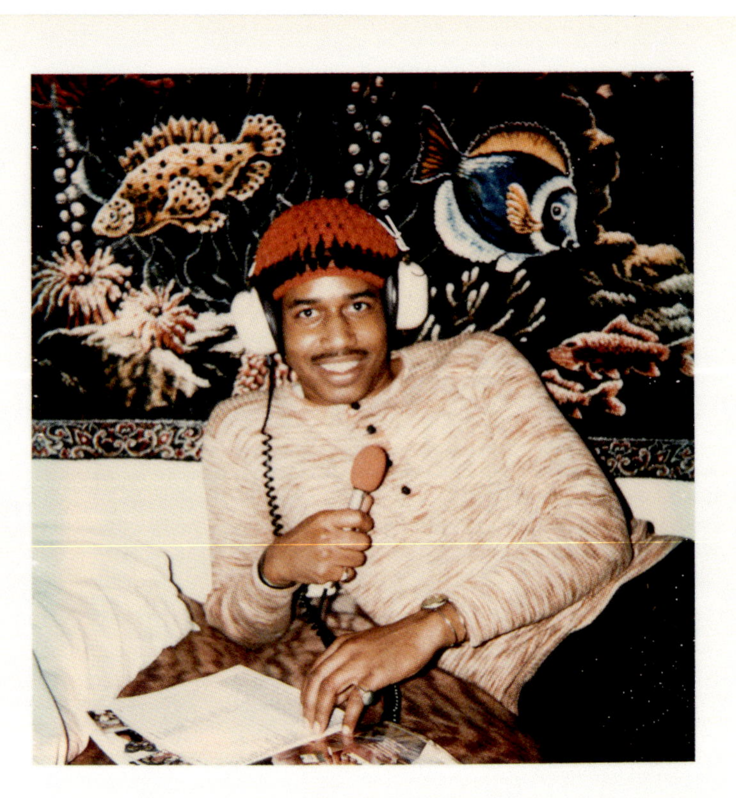

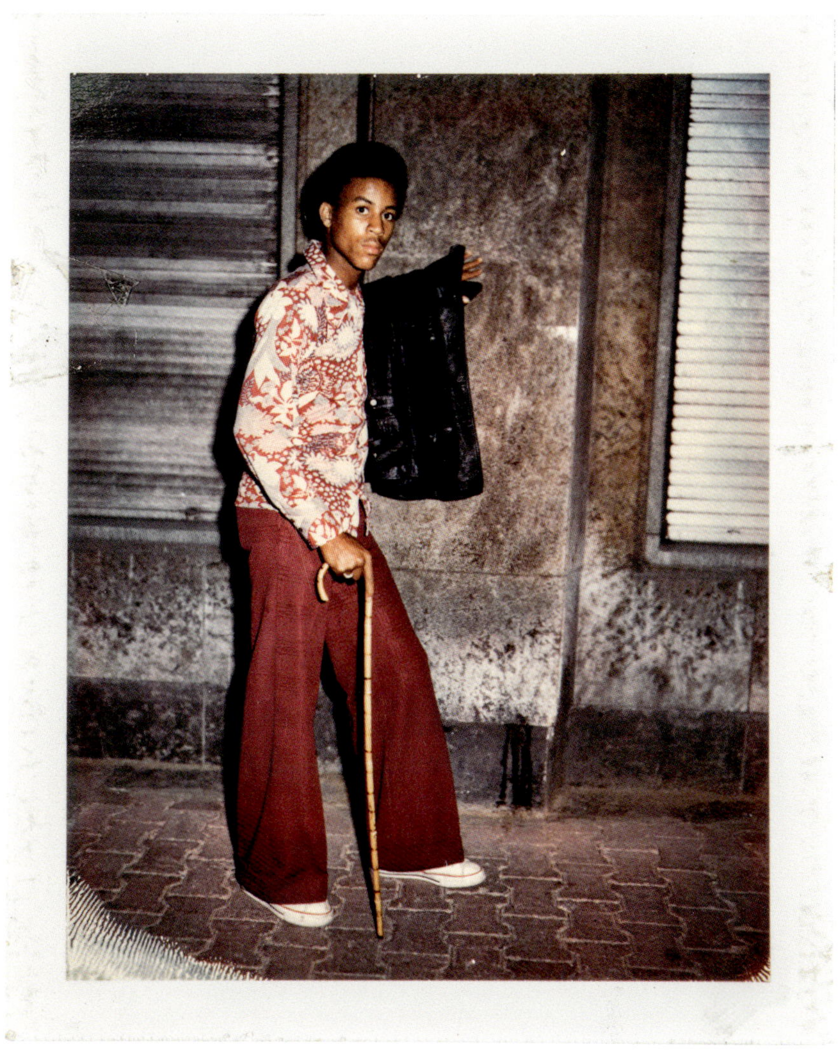

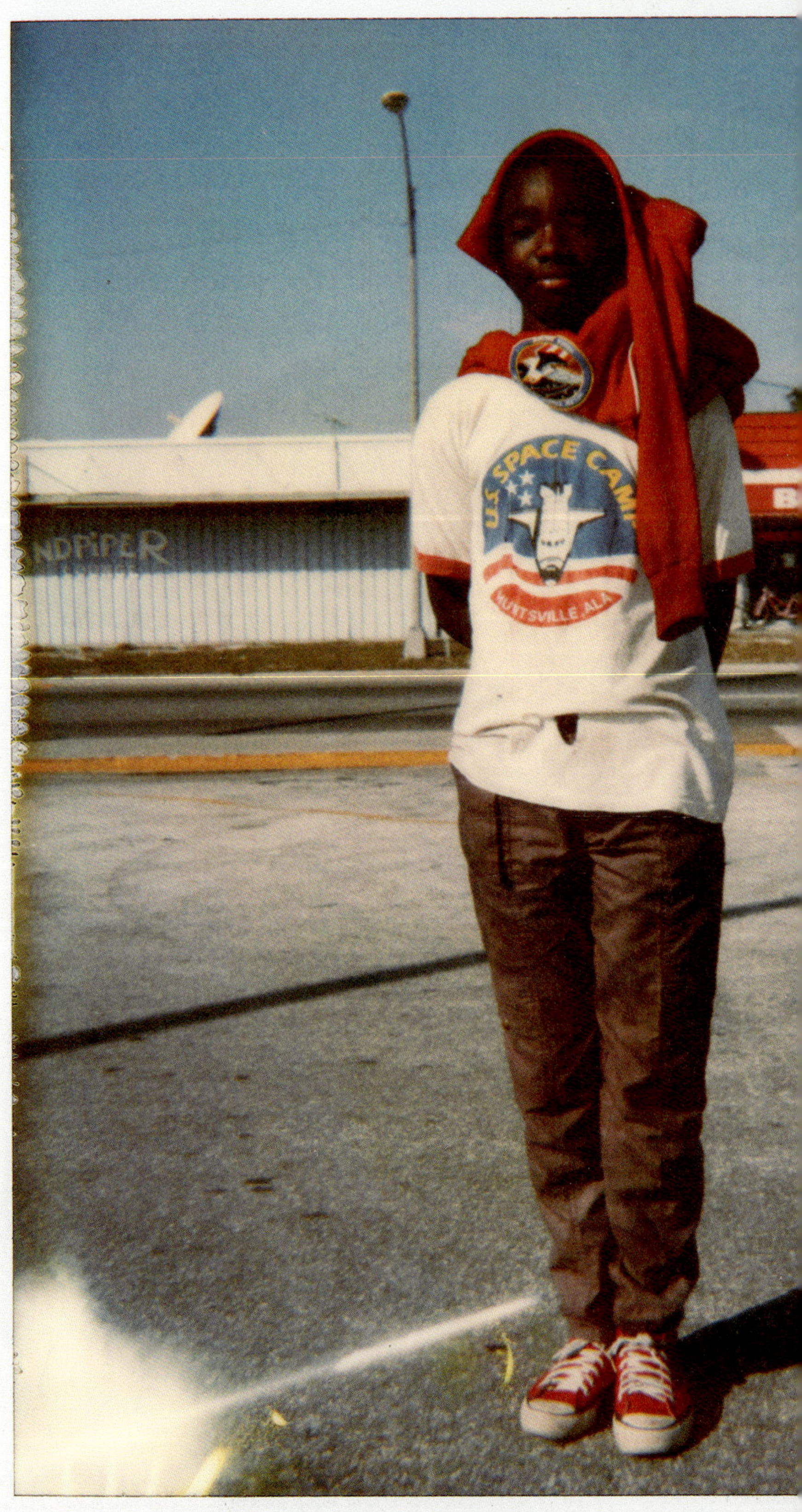

NDPIPER
U.S. SPACE CAMP
HUNTSVILLE, ALA

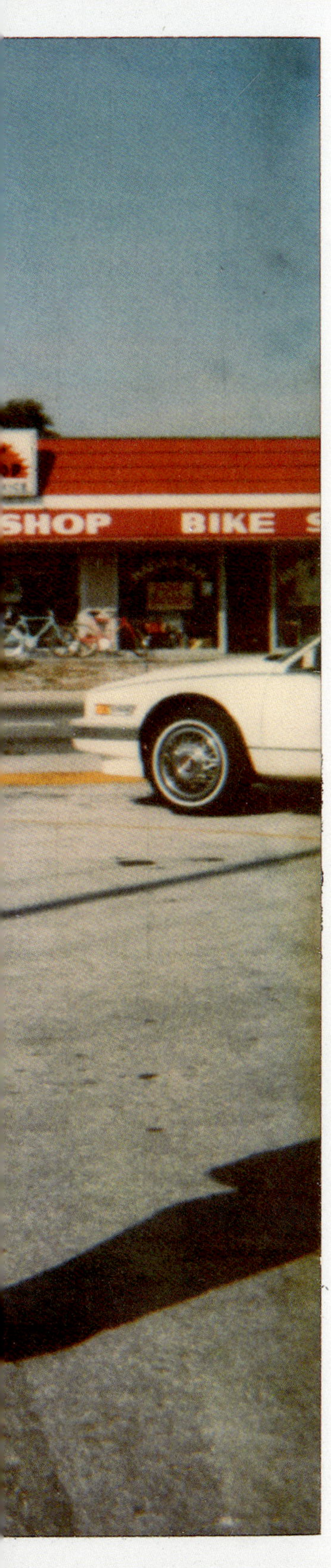

SHOP BIKE S

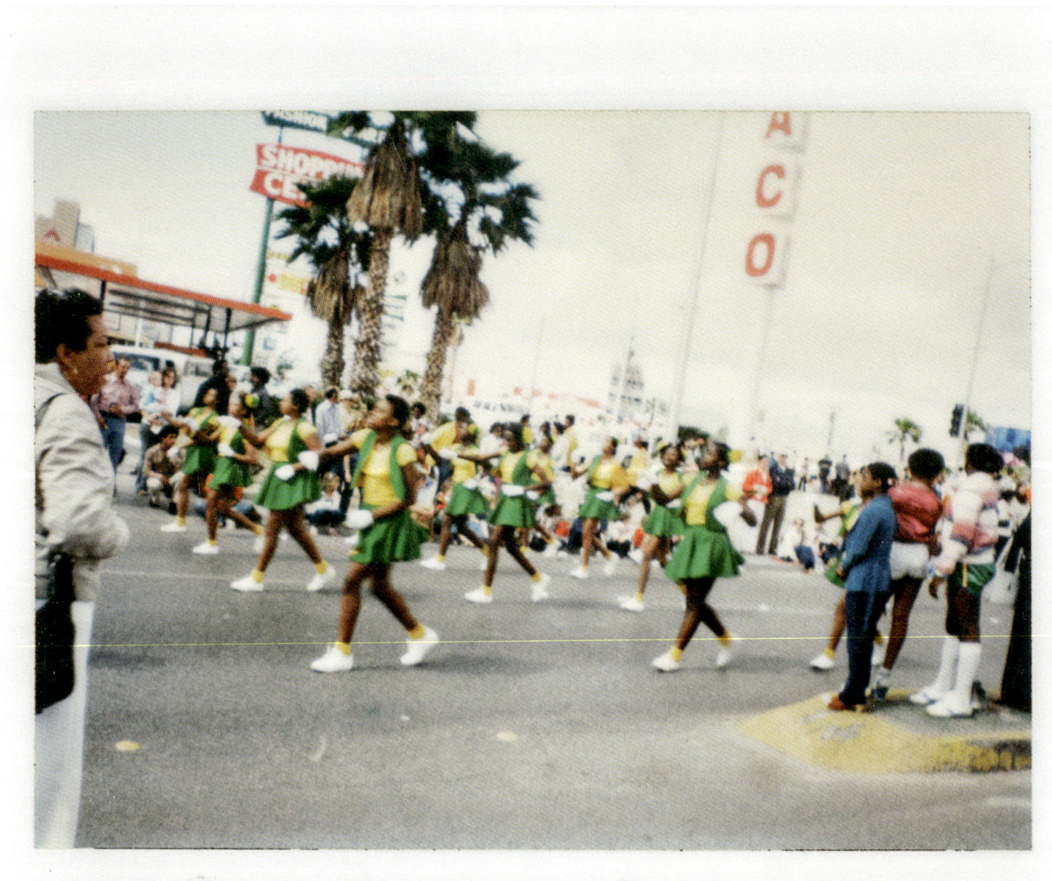

Jordan Highs

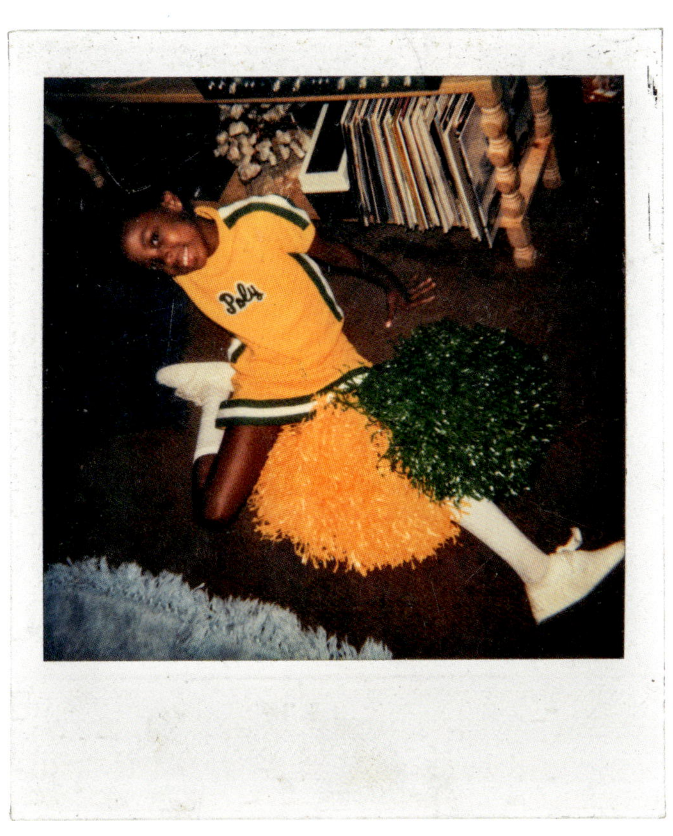

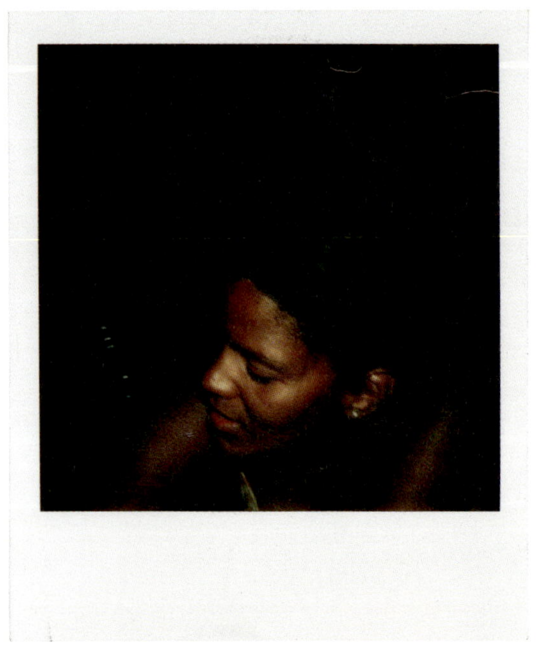 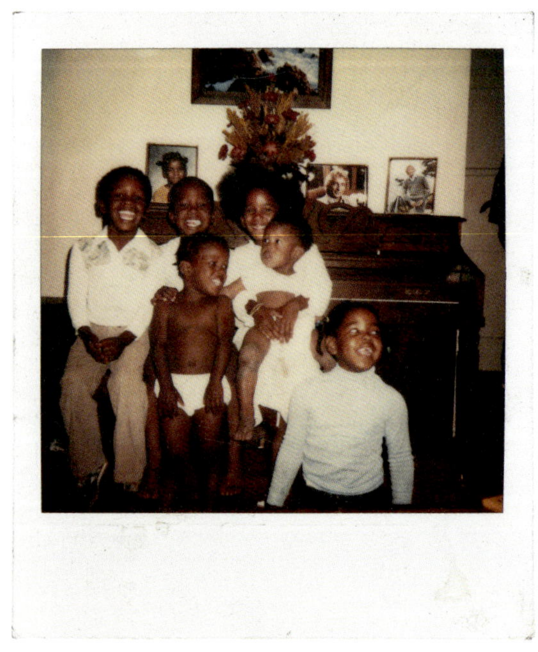

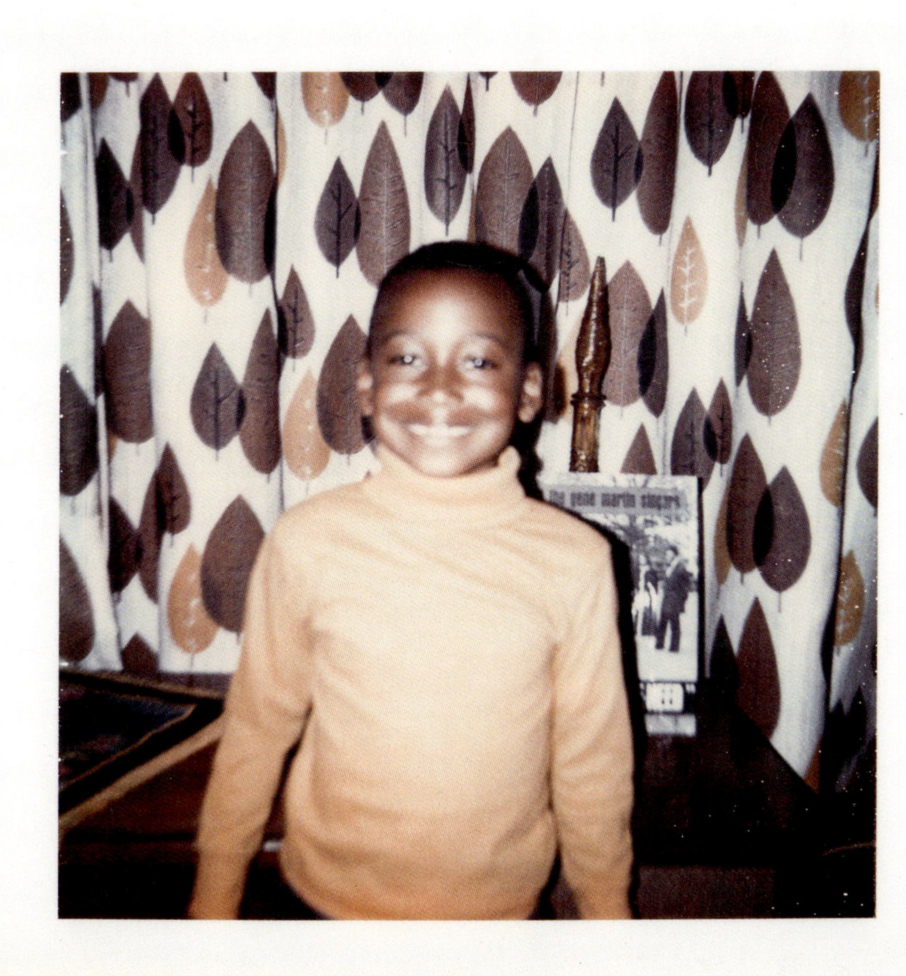

This is when Vickie and them was here
still in their night clothes. We all had
that gold couch, we all went to war.
Her name's a number in Anchorage,
Alaska. Boarding the tour bus and to
_______ with love. You simply
cannot know a Blackness undefined.
No claim toward Blackness made. If
the photo is a long song it is not the
blues. Instead, I'll be home soon so be
sweet and be faithful. Hold that space
for me.

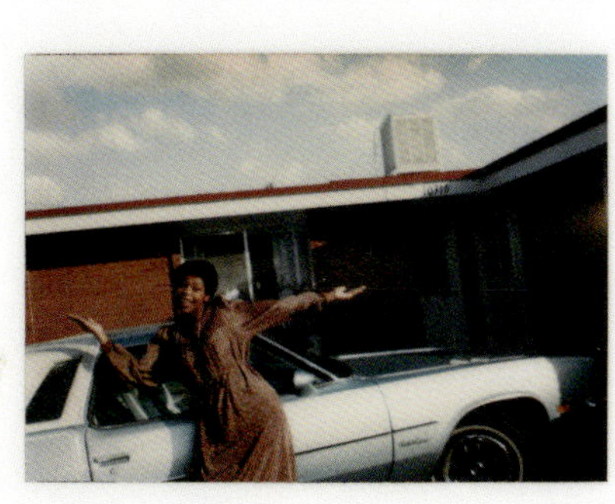

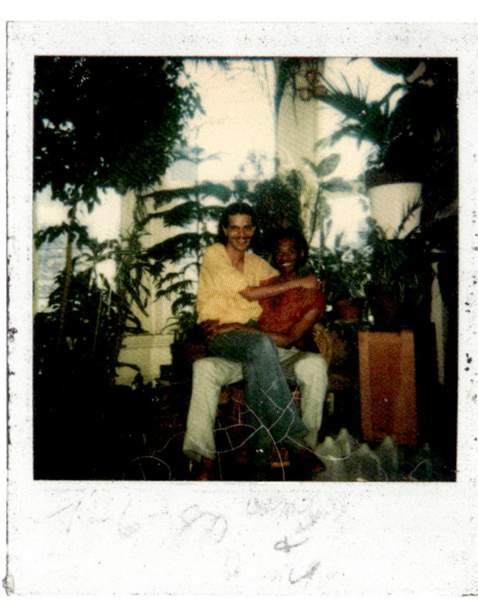

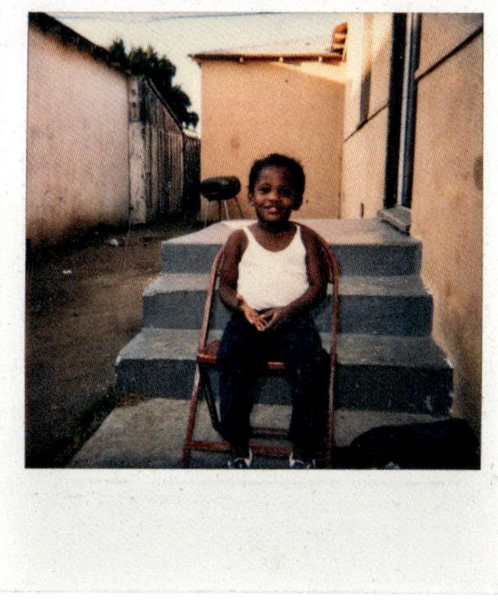

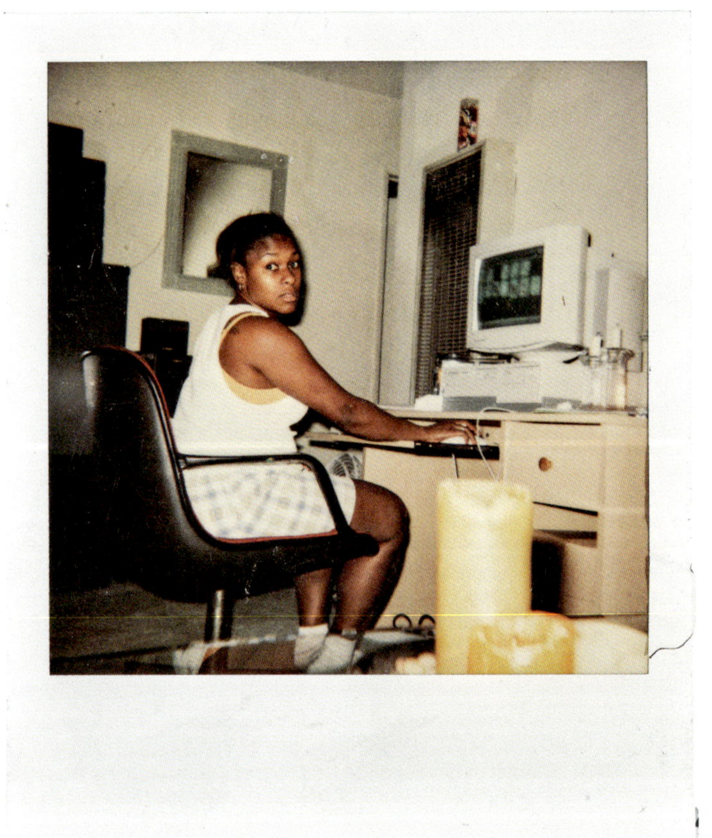

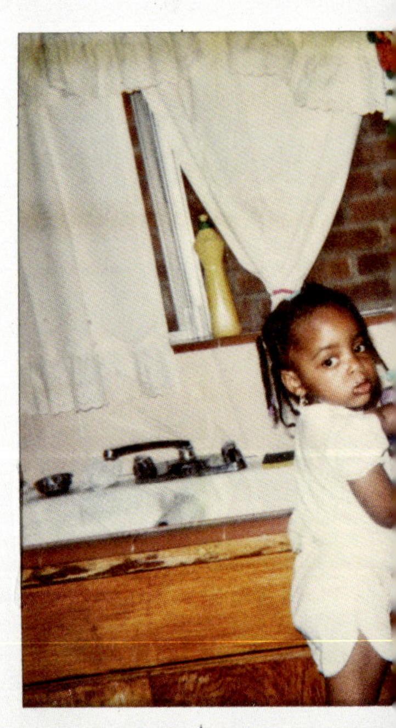
9/12/90
Eating out 07

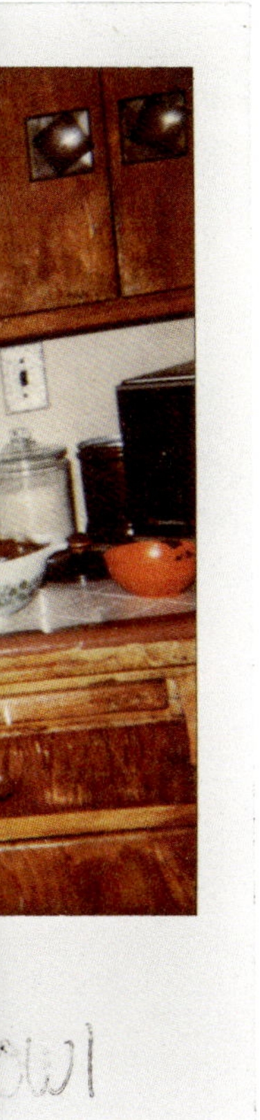

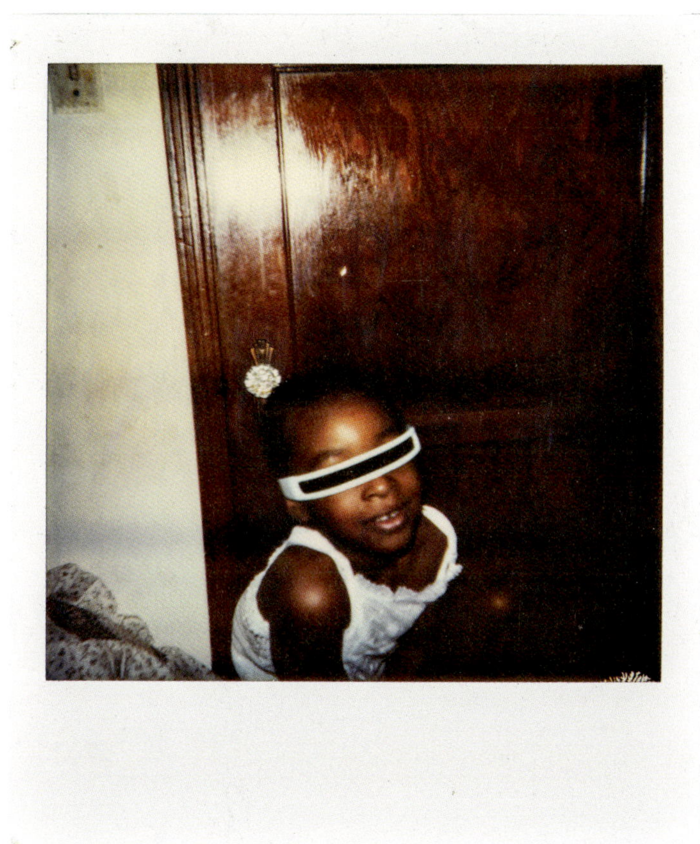

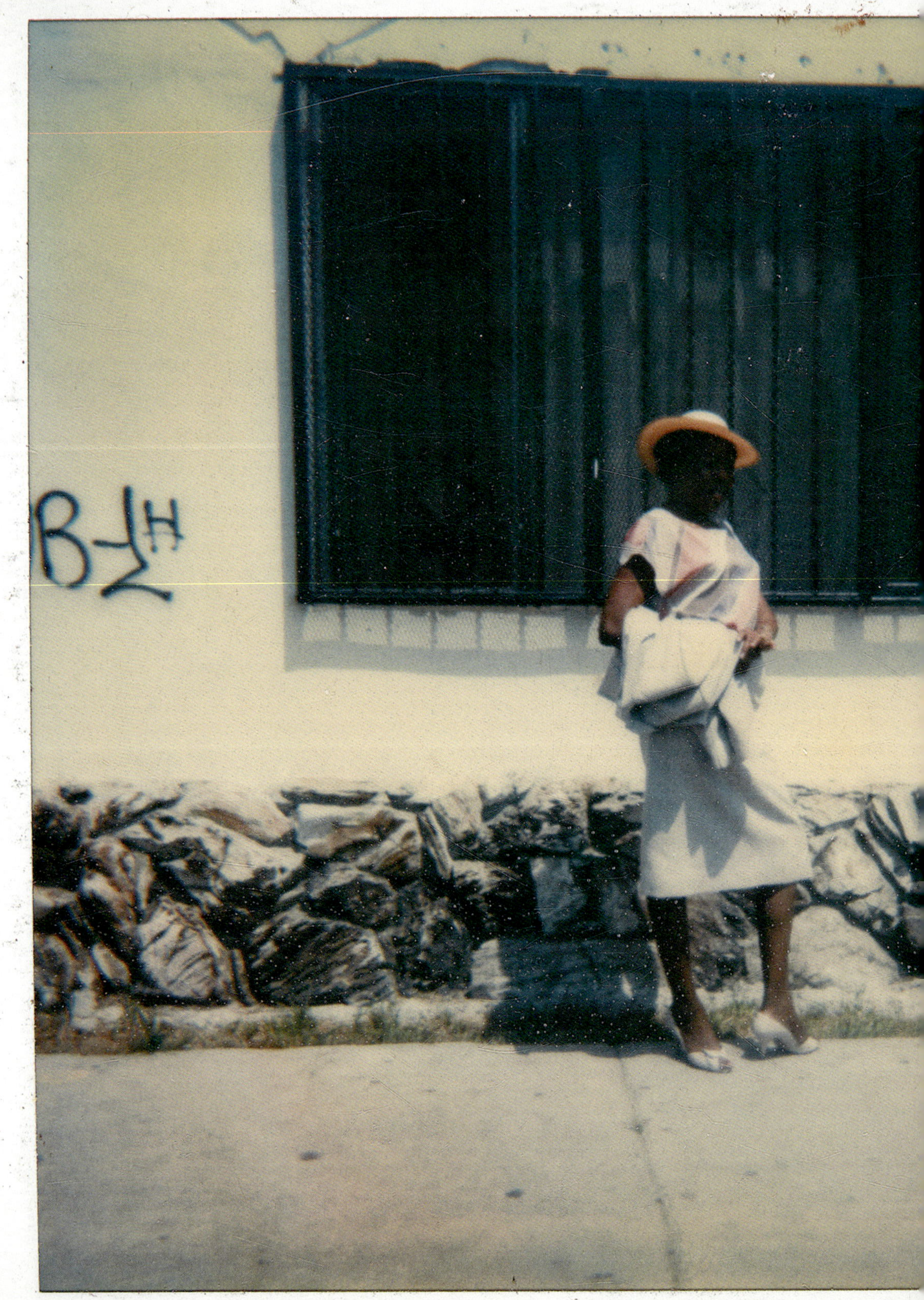
B

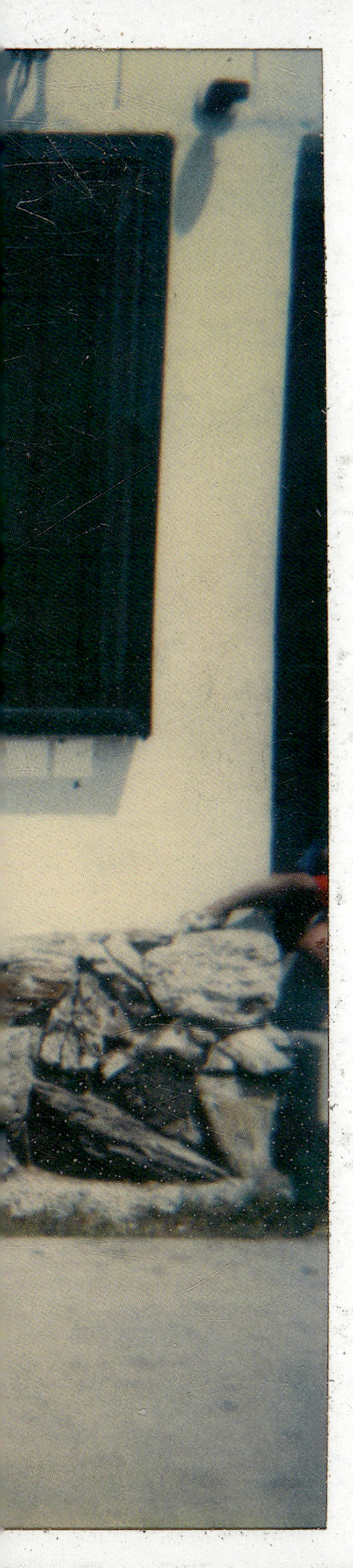

Photographs of Black Life

Dec. 3, 1984.
2018/99

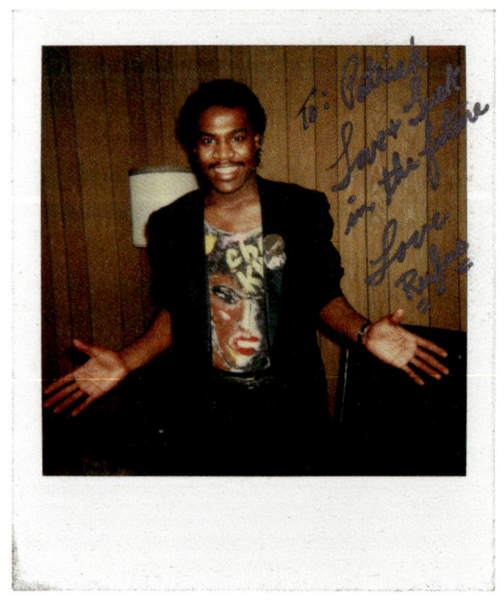
To: Patrick

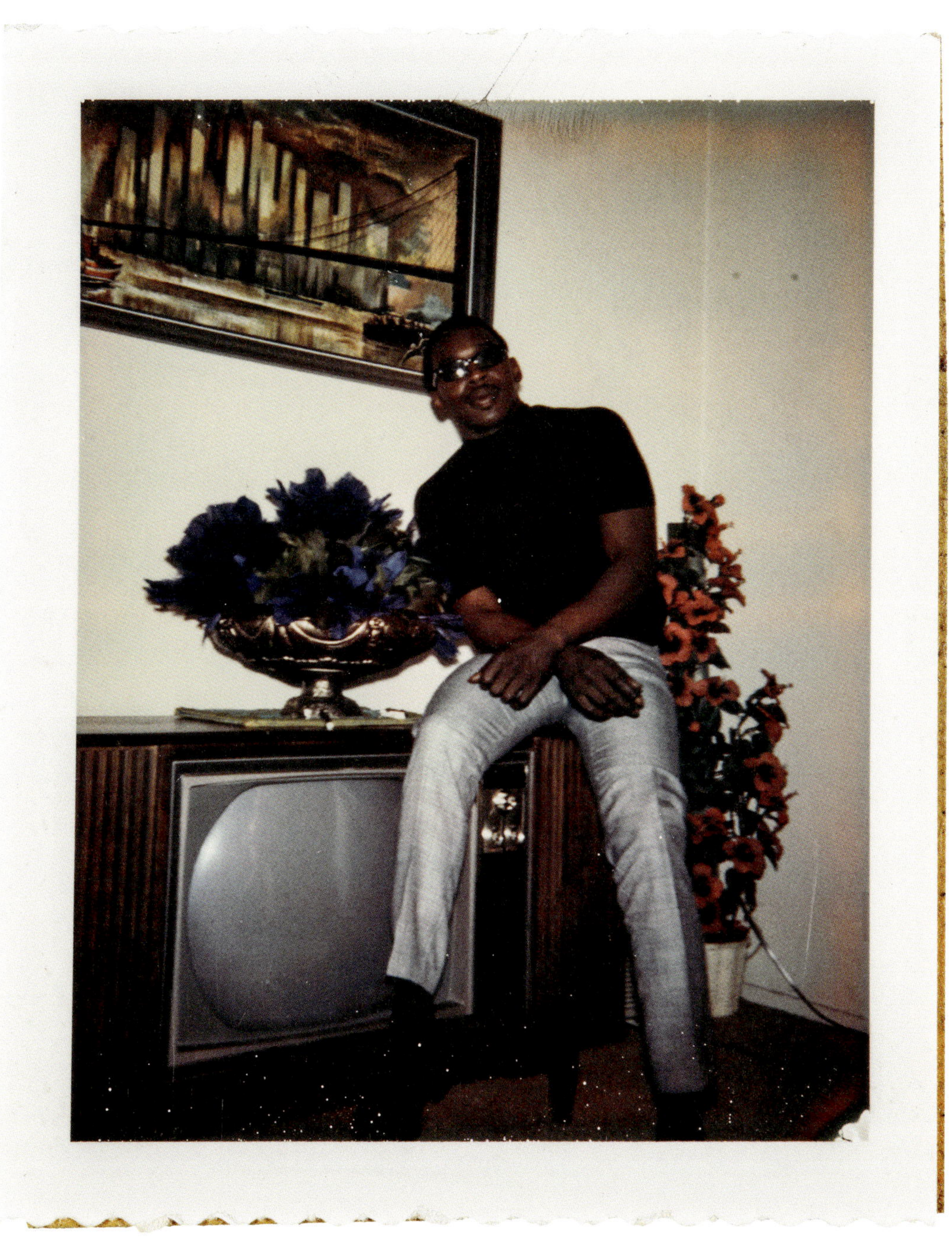

Photographs of Black Life

To Caelyn
With
Love, Hope and
Respect.

Tina Turner

Good things come
to those who
Wait. I've been
Waiting long enough

Smile

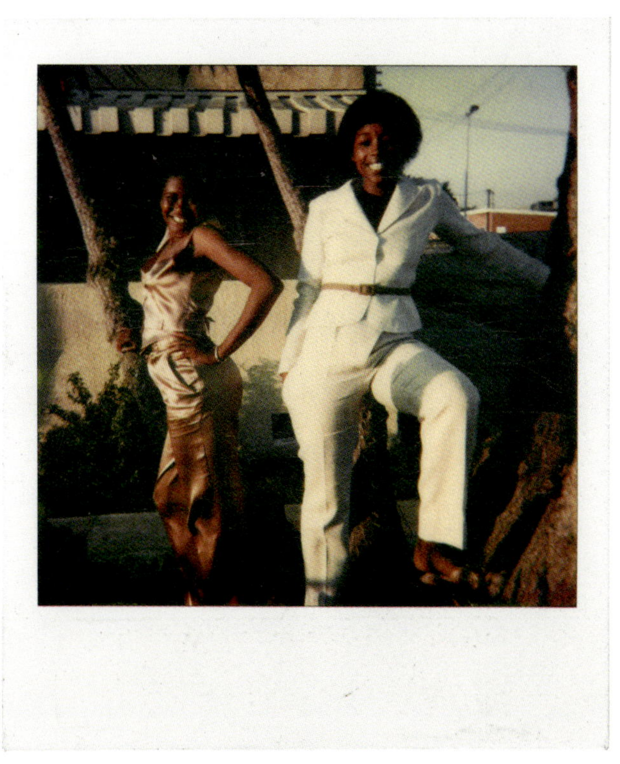

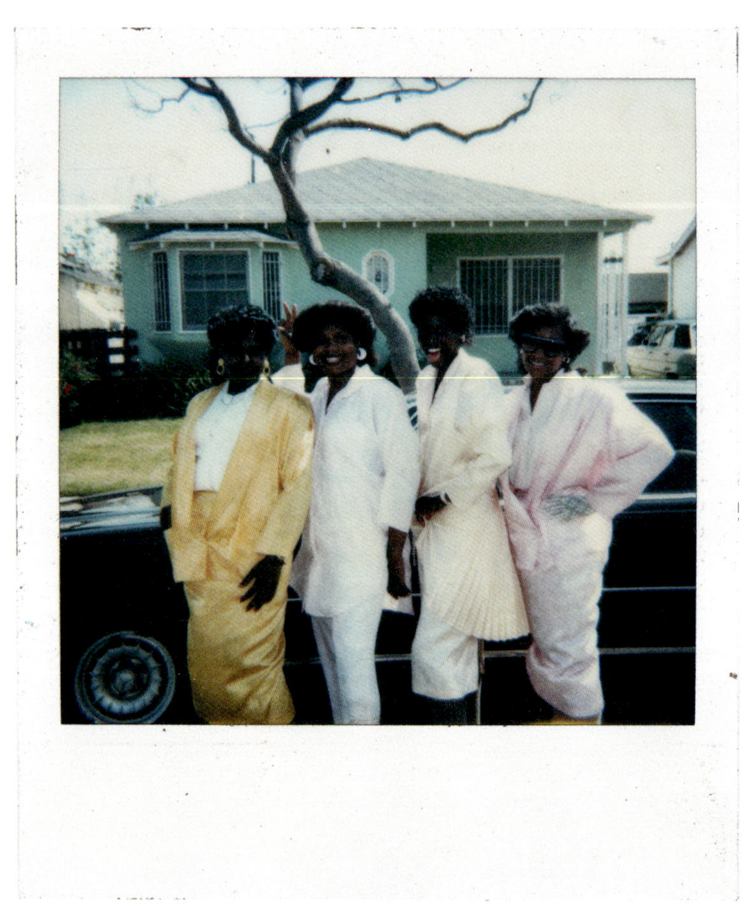

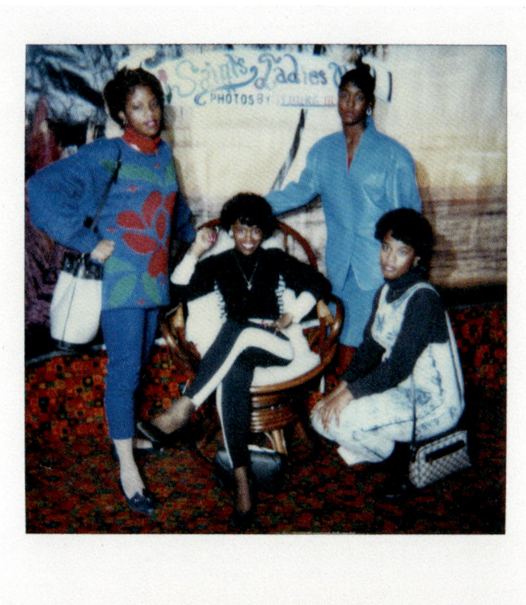

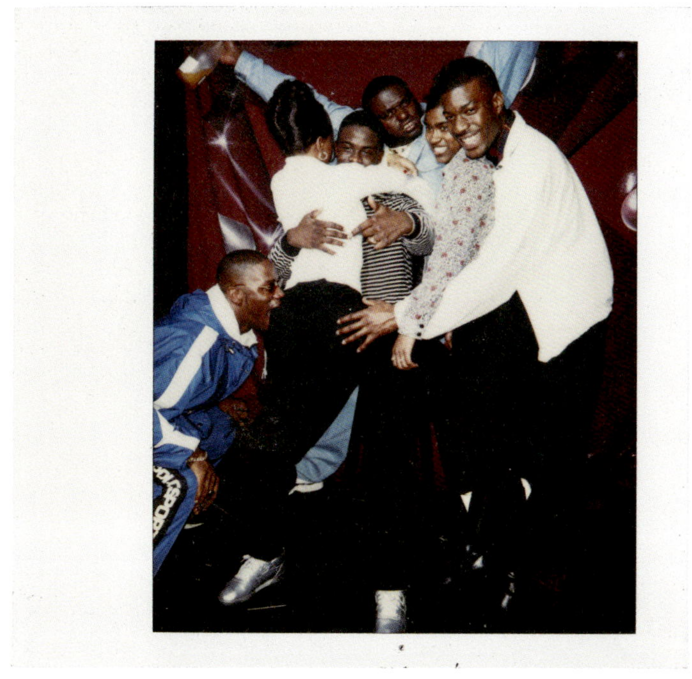

Photographs of Black Life

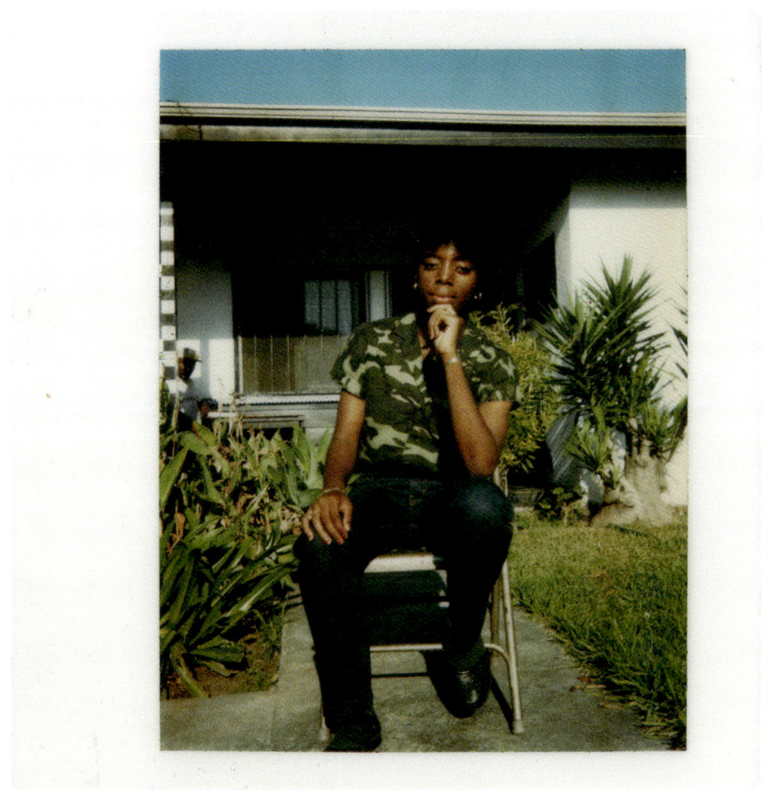

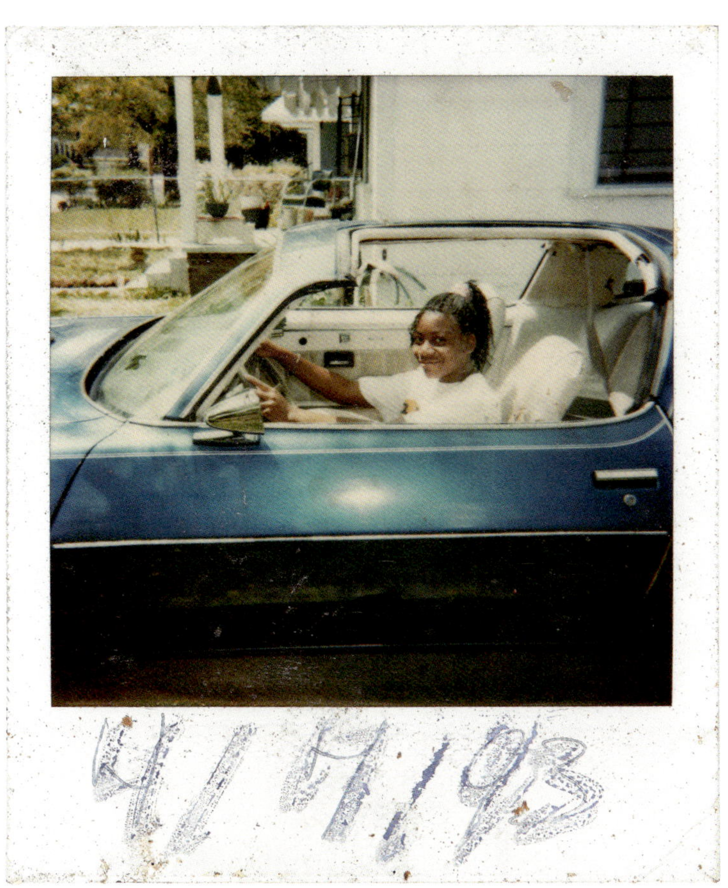

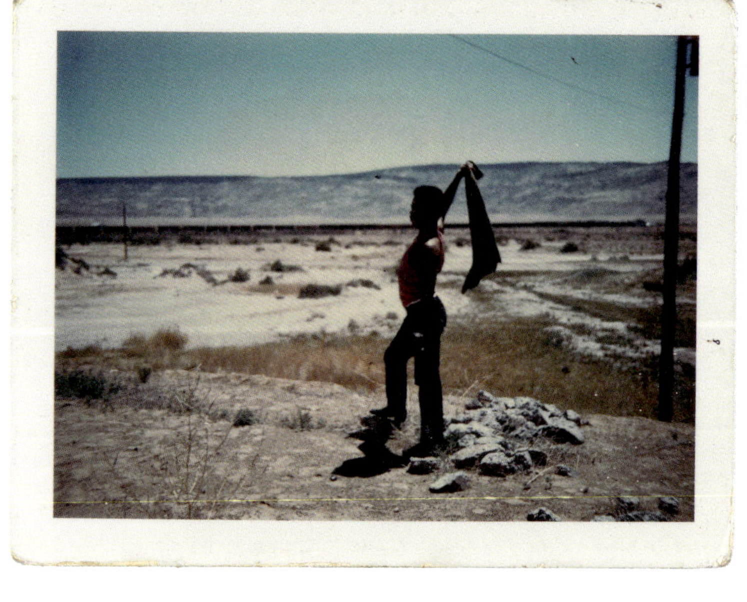

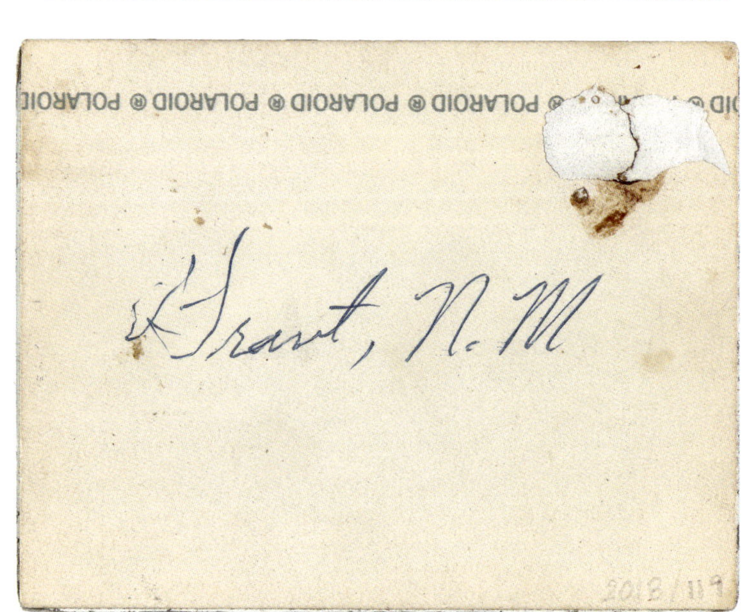
Grant, N. M

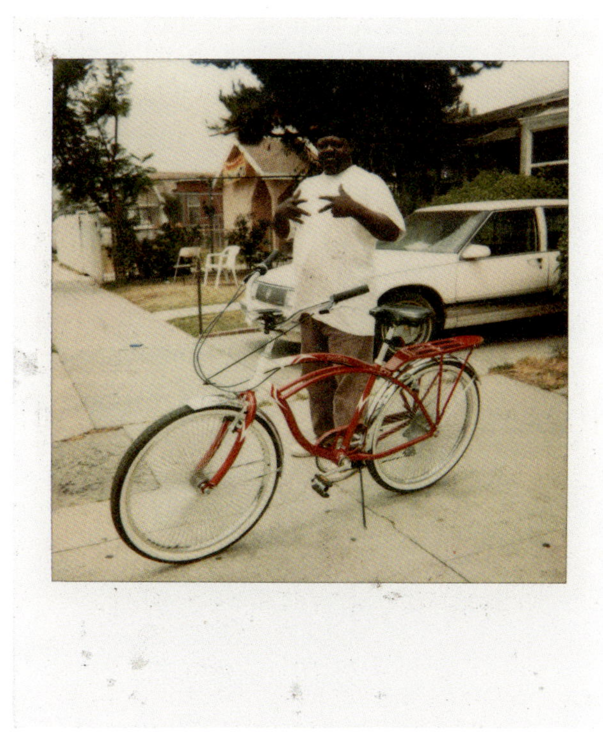

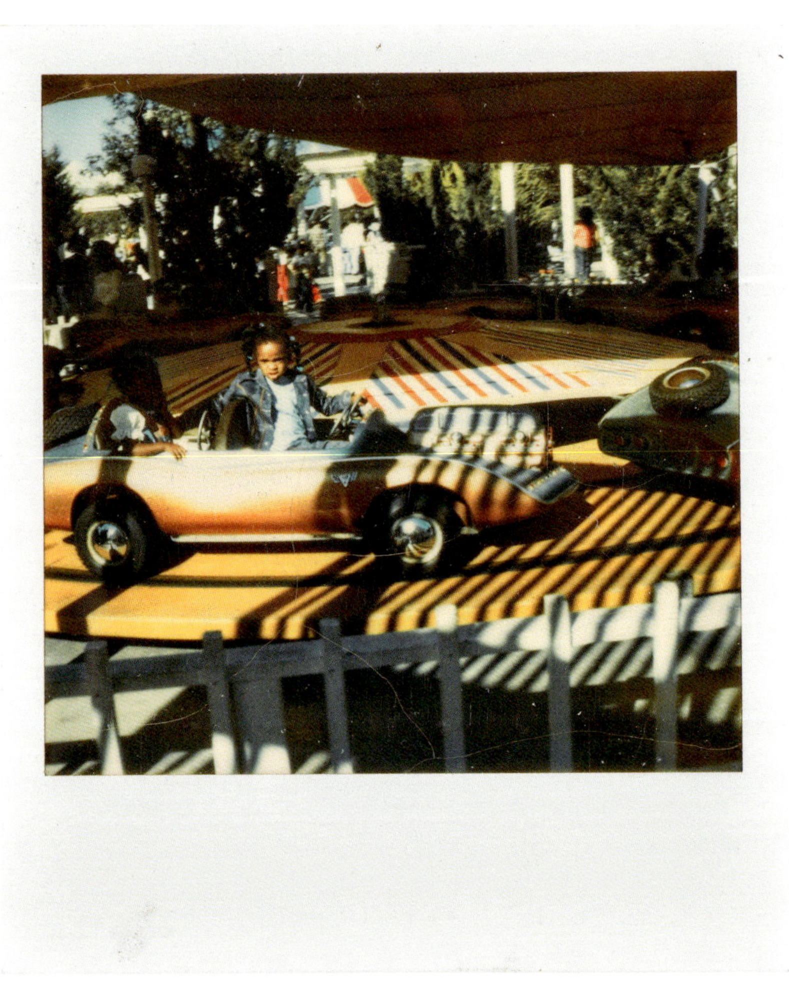

In (joying) where they lent a lab art
thing / a hallelujah in the baptism
bath / a labyrinth / laissez-faire /
lasso / a way into a way out / no
coming fire / or fistula / rather, the
whole moons / only light / what flash
allows / its flicker / rogue route
epistemes / our bodies made
daydream / looking in the sunset age
6 / him posturing around the tree /
the hands—the hands so delicate /
hands in grace, folded, hands' signs
signalling the / holy holiday spirit /
our real names / bedside table with
pills and tissue / breath that heaves,
into a depth so black we cannot
reach it—

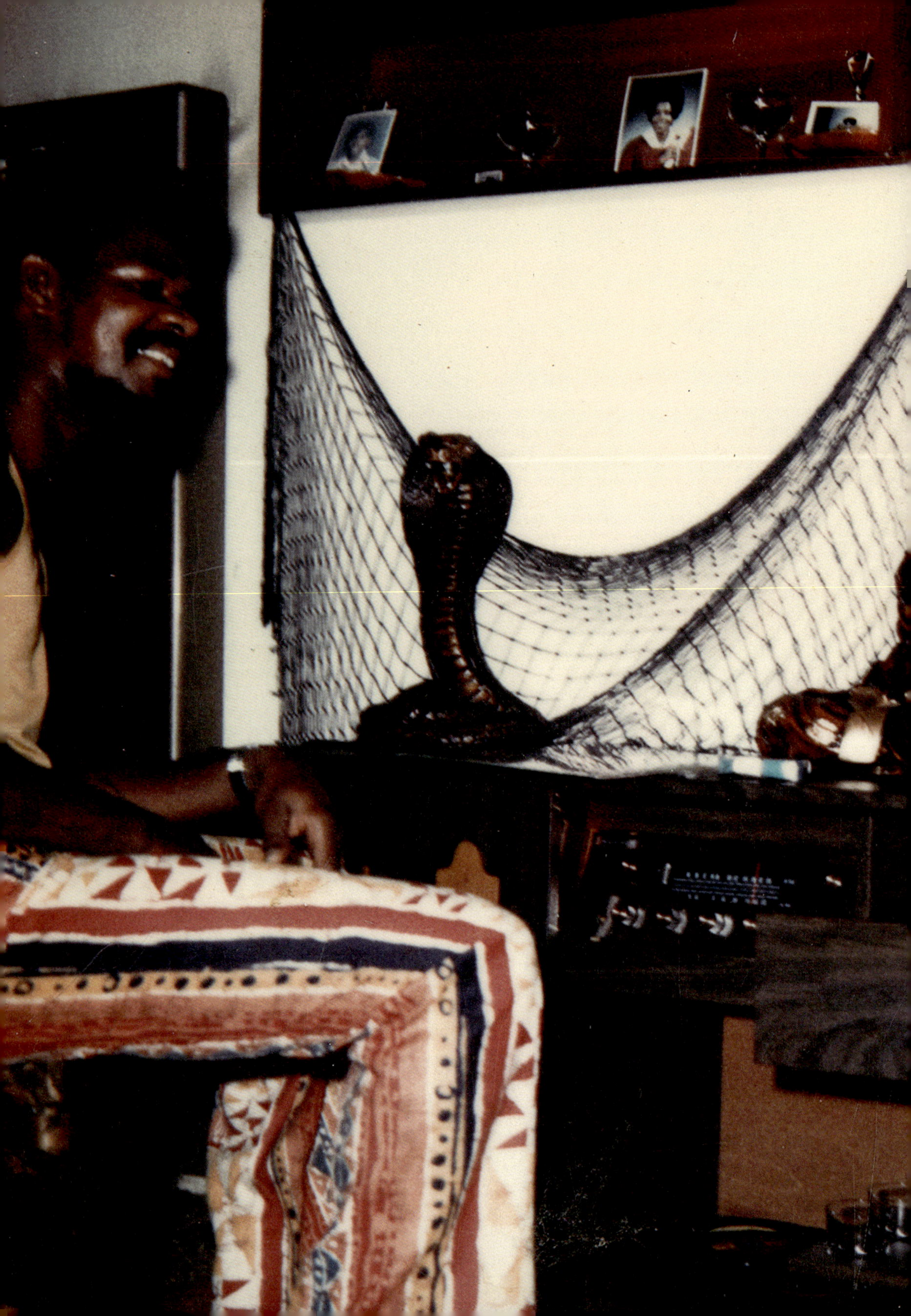

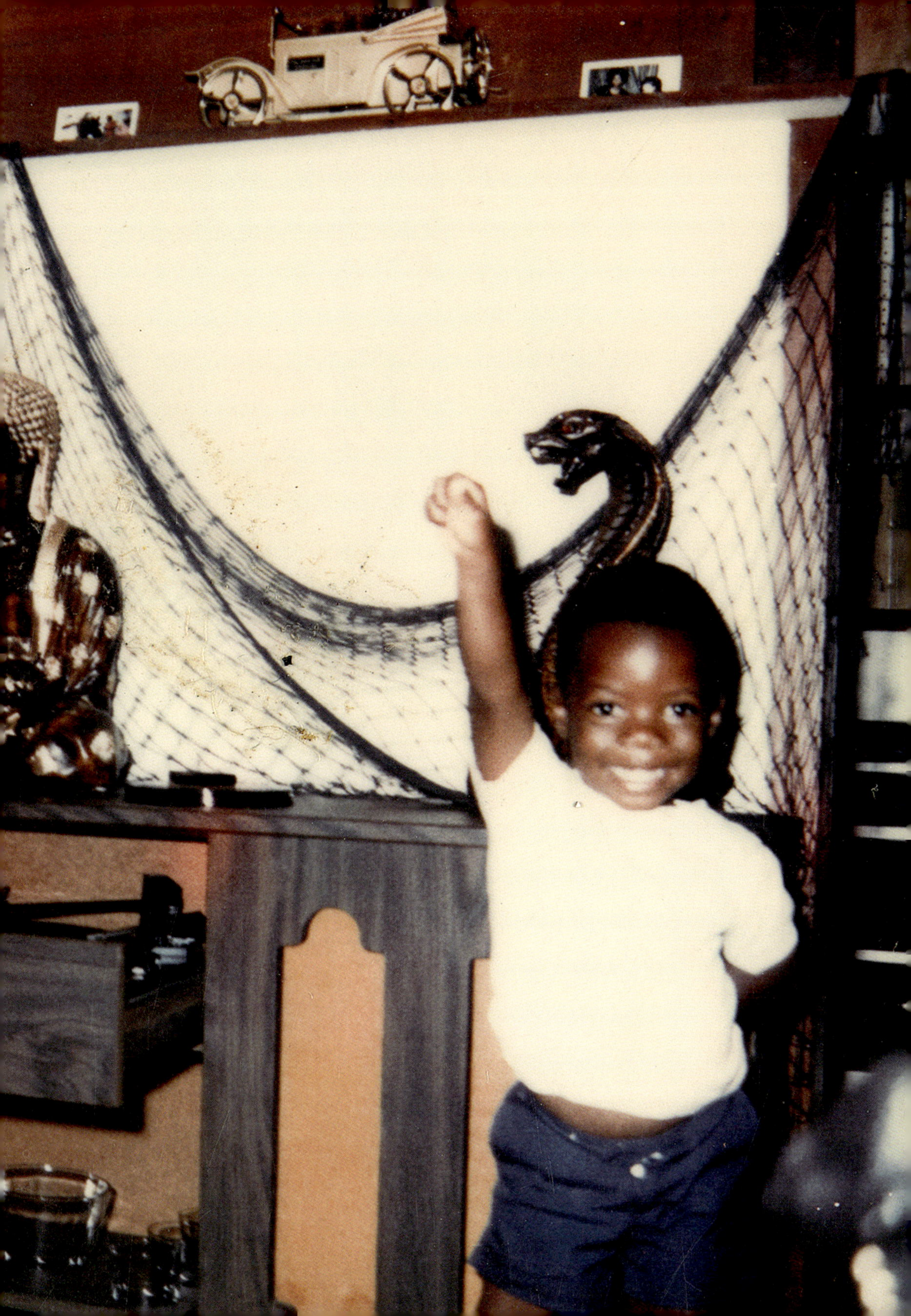

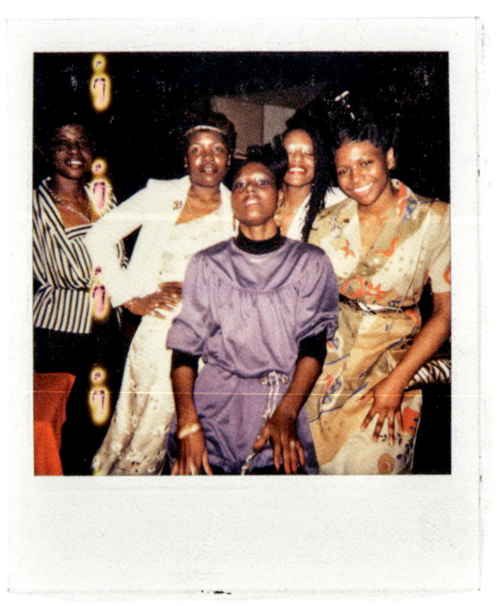

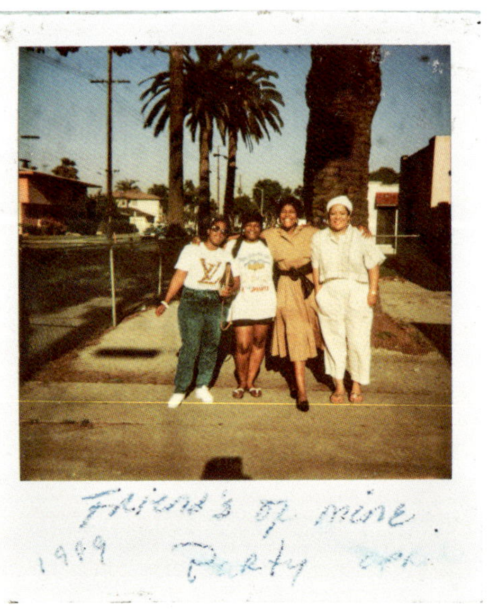
Friend's of mine.
1989 Party

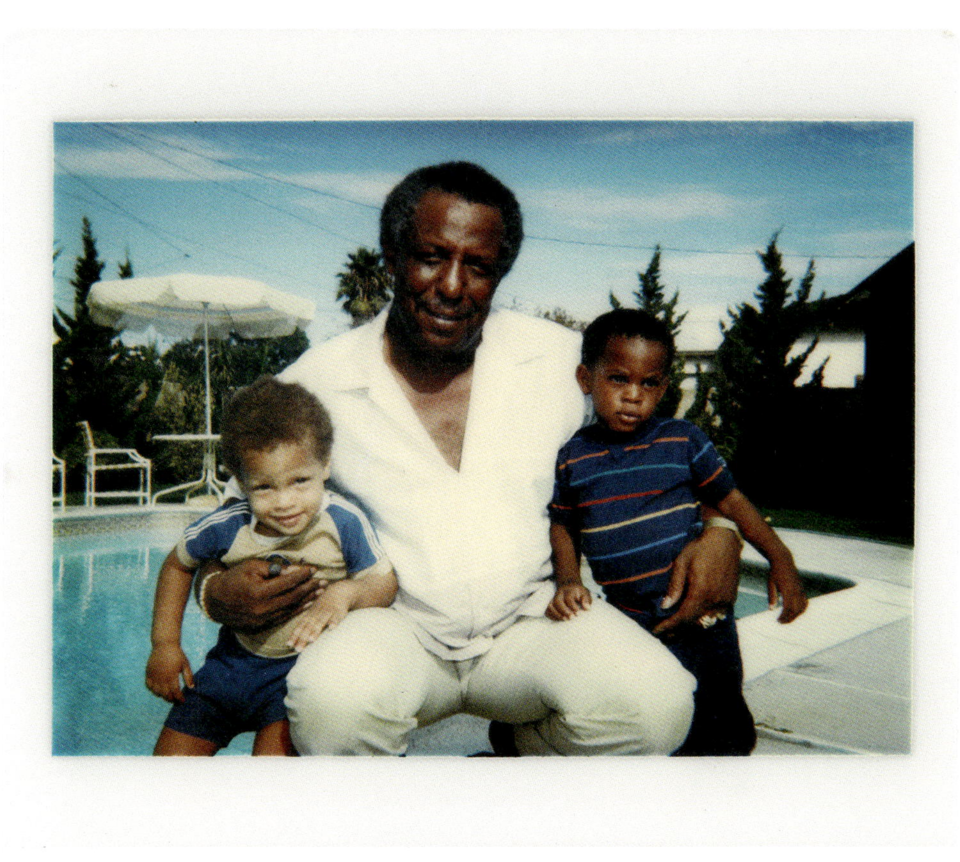

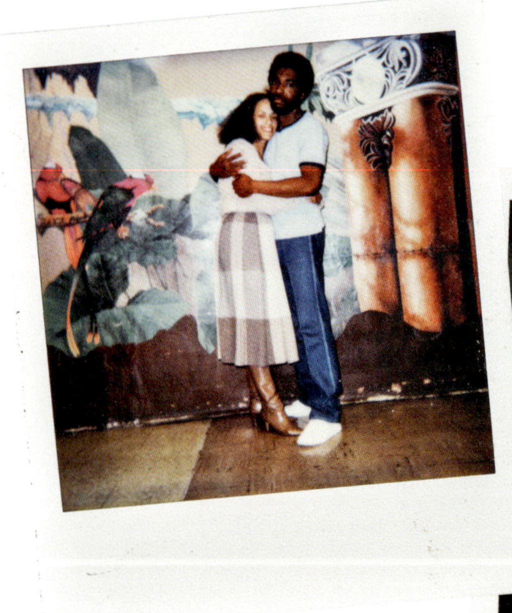

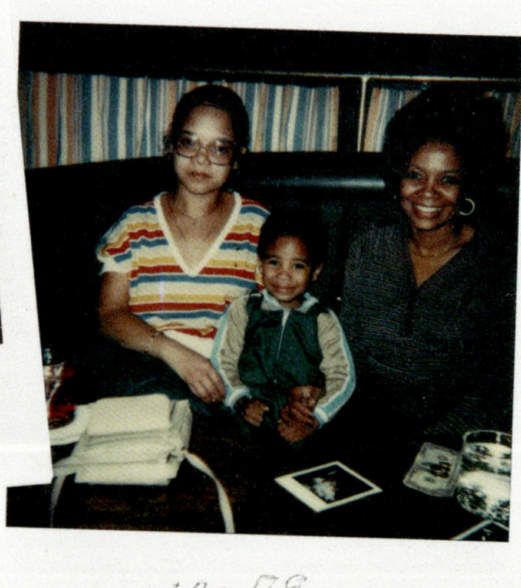

> *here go a box with a lid on it.*
> *if you open it you can come*
> *into our world.*
>
> —Fred Moten

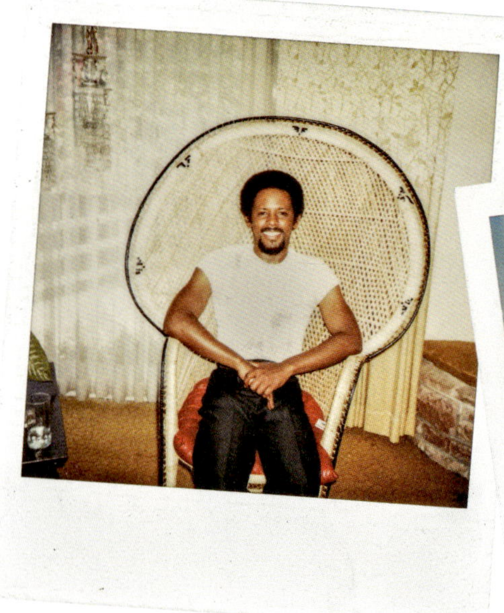

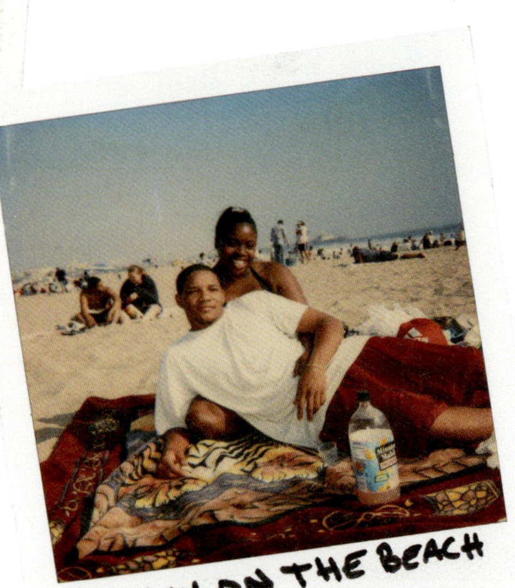

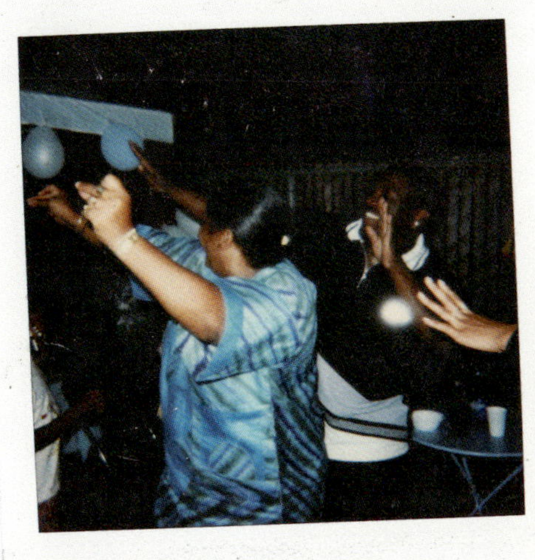

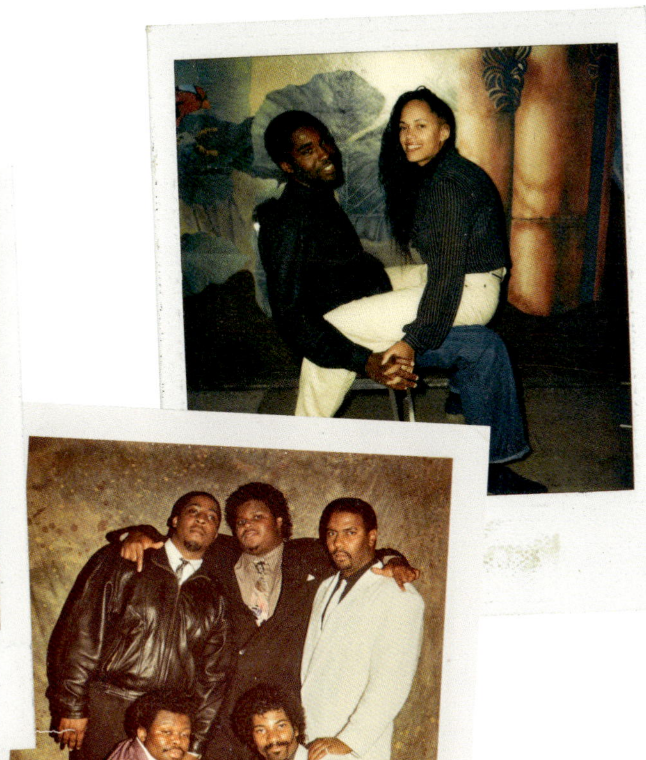

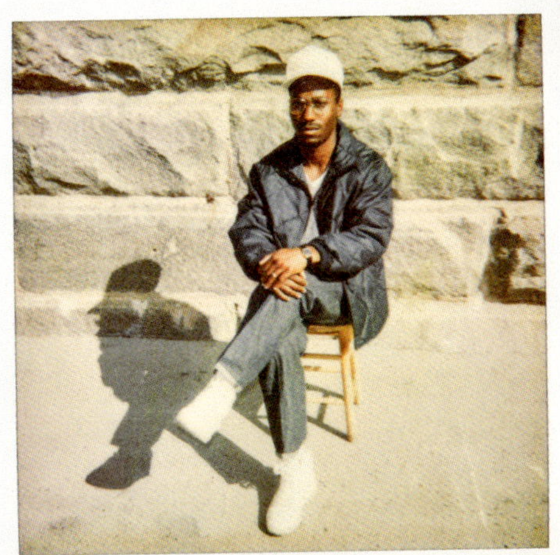

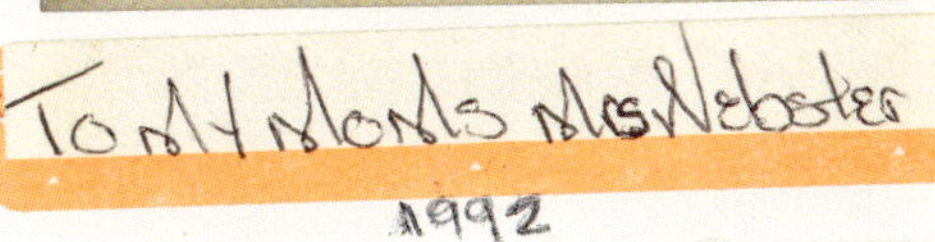
To My Moms Mrs Webster
1992

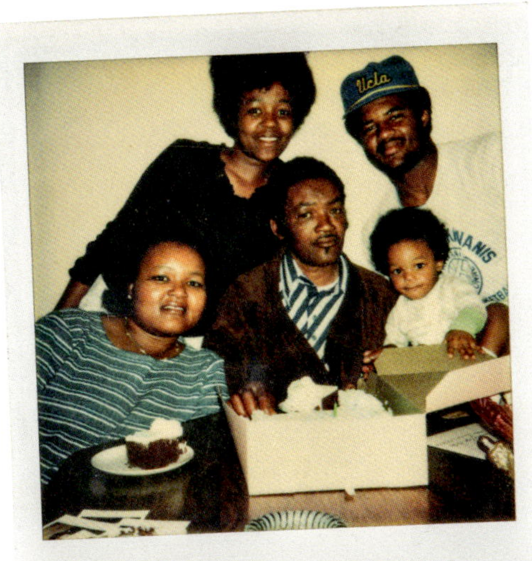

What Outlasts

SOPHIE HACKETT

For many of us, family snapshots mark our first engagements with the medium of photography. We learn the rituals of how they are made; we absorb their meaning as personal keepsakes to hold close. We learn to pore over their details, to share them. Of course, these formative experiences typically involve the photographs of our own families and friends. But what does it mean to engage with family photographs when we have no direct connection to the people in them?

The origins of the *Fade Resistance* collection lie in what is now a well-told set of facts: in December 2012, Zun Lee was working in Detroit when he found a set of Polaroids on the street. Hoping to return the photographs to their owners, he knocked on doors in the neighbourhood, with no success. This sparked a new project—a collection—through which Lee sought to reckon with the loss of this visual history.

In many ways, what Lee found in Detroit—and in the thousands of photographs he would ultimately collect over the next six years—was typical of so many North American family snapshots. Milestones like weddings, birthdays, and graduation ceremonies were chronicled alongside quieter daily moments: doing hair, having a nap, hanging out in the backyard. Together, however, these images define something highly specific—because of when they were created; because they were mainly created by, of, and for African American families. Attuned to the structural issues that continue to shape and regulate Black life, Lee recognized in these orphaned photographs what theorist Saidiya Hartman has called the "afterlife of slavery."[1]

1 Saidiya Hartman, *Lose Your Mother: A Journey Along the Atlantic Slave Trade Route* (New York: Farrar, Straus and Giroux, 2006), 6.

2 Zun Lee, "Fade Resistance," accessed July 4, 2022. zunlee.com/faderesistance.

3 Teju Cole, "On Photography: The Digital Afterlife of Lost Family Photos," *The New York Times Magazine*, April 26, 2016, accessed July 4, 2022. nytimes.com/2016/05/01/magazine/the-digital-afterlife-of-lost-family-photos.html.

4 *Zun Lee: Fade Resistance*, The Gladstone Hotel, Toronto, Feb. 1–28, 2016; *Representing*, Portland Art Museum, July 29 – Dec. 3, 2017.

5 Among others, *Reframing Family Photography* (Toronto, 2017); Art Gallery of Ontario artist-in-residence (Toronto, 2017); *BlackPortraitures V* (New York, 2019); John Simon Guggenheim Memorial Foundation fellow (2020).

The collection, which Lee dubbed *Fade Resistance* (a nod to the "fade-resistant" tag on some garments), grew to include some 2,975 instant prints and 1,384 related gelatin silver and chromogenic prints, dating from the 1950s to the early 2000s. For Lee, this work is rooted in a desire to "reflect the way Black people saw themselves on their terms—without the intention of being seen, or judged, by others."[2] It is a collection formed against Black invisibility; formed to enshrine Black joy and kinship, to emphasize "Black life mattering." And what began as an alternative visual history to counter the distortions in mainstream narratives has evolved into both a symbol and a symptom of systemic violence against and dispossession of African Americans in the United States.

As Lee amassed the *Fade Resistance* collection, he engaged with the photographs in an effort to understand what they could mean now. He digitized and shared images on social media.[3] He curated and loaned works to exhibitions.[4] He participated in conferences, fellowships, and residencies.[5] He led workshops and mentored younger artists. Perhaps most significantly, Lee talked to people, often showing them the box of Polaroids he had begun carrying with him. The photographs easily sparked discussions on family, lived experience, and visual history. These conversations have profoundly affected Lee's own practice—his primary focus has now shifted from making photographs to participating in projects that encourage communities to define and tell their own stories.

For instance, in Charlotte, North Carolina's Camp Greene neighbourhood, Lee collaborated with Muddy Turtle Talks to

6 Bryant Carter, "Q&A with Hannah Hasan, artist/activist bringing Charlotte's Enderly Park to the stage," *QCity Metro*, Sept 13, 2018, accessed July 4, 2022. qcitymetro.com/2018/09/13/qa-with-hannah-hasan-artist-activist-bringing-charlottes-enderly-park-to-the-stage/. The Muddy Turtle Talks were co-founded by Hannah and Shardae Hasan and hosted by QC Family Tree. Lee lived in Charlotte for six months in 2018 as the inaugural artist-in-residence with The Roll Up CLT.

7 Lee has been working in partnership with UNC Greensboro and the Historic East Baltimore Community Action Coalition, as part of the Gates Foundation's Voices for Economic Opportunity Grand Challenge. See: gatesfoundation.org/ideas/media-center/press-releases/2020/06/changing-the-national-conversation-about-poverty-and-economic-mobility.

8 *Pop Photographica: Photography's Objects in Everyday Life* (2003); *Album* (2012); the Casa Susanna photographs in *Outsiders: American Photography and Film, 1950s–1980s* (2016); and *Free Black North* (2017).

record stories of Black life in the area, a practice the group has described as "social-impact story-sharing."[6] During performance events in 2018 and 2019, Lee projected images from the *Fade Resistance* collection behind participants as they spoke, animating each presentation in a new way. This context also brought new life to the images, cementing them as part of a longstanding, living visual history. Most recently, Lee has been working with young Black men in Baltimore to record their stories in photographs and interviews, as a way of affirming "the humanity of young Black men and [deepening] awareness about root causes and barriers to their economic mobility."[7] The *Fade Resistance* collection has thus fed Lee's commitment to use photography to witness, to advocate, and to empower, all while continuing to question whose stories are valued.

The Art Gallery of Ontario has long collected and exhibited vernacular photographs, a reflection of the Gallery's expansive approach to the history of the medium. The acquisition of the *Fade Resistance* collection in 2018 was part of this commitment, and it meant that the Gallery gained a significant group of photographs of Black families by Black photographers, makers, and subjects—all historically underrepresented in the permanent collection.

It's not unusual for a photography collection in a gallery or museum to include family photographs. But over time, there has been an evolution in what these photographs stand for in such contexts. Early on, they were examples of a medium or format of the nineteenth century—the daguerreotype, the carte-de-visite; in later decades, they were admired for their technical accidents, as a parallel to—or shadow of— the twentieth century's modernist avant-gardes. More recently, family photographs have been cast as a challenge to the history of photography itself, their ubiquity (and, for some, banality) the flood that exceeds the canon's narrow riverbanks.

The *Fade Resistance* collection presents yet another opportunity to think anew about the role of family photographs in a public art institution. In past projects at the AGO, our curatorial aim has been to present these works in ways that resonate with the circumstances of their creation.[8] We have also endeavoured to illuminate how and why family photographs have functioned and continue to function in forming communities—whether those communities are bound by affection or by identity. This underscores that the meaning of family photographs continues to evolve. They are not fixed or homogeneous entities, and thus neither is their significance.

Lee's work with the *Fade Resistance* collection is anchored in the following proposition: what if we relate to the Polaroids not simply as artifacts but as objects that are inseparable from the Black social contexts in which they were created? This throws equal emphasis on the makers and viewers—which is to say, any Black maker or viewer, then and now. It means placing Black experience at the centre of all decisions.

We scheduled this project well before the pandemic, and the poignancy of the *Fade Resistance* collection—its difficulty, even—has only increased over the last two years as, here in North America, we have borne close witness to the ongoing legacies of brutal inhumanity toward racialized bodies. For all the joy present in the photographs, these histories cast a long shadow. The challenge now is how to present this collection, created by a Black artist, for a Black audience, in all its distinctiveness and richness, but with an invitation, as Lee puts it, to "feel together with us."[9]

The Polaroids themselves help to point the way: we shake an instant print as the image emerges, discuss the merits of the picture, perhaps make another. This is not just a formal or technical process, but also a social one. Touch and storytelling are built in.

When Lee and I began to discuss the future of his collection in 2017, he wanted to ensure that he was working with an institution that would place as much emphasis on proactive strategies for connecting audiences as on the preservation and presentation of the photographs. In turn, we secured funds for public engagement initiatives to encourage open-ended inquiry. What can the humbleness of *Fade Resistance* stand for and what can it achieve, culturally and politically? What shape can care take—for these photographs, for their subjects, for their audiences. Can seeing private pictures in a public context have a broader social purpose?

[9] See Lee's essay in this volume, page 172.

In December 2019, the AGO hosted *Ways of Caring*, an inaugural round table with Lee, moderator Kimberly Juanita Brown, artists Deanna Bowen and Michèle Pearson Clarke, and cultural theorists Stefano Harney and Fred Moten. It was a generative and at times highly charged discussion, one that underscored the high stakes in play at a time when arts institutions contend with urgent calls to face histories of racism and enact real change, processes that are necessary and ongoing.

During a break in the round table, I was approached by Evelyn Auchinvole, historian of Hamilton's Stewart Memorial Church, home to the city's oldest Black congregation. She felt strongly that, for many, seeing photographs of Black family life in a space like the AGO would be important. It was a meaningful reminder that, for many members of marginalized groups, even baseline visibility is not a given. Auchinvole herself serves as a community archivist, offering the church as a new home for photographs that families no longer feel connected to as relatives die and direct kinship ties fade. The significance of collections like this can shift and expand over time: they can stand for something as simple as presence, as facts of existence, or they can unfurl and feed so many other narratives.[10]

[10] As an example, the AGO exhibition *Free Black North*, curated by Dr. Julie Crooks in 2017. Evidence of Black presence in Ontario in the nineteenth century, the tintypes and cabinet cards in Rick Bell's collection served to expand narratives around Canadian history—and around how photography was used in this context.

Other people's family photographs have been one constant in my own curatorial career. I remain drawn to their mystery, to what I can see—worlds of time, place, and experience outside my own—and what I cannot ever know. There is a Polaroid I keep coming back to, one with a deep blue velvet glow: a figure sits, pensive, forehead resting on his right hand. He is so bathed in the gloaming that he is hard to perceive. The question of who is there in the photograph, of what prompted someone to press the camera's shutter, will likely never be answered, and yet life—*aliveness*—is evident. We become witness to the honouring of a life. Indeed, *Fade Resistance* includes thousands of such instances, honouring thousands of lives. These images hold a collective power, too, enduring as they have in the face of the world's convulsions.

That experience, in turn, reminds me of a poem. During one of our gatherings with the team that made this book, Dawn Lundy Martin told us about Aracelis Girmay's "Ode to the Watermelon" (2007).[11] In the final lines, Girmay writes:

¹¹ Aracelis Girmay, *Teeth* (Evanston, IL: Curbstone Press, 2007).

Sandía, día santo,
yours is a sweetness
to outlast slaughter:
Tongues will lose themselves inside you,
scattering seeds. All over,
the land will hum
with your wild,
raucous blooming.

Whether people find in them seeds for study, reflecting pools, spectres of anti-Black violence, catalysts for empathy, an index of loss—or experience them, over time, as thousands of private homecomings, individual and irreducible—may these photographs outlast us all.

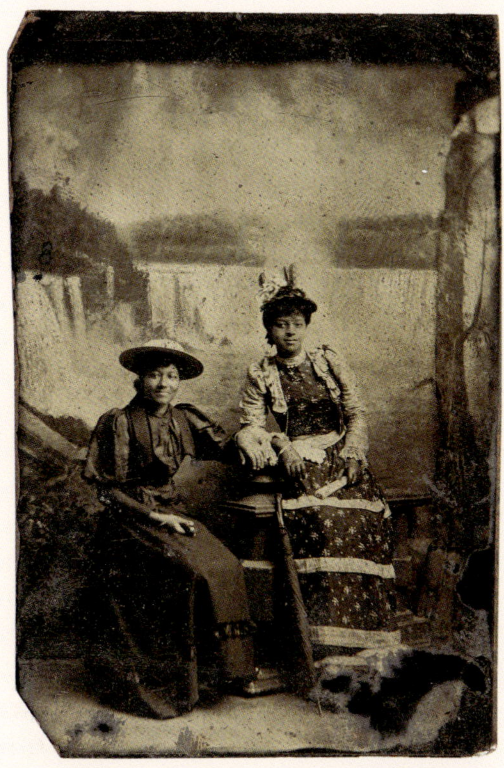

Unknown, [Unidentified women with Niagara Falls backdrop], c.1875. Tintype photograph, 9 x 6 cm. Rick Bell Family Fonds – RG 63, Archives & Special Collections, Brock University Library. Digital image: © 2017 Art Gallery of Ontario.

A Whole Mess and a Half:
The Matter of Most

ZUN LEE *Dagmaris walking away on the beach.*
Asunción, her fan, her trim do.
Gloria two days before dying.
Roberto, pointing to nothing.
Idermis behind Oscar, after Jorge.

I so far away I almost cannot make myself out.
My brother wasting a smile.
My aunt as ugly as the word itself.
Grandmother in her best days.
Grandfather with a festive tie.
My father drunk again.
My mother like a distantly spilled perfume.

—Jesús Cos Causse[1]

here go a box with a lid on it. if you open it you can come into our world.

—Fred Moten[2]

As the pandemic blur of the past two years wears on, I've settled into an uneasy rhythm without a familiar playbook; not a "new normal" but certainly a "new normative" experience—the next instantiation of the same old calculus, the same game of navigating ever-constricting socioeconomic spaces now regulated and surveilled in the name of pandemic mitigation.

The most difficult aspect of this time has been the relentless and ongoing departure of the very kinfolk who would, in other circumstances, help me cope, offer support and comfort, or anchor my sense of belonging in this time of uncertainty. Not being able to travel and gather to sustain relationships disrupted my grieving process. I now understand that I wasn't really processing loss—I was not allowing for grief to fully move through me. I compartmentalized my emotional and mental capacity to care into manageable bits, anticipating yet more bad news and loss. Life started to feel more like I was watching myself standing in front of a flight information board at the airport, row after row of names and dates refreshing with the status "Departed." It no longer was about the disappearance of friends and family; I disappeared, too. I no longer recognized who I was.

I'm not a "photographer," in the sense that my practice doesn't center on the technical aspects of "painting with light," or the materiality of making photographic objects. The visual *poiesis* results from presencing with people with whom I am in entanglement, to engage in study through the sharing of stories, to experiment and embrace uncertainty while letting go of the individuating pressure of feeling too preoccupied with "technique," "style," or "quality." For them to "work," the resulting images have to be a byproduct of such sociality, always a collaborative effort, not a division of labor between the maker and the sitter. The same applies to the purpose behind collecting these found Polaroids:

¹ Jesús Cos Causse, "Miranda Fotos," trans. John Keene, Academy of American Poets, accessed September 24, 2021, poets.org/poem/looking-photos.

² Fred Moten, "fortrd. fortrn," in *The Little Edges* (Middletown: Wesleyan University Press, 2014), 3.

they are not *of* Black sociality, but a matter of Black sociality surrounding and animating them. I've spent the past ten years not only gathering these artefacts but gathering with fellow artists, friends, and strangers to sit with these images and listen to the questions they invite: What does one make of the idea that the refusal of these images to respond to a reductive gaze strains against their violent dispossession? That this very refusal relies on our complicity in something taken, not granted? What exactly is the work the images in this collection perform beyond this unintended framing? How do we sustain a level of care for a work when the matter of what needs preservation cannot be decoupled from its ongoing material decomposition?

Attempting to engage with these questions amid collective pandemic exhaustion came under duress; not because the images themselves lost their vitality in rejecting their dehumanization (how could they?), but rather because the people with whom I would practice this kind of study were no longer around, or were unable to be with me, to feel summoned by these questions in order to answer to the unanswerable. Yet in these moments of pressure, something tends to burst open along familiar scars (and rather ferociously so) like a jolt to the heart and a giant thud to the forehead. Not-so-gentle reminders of what matters most.

I recently received a box of everyday belongings that my friend CJ (we called him "Toots") had wanted me to have but never had a chance to send. Toots had passed away a few months prior, in late 2021, and his mother had mailed this inconspicuous cardboard box with a customs value declaration of $15. No note or letter came with it. I recognized the box. I vaguely recalled its contents. It took me a while to muster the courage to open and unpack it.

Among the many US Army soldiers stationed in my hometown of Frankfurt, Germany, who were part of my inner circle, Toots was my ride-or-die; the kind of companion you are fortunate to have one or two of at any point in your life. In German, we'd say Toots was *jemand, mit dem man Pferde stehlen kann*, or "someone with whom you could go steal horses." German is rarely a suitable language for me to express myself in, but "to steal horses" invites a reading of waywardness, criminality, and insubordination into the idea of a trusted relationship. Ours wasn't about living an unruly existence as much as it was about a shared refusal to be governed—a way to fashion ourselves outside of the *"Spießer"*[3] society that sought to regulate us.

Our army brat friendship unfolded within the liminality of the final years of the Reagan administration, the last gasp of the Cold War in Allied-occupied Germany. In the hold of Toots's sparsely decorated barracks room (a partitioned space inside a larger hall), we dreamed up a whole universe of "otherwise possibility," as Ashon Crawley would say.[4] Toots and I would spend hours listening to albums produced by Jimmy Jam and Terry Lewis with their signature Minneapolis Sound, the S.O.S. Band being our favorite group. Toots would share stories of a magical place called Paradise Garage in New York City, read me works by a poet named Essex Hemphill from a chapbook called *Earth Life*, and tell me of a wondrous city named Atlanta that he'd suggested I move to.

Toots's box of improvised, mostly handmade curios contained, among other things:

- A rusty Acura keychain Toots had remade into a bracelet by adding a strap.

- A dreadlock he saved after shaving his head when he joined the military.

- Little ribbons cut from an old t-shirt and stapled to small branches of pussy willow to make Easter ornaments.

- A small plastic bag filled with cherimoya seeds (a fruit he had often mentioned but that I personally hadn't tasted until 2019).

- Old Polaroids of him and his "other half" Virgil (Toots had many real and imagined "other halves").

- An old birthday card he had written to me. It reads: "To Zun: You're a whole mess and a half. Never change. Love, Toot Toot."

- A vinyl LP label he had drawn for the imaginary music album he had always dreamt of producing. It featured some of the insignia of our favorite record label:

---

[3] A slightly pejorative German term that describes a particular kind of citizen, regardless of class, who is characterized by extreme conformity/normativity, narrow-mindedness, resistance to change, and fear of "the other."

[4] Ashon T. Crawley, *Blackpentecostal Breath: The Aesthetics of Possibility* (New York: Fordham University Press, 2016).

"Flyte Tyme Productions. Tabu Records. The earth has music for those who listen."

"The earth has music for those who listen"—the poignant motto of the legendary Tabu Records. How many readings this aphorism now invites when thinking through the notion of "what matters most." Sonic entanglement in, or as, study. Listening as, or with, care. Instructions for care for those called upon to respond (which really means anyone). Collective cultivation versus cultural production. My engagement with these objects continued as if it had never been disrupted.

As intense as the re-encounter with these objects was, it was the smell emanating from that box, at once faint and intense, that nearly made me lose my composure in the moment. Toots' favorite sandalwood incense sticks, the stale aroma of the hallway air in the barracks, the t-shirt he had cut into strips to make ornaments—the box smelled of him. Of us. Of our time together. Of many late-night moments we spent in his room, talking after returning from the clubs, still revved up and our ears still numb from the music. Our daydreams were our preferred way of inhabiting new worlds. They were guide maps that didn't exist before, so we had to draw them ourselves.

The encounter with Toots's keepsakes brought back memories, made me recall names, places, addresses, and phone numbers I hadn't thought about in decades. I momentarily reveled in a kind of nostalgia, considering the sentimentality we attach to a time we deem to have been simpler and more joyful when it was just as monstrous as any other period in our lives. But another realization hit me like a ton of bricks: the familiar smell, this synaesthetic engagement with Toots's box of belongings did more than just take me (a)back. It *remade* me—not just who I *was* but who I can *be*. I didn't just "re-member" what we did. Through registering the scent and touching the objects in the box, I instantly became that person again. A whole mess and a half.

This experience brought into focus what my ten years of practice with these Polaroids had been really about: that what we can "touch" by opening the proverbial box is really the making of worlds: a poetics of shared dispossession *through* dislocated images, not a practice of looking

at images. A practice of feeling that calls us to sit with
questions we have all lived a version of: What can be
crueler than the act of gazing at the material evidence of
personhood reduced to detritus, at subjectivities denied
and dislocated? What can be more affirming than sharing
in a Black aliveness that refuses to be discarded, even if
its material circumstances were? An aliveness that cannot
be contained, indexed, or catalogued, and that—even if
(or because) it was produced by horrific means—never
answers to the horror itself?

The earth has music for those who listen.

None of Toots's objects were meant to be kept in this box.
Toots *used* them, wore them out. The value attached to these
objects came from us using them and the possibilities of
such use, not from their preservation. Just as Toots didn't
discard anything or abandon anybody he cared about, that
little box he left didn't just signify an open invitation—it
came with instructions for careful use, to add and extend my
care onto these objects by using them as tools to build the
"otherwise" we had always imagined, not to hide them away.

It is in the recognition of this shared but irredeemable care,
of hapticality reproduced in the hold, that we are moved
from a "look at them" to a "look at us" and a "feel together
with us." Can we look at them to be able to feel with us?
I argue that we can and we must. Not as an imposition or by
way of a permission that can never be granted anyway, but
in the recognition that Black sociality refuses capture—even
in images—and thus can neither be reduced nor boxed in.
Sitting with the ineffable does not equate to being imprecise
about how we feel about it. We can sustain a space where
being and becoming can thrive, not in response to negation
but as an affirmation of undercommunal entanglement.
We can gather to try and figure out some things, but this
gathering requires an orientation toward risk. Worldmaking
isn't always pretty; in fact, it can be downright messy.
Yet, the mess(i)ness doesn't mean we don't care. We care
deeply and demand to be cared for deeply. Much like Toots's
memorabilia, the Polaroids in this collection are tools for
worldmaking that demand to be touched and used. They are
marked by wear and tear but also gathered in honor of their
refusal to be discarded.

To recognize the one-of-a-kindness of Polaroids, their intense photographic beauty, and their charm is to also recognize the fact that what matters most spills beyond the edges of the object itself: the images were handled, written on, rubbed, cut, torn, taped, stained, or breathed into—literally "in-spired." What survives (and thus what ought to be preserved) isn't necessarily their objectness, but rather it is the transformation given to us as their permanence is taken by decay and decomposition.

Herein lies the double paradox: the need for institutional archival preservation of the Polaroids removes them from our ability to touch, yet what survives—what matters most—can only be constituted through touch and shared use. And further, such communal use and touch cannot be upheld where it needs to manifest—in this case, the Black homes where this practice lives—because of the ongoing dispossession and dislocation enacted by an antiBlack world. An institution was invoked to provide custodial care, to offer the home that the dispossessed have been refused.[5]

The preciousness inherent in these keepsakes was never meant to be found in a book or displayed in a museum, especially if it removes the images from shared use and touch. But institutional custodianship might assist in reminding those who are called on to respond with care that the daily cultivation of aliveness and worldmaking continues under duress; that the practice and muscle memory of shared care continues to regenerate itself from the remnants of decay, and that what is salvaged is not an object and its place in time but instead a placelessness that refuses displacement—a dispossession that refuses the idea of ownership in general. If we can be reminded of who we are, who we become, and how we enact a care that expands the idea of *gazing at* into a vibrant, entangled *feeling-with*, holding space for all these beautiful, horrific contradictions may constitute a gift some of us may be able to honor.

I'm deeply inspired by Audre Lorde's exploration of feeling and worldmaking in her essay "Poetry Is Not a Luxury." Similar to her deliberations on the erotic, Lorde invokes feeling(s) not as "idle fantasy" but as loci of "hidden sources of power," and poetry as a transformational tool to express into knowledge "the revelation or distillation of experience."[6]

[5] In 2018, the Art Gallery of Ontario acquired the *Fade Resistance* collection, which documents African American family life from the 1950s to the early 2000s.

[6] Audre Lorde, "Poetry is Not a Luxury," in *Sister Outsider: Essays and Speeches* (Berkeley: Crossing Press, 1984), 36–39.

"Poetry [...] forms the quality of the light within which we predicate our hopes and dreams toward survival and change, first made into language, then into idea, then into more tangible action," says Lorde.[7] I especially love Kevin Quashie's reading of Lorde's poetry as illumination in his book *Black Aliveness, or A Poetics of Being*, in which he posits that "the manner and sensation of how we pay attention to our being constitute our being itself, as well as what our being is/becomes in the world," thereby connecting the idea of inseparability of interiority, embodiment, and feeling when conceptualizing aliveness as (a) poetic. How we feel makes who we are or will become.

Is there a better way to sit with these Polaroids and their leakage of scent, pigment, and light? The idea of poetry as illumination moves us away from *looking at* and allows us to feel what cannot be framed: the dislocated archive as haptic *rasanblaj*, not accessed via aesthetic considerations but in reclaiming our capacity "to become." By allowing this force to move us into action, we mess ourselves up into the kind of life that instantiates our imagination as a new reality.

Toots's presence is still felt through the objects he once made and touched. The jolt I experienced when opening that box was the same overwhelming feeling that I experienced ten years ago when I stumbled across my first few orphaned Polaroids in Detroit. It took this intervention to become a whole mess and a half again and to remember what matters most.

List of Works

Fade Resistance collection. Art Gallery of Ontario. Purchase, with funds donated by Martha LA McCain, 2018. Digital images: © Art Gallery of Ontario.

Inside front cover: [Teenage boy with his arm around teenage girl in a grey hoodie], 2000. Instant print (Polaroid Type 600), 10.8 × 8.8 cm. 2018/2532

Inside front cover: Alondra Park, 15 mos, September 9, 1979. Instant print (Polaroid SX70), 10.8 × 8.8 cm. 2018/2404

Inside front cover: [Bride, groom, and others standing in decorated room], 1978. Instant print (Polaroid SX70), 10.8 × 8.8 cm. 2018/2081

Inside front cover: [Two people posing, one in red stripes and one in black outfit], 1982. Instant print (Polaroid SX70), 10.8 × 8.8 cm. 2018/2546

Inside front cover: [Woman and two girls dressed up and posing in front of car], 1983–1993. Instant print (Polaroid Type 600), 10.8 × 8.8 cm. 2018/2501

Inside front cover: [Group of four standing outside on deck], 1984–1994. Instant print (Polaroid SX70), 10.8 × 8.8 cm. 2018/2401

Inside front cover: Grace & Peas on the Hudson River, 1997. Instant print (Polaroid Type 600), 10.8 × 8.8 cm. 2018/520

Inside front cover: [Woman in stripes standing between two dapper men], 1981–1991. Instant print [Polaroid SX70], 10.8 × 8.8 cm. 2018/2452

Inside front cover: [Bride standing with three women in formal wear], 1981–1997. Instant print (Polaroid SX70), 10.8 × 8.8 cm. 2018/2409

Inside front cover–page 1: Monique just knowing she is so damn fine, 1986–1996. Instant print (Polaroid Type 600), 10.8 × 8.8 cm. 2018/2094

Page 1: [Group of six children smiling on front steps], 1988–1998. Instant print (Polaroid Type 600), 10.8 × 8.8 cm. 2018/2420

Page 1: [Two men dressed up, one with his arm around the other], 1980. Instant print (Polaroid SX70), 10.8 × 8.8 cm. 2018/2500

Page 1: [Children crowded together inside], 1976–1985. Instant print (Kodak), 9.7 × 10.2 cm. 2018/2228

Page 2: [Children standing outside in white graduation caps and gowns], 1988. Instant print (Polaroid Type 600), 10.8 × 8.8 cm. 2018/2969

Page 2: [Little girl smiling, woman sitting on couch behind], 1988. Instant print (Polaroid Type 600), 10.8 × 8.8 cm. 2018/3483

Pages 2–3: [Boy smiling and holding adult's hand], 2006. Instant print (Polaroid Type 600), 10.8 × 8.8 cm. 2018/2451

Page 2: [Woman holding Polaroid in park], 1978. Instant print (Polaroid SX70), 10.8 × 8.8 cm. 2018/3541

Page 2: [Woman and children outside with balloons], 1960s–1990s. Instant print (Polaroid SX70), 10.8 × 8.8 cm. 2018/2881

Pages 2–3: [Woman with elderly man in bed], 1984–1994. Instant print (Polaroid SX70), 10.8 × 8.8 cm. 2018/2502

Page 2: JD & Jay eating meat sticks, 9 mos old [Man smiling and feeding baby], January 6, 1980. Instant print (Polaroid SX70), 10.8 × 8.8 cm. 2018/2509

Page 2: Eleanor & J.D., Tuesday Morning [Woman in glasses hugging man from behind], April 30, 1991. Instant print (Polaroid Type 600), 10.8 × 8.8 cm. 2018/2516

Pages 2–3: [Two women dressed up standing outside with their arms around each other], 1960s–1990s. Instant print (Polaroid SX70), 10.8 × 8.8 cm. 2018/2520

Page 2: [Three women dressed up in pastel colours standing together and smiling], 1979. Instant print (Polaroid SX70), 10.8 × 8.8 cm. 2018/2558

Page 2: Evan (Gloria's son) [Man in blue jacket by wood door], December 21, 1984. Instant print (Polaroid Type 600), 10.8 cm x 8.8 cm. 2018/322

Pages 2–3: Eric Jr. + Kenny, September 21, 1989. Instant print (Polaroid Type 600), 10.8 × 8.8 cm. 2018/2570

Page 3: [Woman in glasses sitting at table full of food], 1976. Instant print (Polaroid SX70), 10.8 × 8.8 cm. 2018/2165

Page 3: Juviya, Gloria, Yolanda, Aunt Mattie [Three women and baby posing together], 1982–1992. Instant print (Polaroid SX70), 10.8 × 8.8 cm. 2018/2218

Page 3: [Man and woman with baby on rocking horse], 1984–1994. Instant print (Polaroid SX70), 10.8 × 8.8 cm. 2018/2508

Page 3: [People around dining room table with large spread of food], 1987–1997. Instant print (Polaroid Type 600), 10.8 cm × 8.8 cm. 2018/339

Page 3: 12-16-78, 1978. Instant print (Polaroid SX70), 10.8 × 8.8 cm. 2018/859

Page 3: [Group of three posing together in red room with party streamers], 1980–1997. Instant print (Polaroid SX70), 10.8 × 8.8 cm. 2018/2085

Page 3: [Three adults and two children posing together inside home], 1978. Instant print (Polaroid SX70), 10.8 × 8.8 cm. 2018/697

Page 4: [Young woman sitting in armchair, two men standing behind her], 1980–1990. Instant print (Polaroid SX70), 10.8 × 8.8 cm. 2018/1646

Page 4: [Woman in purple graduation cap and gown with another woman], 1982–1992. Instant print (Polaroid SX70), 10.8 × 8.8 cm. 2018/1789

Page 4: [Woman and two boys posing in garden], 1990. Instant print (Polaroid Type 600), 10.8 × 8.8 cm. 2018/843

Pages 6–7: Detail of [Two women in the sunlight], 2001. Instant print (Polaroid Captiva), 6.4 × 11 cm. 2018/2011

Page 17: [Woman in bikini wading in water], 1986–1996. Instant print (Polaroid Type 778), 10.8 × 8.8 cm. 2018/645

Page 21: [Looking at Polaroids], 1980. Instant print (Polaroid SX70), 10.8 × 8.8 cm. 2018/1113

Page 26: Sammy's Baptism, July 19, 1998. Instant print (Polaroid Type 600), 10.8 × 8.8 cm. 2018/3499

Page 26: GiGi Rose, Gran Barbara, Mommy, Aunt Nora, Uncle Matt, Aunt Jackie, Aunt Juanita, Logan + Sammy, July 19, 1998. Instant print (Polaroid Type 600), 10.8 × 8.8 cm. 2018/2229

Page 27: San Francisco, October 3, 1975. Instant print (Polaroid SX70), 10.8 × 8.8 cm. 2018/384

Page 28: [Woman holding boy on roof of car], 1986–1996. Instant print (Polaroid SX70), 10.8 × 8.8 cm. 2018/806

Page 28: [Girl with ball posing in driveway], 1970s. Instant print (Polaroid SX70), 10.8 × 8.8 cm. 2018/2090

Page 28: [Little girl in pink sweater], 1960s–1990s. Instant print (Polaroid SX70), 10.8 × 8.8 cm. 2018/831

Page 28: Age 6, June 19, 1988. Instant print (Polaroid Type 600), 10.8 × 8.8 cm. 2018/809

Page 28: [Woman sitting with child in cowboy boots], 1985–1995. Instant print (Polaroid Type 600), 10.8 cm × 8.8 cm. 2018/246

Page 29: [Little boy standing on lawn with Easter basket], 1960s–1990s. Instant print (Polaroid SX70), 10.8 × 8.8 cm. 2018/833

Page 29: [Little girl in white dress with clips in her hair], 1986–1996. Instant print (Polaroid Type 600), 10.8 × 8.8 cm. 2018/832

Page 29: [Woman and girl sitting on brown couch], 1977. Instant print (Polaroid SX70), 10.8 × 8.8 cm. 2018/692

Page 29: Neicy, Donta, 1990. Instant print (Polaroid Type 600), 10.8 cm × 8.8 cm. 2018/284

Page 29: [Group sitting around a red picnic table], 1976–1985. Instant print (Kodak), 9.7 × 10.2 cm. 2018/395

Page 30: [Woman leaning on couch cushion], 1986–1996. Instant print (Polaroid SX70), 10.8 × 8.8 cm. 2018/2899

Page 31: [Woman with wine glass and making "Call Me" gesture], 2000. Instant print (Polaroid Type 600), 10.8 × 8.8 cm. 2018/2490

Page 32: [Man sitting in armchair, holding Polaroids], 1978. Instant print (Polaroid Type 88), 8.5 × 8.2 cm. 2018/624

Page 33: [Man lying on bed with two children], 1979. Instant print (Polaroid SX70), 10.8 × 8.8 cm. 2018/2586

Page 33: Foster III, Foster IV, 1978. Instant print (Polaroid SX70), 10.8 × 8.8 cm. 2018/2585

Page 33: 101178, 1978. Instant print (Polaroid SX70), 10.8 × 8.8 cm. 2018/2584

Page 33: Dominique, Foster, November 18, 1978. Instant print (Polaroid SX70), 10.8 × 8.8 cm. 2018/2587

Page 34: [Man in party hat holding camera], 1990–2000. Instant print (Polaroid Spectra), 10.2 × 10.3 cm. 2018/110

Page 36: [Group of men standing in a semi-circle], 1976–1985. Instant print (Kodak), 9.7 × 10.2 cm. 2018/3035

Page 36: [Woman and girl lying on the floor], 2000. Instant print (Polaroid Type 600), 10.8 × 8.8 cm. 2018/1367

Page 37: [Group gathered inside looking at Polaroids], 1963. wInstant print (Polaroid Type 107), 8.5 × 10.8 cm. 2018/982

Page 38: [Twin boys smiling with their arms around each other], 1980–1990. Instant print (Polaroid SX70), 10.8 × 8.8 cm. 2018/2316

Page 39: [Twin boys smiling with a dog], 1982–1992. Instant print (Polaroid SX70), 10.8 × 8.8 cm. 2018/2542

Page 39: [Man with moustache crouching and hugging twin boys], 1980–1990. Instant print (Polaroid SX70), 10.8 × 8.8 cm. 2018/2576

Page 40: [Shirtless man at sink looking in the mirror], 1976–1985. Instant print (Kodak), 9.7 × 10.2 cm. 2018/2163

Page 41: To Dad, Love Butch, December 16, 1977. Instant print (Polaroid SX70), 10.8 × 8.8 cm. 2018/2160

Page 42: [Two women in matching dresses standing with two men in a kitchen], 1986–1996. Instant print (Polaroid Type 600), 10.8 × 8.8 cm. 2018/3453

Page 42: [Two women in matching tops standing inside], 1981–1991. Instant print (Polaroid Type 600), 10.8 × 8.8 cm. 2018/822

Page 43: [Two women laughing], 1982–1992. Instant print (Polaroid Type 600), 10.8 × 8.8 cm. 2018/1355

Page 43: [Two boys in matching plaid shirts sitting on bed], 1963–1970. Instant print (Polaroid Type 108), 8.5 × 10.8 cm. 2018/825

Pages 44–45: [Young woman and two girls in matching red dresses], 1981–1991. Instant print (Polaroid SX70), 10.8 × 8.8 cm. 2018/823

Page 46: Geoffrey Grandma Hall, Mother & Dr. Basu, May 13, 1984. Instant print (Polaroid Type 600), 10.8 × 8.8 cm. 2018/2013

Page 47: Geoffrey, 62 days old, 1180 gms = 2 lbs., 9 1/2 oz., 1984. Instant print (Polaroid Type 600), 10.8 × 8.8 cm. 2018/2016

Page 47: Ashley, Mom & Dad, 9 weeks old, 1984. Instant print (Polaroid Type 600), 10.8 × 8.8 cm. 2018/1772

Page 48–49: Pamela & Mauricée Noel, Age 4 Months [Woman in straw hat holding baby outside], 1976. Instant print (Polaroid Type 108), 10.8 × 8.5 cm. 2018/770

Page 51: Otha and Pam, Herman Desiree [Two couples posing], December 28, 1975. Instant print (Polaroid SX70), 10.8 × 8.8 cm. 2018/763

Page 51: To a Very Special Woman from the Prince Bright Days Ahead, December 24, 1982. Instant print (Polaroid Type 600), 10.8 × 8.8 cm. 2018/2282

Page 51: Verso of 2018/322 (page 2).

Page 52: [Man and woman hugging outside by tree], 1960s–1990s. Instant print (Polaroid SX70), 10.8 × 8.8 cm. 2018/780

Page 53: [Man and woman with arms around each other standing on lawn], 1988–1992. Instant print (Polaroid Type 600), 10.8 × 8.8 cm. 2018/2038

Page 53: [Man and woman on motorcycle], 1982–1992. Instant print (Polaroid Type 600), 10.8 × 8.8 cm. 2018/828

Page 54: [Family visit: woman holding hands with crouching man], 1984–1994. Instant print (Polaroid Type 600), 10.8 × 8.8 cm. 2018/2285

Page 55: [Family visit: woman standing behind seated man in front of backdrop], 1982–1992. Instant print (Polaroid Type 600), 10.8 × 8.8 cm. 2018/1743

Page 55: [Family visit: man and woman in glasses hugging in front of backdrop], 1984–1994. Instant print (Polaroid Type 600), 10.8 × 8.8 cm. 2018/1750

Page 55: [Family visit: man and woman posed in profile in front of backdrop], 1983–1993. Instant print (Polaroid Type 600), 10.8 × 8.8 cm. 2018/1735

Page 55: [Family visit: man hugging woman in white pants in front of backdrop], 1983–1993. Instant print (Polaroid Type 600), 10.8 × 8.8 cm. 2018/2284

Page 56: [Family visit: two men standing in front of backdrop], 1984–1994. Instant print (Polaroid Type 600), 10.8 × 8.8 cm. 2018/2286

Page 56: [Family visit: man with knee on chair, holding baby], 1984–1994. Instant print (Polaroid Type 600), 10.8 × 8.8 cm. 2018/1734

Page 56: [Family visit: two couples posing with arms around each other], November 10, 1984. Instant print (Polaroid Type 600), 10.8 × 8.8 cm. 2018/1751

Page 56: Verso of 2018/2282 (page 51).

Page 57: [Family visit: man standing with jacket on one arm in front of backdrop], 1984. Instant print (Polaroid Type 600), 10.8 × 8.8 cm. 2018/1752

Page 58: [Woman in yellow dress posing next to brown car], 1983–1993. Instant print (Polaroid Type 600), 10.8 × 8.8 cm. 2018/2385

Page 59: [Girl in white dress making peace sign in front of brown car], 1983–1993. Instant print (Polaroid Type 600), 10.8 × 8.8 cm. 2018/2200

Page 59: [Three girls posing in front of car], 1986–1996. Instant print (Polaroid Type 600), 10.8 × 8.8 cm. 2018/2078

Page 59: [Boy posing with arms crossed in front of brown car], 1983–1993. Instant print (Polaroid Type 600), 10.8 × 8.8 cm. 2018/2371

Page 60: [Woman and two children by car], 1970s–1990s. Instant print (Polaroid), 8.7 × 8.8 cm. 2018/53

Page 61: [Young man shirtless wearing blue shorts in army barracks], 1978. Instant print (Polaroid SX70), 10.8 × 8.8 cm. 2018/2629

Page 61: [Three men posing together in army barracks], 1978. Instant print (Polaroid SX70), 10.8 × 8.8 cm. 2018/694

Page 62: Nuchie & Daddy, November 18, 1978. Instant print (Polaroid SX70), 10.8 × 8.8 cm. 2018/829

Page 62: [Girl smiling with hands on hips in front of TV set], 1990. Instant print (Polaroid Type 600), 10.8 × 8.8 cm. 2018/3428

Page 62: Church Day Stephen and Mom, February 26, 1994. Instant print (Polaroid Type 600), 10.8 × 8.8 cm. 2018/864

Page 62: [Boy on bicycle near red car], 1960s–1990s. Instant print (Polaroid SX70), 10.8 × 8.8 cm. 2018/2189

Page 62: [Two teenagers in backseat of car, one with face in hands], 1998. Instant print (Polaroid Type 600), 10.8 × 8.8 cm. 2018/2421

Page 63: [Woman in white hat in front of "Kodak Instant Camera" poster], July 2 1979. Instant print (Kodak), 9.7 × 10.2 cm. 2018/1823

Page 63: [Three girls posing in living room], 1990. Instant print (Polaroid Type 600), 10.8 × 8.8 cm. 2018/695

Page 63: 10/31/90 [Man holding toddler in tiger costume], 1990. Instant print (Polaroid Type 600), 10.8 × 8.8 cm. 2018/830

Page 97: [Man holding girl, sitting in armchair (fist bump)], 1988. Instant print (Polaroid Type 600), 10.8 × 8.8 cm. 2018/846

Page 98: [Woman in red laughing], 1998. Instant print (Polaroid Type 600), 10.8 × 8.8 cm. 2018/810

Page 98: [Three children posing with fists stacked], 1978. Instant print (Polaroid SX70), 10.8 × 8.8 cm. 2018/1348

Page 99: [Young woman posing in front of white car in driveway], 1976–1985. Instant print (Kodak), 9.7 × 10.2 cm. 2018/396

Page 101: [Person sitting in chair in dark room], 1976–1985. Instant print (Kodak), 9.7 × 10.2 cm. 2018/173

Page 102: [Girl holding plush panda above man's head], 1985–1995. Instant print (Polaroid SX70), 10.8 × 8.8 cm. 2018/2569

Page 102: [Two women sitting on bed smiling], 1990. Instant print (Polaroid Type 600), 10.8 × 8.8 cm. 2018/2566

Page 102: [Man in cowboy hat smiling at woman beside him], 1981–1991. Instant print (Polaroid SX70), 10.8 × 8.8 cm. 2018/2637

Page 102: [Young man holding baby cheektocheek], 1983–1993. Instant print (Polaroid Type 600), 10.8 × 8.8 cm. 2018/2592

Page 102: [Two boys hugging in matching white tank tops], 1999. Instant print (Polaroid Type 600), 10.8 × 8.8 cm. 2018/2178

Page 102: [Man standing beside woman in wicker chair in red room], 1967–1977. Instant print (Polaroid Type 108), 10.7 × 8.5 cm. 2018/2667

Page 103: [Boy and girl in roller skates on sidewalk], 1981–1997. Instant print (Polaroid Type 600), 10.8 × 8.8 cm. 2018/2266

Page 103: [Woman wearing beaded necklace sitting with man], 1980–1997. Instant print (Polaroid SX70), 10.8 × 8.8 cm. 2018/2657

Page 103: [Man with two toddlers in pink toy car], 1988. Instant print (Polaroid Type 600), 10.8 × 8.8 cm. 2018/2098

Page 103: [Boy and girl with school bags smiling outside], 1986–1996. Instant print (Polaroid Type 600), 10.8 × 8.8 cm. 2018/2179

Page 103: [Man in glasses sitting with woman in a tan hat], 1984–1994. Instant print (Polaroid Type 600), 10.8 × 8.8 cm. 2018/2664

Page 103: [Two women dressed up and standing outside door], 1984–1994. Instant print (Polaroid Type 600), 10.8 × 8.8 cm. 2018/2725

Page 104: Mr. Money Monroe & Gerald Scearg at Nito & Fatima's "77" [Two men posing with hands on hips], 1977. Instant print (Polaroid Type 88), 8.5 × 8.2 cm. 2018/107

Page 105: [Man and woman sitting at table, his arm around her waist], 1963–1970. Instant print (Polaroid Type 108), 8.5 × 10.8 cm. 2018/890

Page 106: Sebastian Virgil, Kyla Amonette, Namaste Tara, Cousins to Kyla, December 30, 1987. Instant print (Polaroid Type 600), 10.8 × 8.8 cm. 2018/3431

Page 107: 10-15-71 [Three girls in white Compton sweatshirts sitting on a couch with a baby], 1971. Instant print (Polaroid Type 108), 10.8 × 8.5 cm. 2018/756 (recto and verso)

Page 108: [Woman in gloves and shiny dress striking a pose], 1960. Instant print (Polaroid Type 47), 10.5 × 8.2 cm. 2018/2694

Page 109: [Woman smiling and standing by a man on the phone], 1970–1980. Instant print (Polaroid Type 108), 10.8 × 8.7 cm. 2018/2642

Page 110: To: My Son, Daddy loves you Shamar, 2005. Instant print (Polaroid Spectra), 10.8 × 10.2 cm. 2018/2092

Page 111: [Boy with glasses snapping his fingers], 1988. Instant print (Polaroid Type 600), 10.8 cm × 8.8 cm. 2018/79

Page 111: [Man lying in bed with a smiling baby], 1981–1991. Instant print (Polaroid Type 600), 10.8 × 8.8 cm. 2018/3490

Page 112: [Baptism], 1982–1992. Instant print (Polaroid Type 600), 10.8 × 8.8 cm. 2018/2089

Page 113: [Man and woman in hats holding hands and smiling], 1966–1976. Instant print (Polaroid Type 108), 10.7 × 8.5 cm. 2018/159

Page 113: [Person wearing a white top and shorts in the dark], 1976–1985. Instant print (Kodak), 9.7 × 10.2 cm. 2018/3033

Page 114: [Man standing by picnic area], 1983–1993. Instant print (Polaroid Type 600), 10.8 × 8.8 cm. 2018/877

Page 115: [Two men sitting together and laughing], 1982–1992. Instant print (Polaroid Type 600), 10.8 cm × 8.8 cm. 2018/162

Page 116: [Woman doing elderly woman's hair in living room], 1980. Instant print (Polaroid SX70), 10.8 × 8.8 cm. 2018/2201

Page 117: Ola Mae Bradly, "What did you say darling," 2000. Instant print (Polaroid Type 600), 10.8 × 8.8 cm. 2018/2631

Page 118: [Man posing in front of yellow taxi], 1978. Instant print (Kodak), 9.7 × 10.2 cm. 2018/65

Page 119: [Woman in yellow pants with hands on hips], 1976–1985. Instant print (Kodak), 9.7 × 10.2 cm. 2018/115

Pages 120–121: [Man in black hat and tank top standing in front of black car], 1960s–1990s. Instant print (Polaroid), 8.8 × 8.8 cm. 2018/1231

Page 122: [Woman in red dress sitting on grass], 1976–1985. Instant print (Kodak), 10.2 × 9.7 cm. 2018/2124

Page 124: [Man in glasses with hands in pockets], 1981–1991. Instant print (Polaroid Type 600), 10.8 cm × 8.8 cm. 2018/340

Page 124: [Woman in tan beret with hands on hips], 1976. Instant print (Polaroid SX70), 10.8 × 8.8 cm. 2018/860

Page 125: [Person in white face paint and wig], 1990. Instant print (Polaroid Spectra), 10.2 × 10.1 cm. 2018/804

Page 126: [Woman in wedding dress holding bouquet], 1960s–1990s. Instant print (Polaroid SX70), 10.8 cm × 8.8 cm. 2018/289

Page 127: [Person in nightgown reclining on bed], 1982–1992. Instant print (Polaroid SX70), 10.8 cm × 8.8 cm. 2018/82

Pages 128–129: Bon temps [Man sitting on cot], 1962. Instant print (Polaroid Type 47), 8.3 × 10.7 cm. 2018/2216 (recto and verso)

Page 130: 82684 [Two women sharing patio chair with a baby], 1984. Instant print (Polaroid SX70), 10.8 × 8.8 cm. 2018/2278

Page 130: [Boy in dress shirt by doorway], 1987–1997. Instant print (Polaroid Type 600), 10.8 × 8.8 cm. 2018/2068

Page 130: [Child in white suit beside statue], 1980–1990. Instant print (Polaroid SX70), 10.8 × 8.8 cm. 2018/2199

Page 130: [Two women smiling, in car at night], 1982–1992. Instant print (Polaroid Type 600), 10.8 × 8.8 cm. 2018/2572

Page 130: [Three people in front of red curtain], 1976. Instant print (Polaroid SX70), 10.8 × 8.8 cm. 2018/773

Page 130: [Two women fist bumping in front of graffiti wall], 1984–1994. Instant print (Polaroid SX70), 10.8 × 8.8 cm. 2018/894

Page 131: [Woman in white sweatshirt smiling and holding baby], 1986–1996. Instant print (Polaroid Spectra), 10.1 × 10.3 cm. 2018/2052

Page 131: [Girl in blue graduation gown posing with man in blue cap], 1981–1997. Instant print (Polaroid Type 600), 10.8 × 8.8 cm. 2018/855

Page 131: [Woman posing with red and yellow flowers], 1976–1985. Instant print (Kodak), 9.7 × 10.2 cm. 2018/1494

Page 131: [Woman and man posing in front of yellow cityscape backdrop], 1986–2008. Instant print (Polaroid Spectra), 10 × 8.7 cm. 2018/2568

Page 131: [Woman in floral dress sitting on bed], 1960s–1990s. Instant print (Polaroid SX70), 10.8 × 8.8 cm. 2018/2167

Page 132: 7-17-88, 1988. Instant print (Polaroid SX70), 10.8 × 8.8 cm. 2018/3515

Page 133: [Woman with braided headband sitting on couch], 1982–1992. Instant print [Polaroid SX70], 10.8 × 8.8 cm. 2018/2448

Page 134: [Man smiling in headphones with microphone], 1976. Instant print (Polaroid Type 88), 8.5 × 8.2 cm. 2018/39

Page 135: Frankfut [sic] Germany, Bob Clubinn [Man posing by wall with cane], 1973. Instant print (Polaroid Type 108), 10.7 × 8.5 cm. 2018/416

Pages 136–137: [Boy in U.S. Space Camp t-shirt with red sweatshirt], 1986–1996. Instant print (Polaroid Spectra), 10.8 × 8.8 cm. 2018/781

Page 138: Jordans High, 1976–1985. Instant print (Kodak), 9.7 × 10.2 cm. 2018/616

Page 139: [Girl posing in yellow and green cheerleader outfit], 1981–1991. Instant print (Polaroid Type 779), 10.8 × 8.8 cm. 2018/2894

Page 140: [Profile of woman with a stud earring and bare shoulders], 1974. Instant print (Polaroid SX70), 10.8 × 8.8 cm. 2018/3547

Page 140: Troy, Nate, Jimmy, MeMe, Tasha, Shana [Six children in front of piano], 1981–1991. Instant print (Polaroid SX70), 10.8 × 8.8 cm. 2018/752

Page 141: John A. James Jr. [Boy in turtleneck smiling], 1973. Instant print (Polaroid Type 88), 8.5 × 8.2 cm. 2018/2528

Page 143: [Woman with arms outstretched in front of car], 1976–1985. Instant print (Kodak), 9.7 × 10.2 cm. 2018/3525

Page 143: 7680 [Two men in room full of plants], 1980. Instant print (Polaroid SX70), 10.8 × 8.8 cm. 2018/3456

Page 143: Shawna [Girl on chair in front of steps], 1981–1991. Instant print (Polaroid Type 600), 10.8 × 8.8 cm. 2018/2620

Page 144: [Woman playing Solitaire on computer], 1997–2008. Instant print (Polaroid Type 600), 10.8 × 8.8 cm. 2018/2066

Pages 144–145: Eating out of cake bowl, 1990. Instant print (Polaroid Type 600), 10.8 × 8.8 cm. 2018/2067

Page 145: [Girl wearing costume glasses in front of wooden door], 1982–1992. Instant print (Polaroid SX70), 10.8 × 8.8 cm. 2018/2071

Pages 146–147: [Woman in hat posing in front of a building], 1983–1993. Instant print (Polaroid Type 600), 10.8 × 8.8 cm. 2018/2464

Page 148: To: Patrick, Love + Luck in the future, Love Rufus, December 8, 1984. Instant print (Polaroid SX70), 10.8 × 8.8 cm. 2018/99 (recto and verso)

Page 149–150: Good things come to those who wait [Man in sunglasses leaning on TV set], 1963–1970. Instant print (Polaroid Type 48), 10.8 × 8.2 cm. 2018/797 (recto and verso)

Page 151: [Two women dressed up and posing by tree], 1978. Instant print (Polaroid SX70), 10.8 cm × 8.8 cm. 2018/118

Page 152: [Four women dressed in pastels, in front of a car], 1960s–1990s. Instant print (Polaroid SX70), 10.8 × 8.8 cm. 2018/2226

Page 153: [Four women posing in front
of Saints Ladies backdrop, one sitting
in chair], 1987–1997. Instant print
(Polaroid Type 600), 10.8 × 8.8 cm.
2018/2240

Page 153: [Five men and a woman
posing in front of red backdrop],
1996–2006. Instant print (Polaroid
Spectra), 10.1 × 10.3 cm. 2018/2230

Page 154: [Woman in camouflage shirt
sitting on chair outside], 1976–1985.
Instant print (Kodak), 9.7 × 10.2 cm.
2018/62

Page 155: 4/7/93, 1993. Instant print
(Polaroid Type 600), 10.8 × 8.8 cm.
2018/38

Page 156: Grant, N.M. [Man in rocky
landscape holding shirt above his head],
1963–1970. Instant print (Polaroid
Type 108), 8.6 × 10.8 cm. 2018/119
(recto and verso)

Page 157: [Man posing with red bicycle
in driveway], 2000. Instant print
(Polaroid Type 600), 10.8 cm × 8.8 cm.
2018/121

Page 158: [Little girl in car ride at
amusement park], 1974. Instant
print (Polaroid SX70), 10.8 × 8.8 cm.
2018/662

Pages 160–161: Detail of Johnny [Boy
posing with one arm raised, man sitting
on the left], July 4, 1972. Instant print
(Polaroid Type 108), 8.5 × 10.7 cm.
2018/3486

Page 162: [Five women dressed up for
the night], 1981–1991. Instant print
(Polaroid SX70), 10.8 cm × 8.8 cm.
2018/286

Page 162: Friends of mine [Four women
with their arms around each other],
April 1989. Instant print (Polaroid
Type 600), 10.8 × 8.8 cm. 2018/2678

Page 163: [Man kneeling with two boys
by a pool], 1976–1985. Instant print
(Kodak), 8.8 × 10.2 cm. 2018/150

Page 164: March 85 [Family visit:
man and woman hugging in front
of backdrop], 1985. Instant print
(Polaroid Type 600), 10.8 × 8.8 cm.
2018/1753

Page 164: 1279, 1979. Instant print
(Polaroid SX70), 10.8 × 8.8 cm.
2018/2456

Page 164: [Man in white t-shirt sitting
on wicker chair], 1983–1993. Instant
print (Polaroid Type 600),
10.8 × 8.8 cm. 2018/2812

Page 164: Chillin on the beach, Santa
Monica, April 17, 2005. Instant print
(Polaroid Type 600), 10.8 × 8.8 cm.
2018/771

Page 165: [People dancing with their
arms in the air], 1998. Instant print
(Polaroid Type 600), 10.8 × 8.8 cm.
2018/2339

Page 165: [Five men in suits posing in
front of backdrop], 1981. Instant print
(Polaroid Type 108), 10.2 × 8.5 cm.
2018/623

Page 165: [Family visit: man sitting
with woman on his lap, holding hands],
June 24, 1983. Instant print (Polaroid
Type 600), 10.8 × 8.8 cm. 2018/3399

Page 165: To my moms Mrs. Webster,
1992. Instant print (Polaroid Type
600), 10.8 × 8.8 cm. 2018/2830

Page 165: [Four adults and a baby
posing around a cake in a box], 1977.
Instant print (Polaroid SX70),
10.8 × 8.8 cm. 2018/2896

Page 187: [Child with award beside
woman holding disposable camera],
1983–1993. Instant print (Polaroid
Type 779), 10.8 × 8.8 cm. 2018/139

Page 191: Grandpa and his sweet
thing [Baby sitting on roof of car,
man smiling at her], March 29, 1970.
Instant print (Polaroid Type 108),
8.5 × 10.7 cm. 2018/418

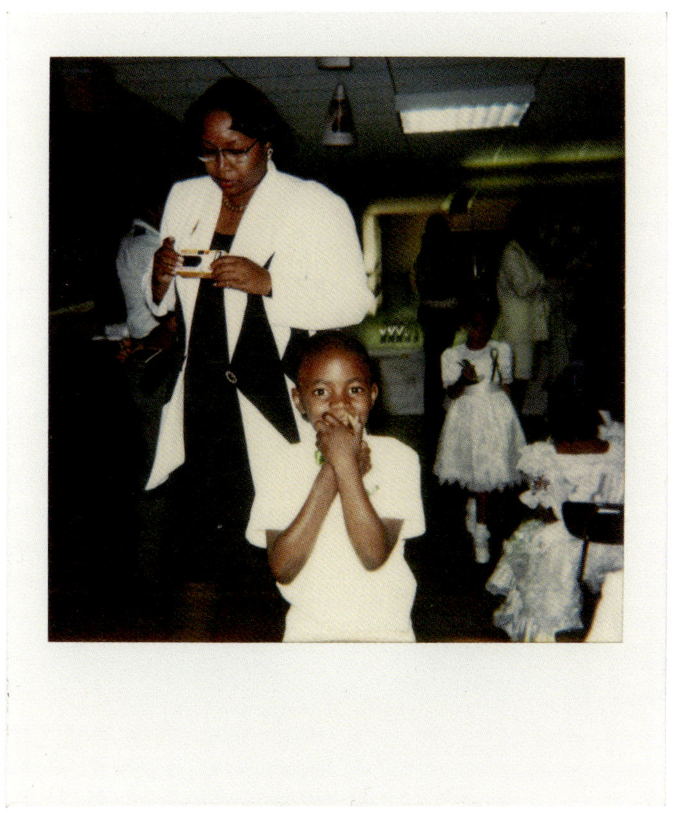

LAND ACKNOWLEDGEMENT

The Art Gallery of Ontario operates on land that is the territory of the Anishinaabe (Mississauga) nation and is also the territory of the Wendat and Haudenosaunee. The Dish with One Spoon Wampum Belt Covenant is an agreement between the Haudenosaunee Confederacy and the Anishinaabe Three Fires Confederacy to peaceably share and care for the resources around the Great Lakes. Toronto is also governed by a treaty between the federal government of Canada and the Mississaugas of the New Credit (Anishinaabe nation). Toronto has always been a trading centre for First Nations.

THANK YOU

Lead Support
David W. Binet

Generous Support
Martha LA McCain

Additional Support
Cindy & Shon Barnett

The Art Gallery of Ontario is partially funded by the Ontario Ministry of Culture.
Additional operating support is received from the City of Toronto, the Department of Canadian Heritage, and the Canada Council for the Arts.
Contemporary programming at the Art Gallery of Ontario is supported by

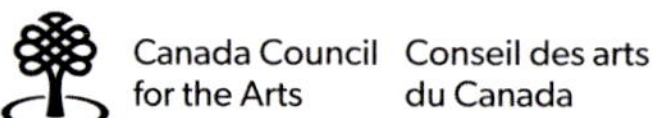

Library and Archives Canada Cataloguing in Publication
Title: *What Matters Most: Photographs of Black Life*
Names: Art Gallery of Ontario, host institution, publisher.
Description: Published on the occasion of the exhibition What Matters Most: Photographs of Black Life, organized by the Art Gallery of Ontario from August 27, 2022 to January 8, 2023.
Identifiers: Canadiana 2022023793X | ISBN 9781942884941 (hardcover)
Subjects: LCSH: African Americans—Social life and customs—Pictorial works—Exhibitions. | LCSH: African American families—Pictorial works—Exhibitions. | LCGFT: Exhibition catalogs. | LCGFT: Photobooks.
Classification: LCC E185.86 .W53 2022 | DDC 779/.99730496073—dc23

Art Gallery of Ontario
317 Dundas Street West
Toronto, Ontario M5T 1G4
Canada
www.ago.ca

DelMonico Books
available through ARTBOOK | D.A.P.
75 Broad Street, Suite 630
New York, NY 10004
artbook.com
delmonicobooks.com

Printed and bound in Belgium
ISBN: 978-1-942884-94-1
10 9 8 7 6 5 4 3 2 1

PUBLICATION

Editors: Zun Lee, Sophie Hackett
Managing Editor: Jim Shedden
Production and Copy Editors: Nives Hajdin, Sarah Liss
Publishing Coordinator: Kathryn Yuen
Researcher: Emily Miller
Designers: Polymode, Los Angeles/Raleigh: Brian Johnson, Silas Munro, and Randa Hadi
Photographers: Craig Boyko, Sean Weaver
Pre-Press and Printing: Type A Print Inc.

EXHIBITION

Deputy Director and Chief Curator: Julian Cox
Curators: Zun Lee, Sophie Hackett
Project Manager: Hillary Taylor
Interpretive Planner: Nadia Abraham
Research & Collections Assistant: Emily Miller
Interns: Alex Arslanyan, Emilie Croning, Shanice Francis, Avery Steel
Editors: Nives Hajdin, Sarah Liss
Exhibition Design: Aleksandra Grzywaczewska
Graphic Design: Tara Keens-Douglas
Production: Malene Hjørngaard, Evelyn Quinn

EXHIBITIONS AND COLLECTIONS

Chief, Exhibitions, Collections, & Conservation: Jessica Bright
Associate Director, Exhibitions: Laura Comerford
Registration: Alison Beckett, Cindy Brouse, Jerry Drozdowsky, Joel Herman, Dale Mahar, Sabine Schaefer, Curtis Strilchuk
Collection Information: Alexandra Cousins, Tracy Mallon-Jensen, Liana Radvak, Joe Venturella, Olga Zotova
Conservation: Katharine Whitman, Margaret Haupt, Maureen Del Degan, John Williams, Curtis Amisich

LOGISTICS AND ART SERVICES

Gregory Baszun, Patric Colosimo, Scott Cameron, Colin Campbell, Brian Davis, Randal Fedje, Tina Giovinazzo, Roland Hardy, Iain Hoadley, Matthew Janisse, Ruth Jones, David Kinsman, Jason Laudadio, Alison Lindsay, Paul Mathiesen, Angelo Pedari, Craig Whiteside, Darin Yorston, Tanya Zhilinsky

EDUCATION & PROGRAMMING

Richard & Elizabeth Currie Chief, Education & Programming: Audrey Hudson
Director, Engagement & Learning: Paola Poletto
Director, Strategic Projects & Operations: Deborah Nolan
Education & Programming: Danah Abusido, Madelyne Beckles, Erica Chan, Maureen DaSilva, Sarah Febbraro, Nathan Huisman, Natalie Lam, Idalette Martins, Kathleen McLean, Zavette Quadros-Evangelista, Annie Roper, Melissa Smith

MEDIA PRODUCTION

Catherine Thomson, Danny Winchester, Matthew Scott

As if before
As if before time

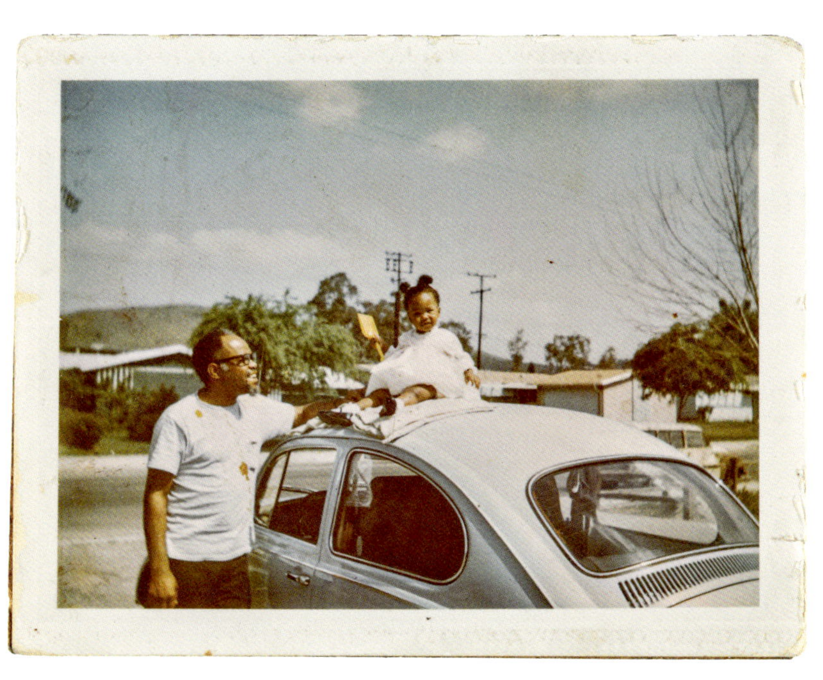

Note on the collection

These photographs are part of the *Fade Resistance* collection, assembled between 2012 and 2018 by Zun Lee. The Toronto-based photographer, visual storyteller, and educator purchased the photographs from various sources, including eBay and yard sales, and found some on the street; he ultimately collected 2,975 instant prints (primarily Polaroids, though some are Kodak) and 1,384 related gelatin silver and chromogenic prints, dating from the 1950s to the early 2000s. For the most part, it is not known what circumstances led to the separation of these items from the families who made them. Based on information in the images, many of the photographs were made in southern California.

In 2018, the Art Gallery of Ontario (AGO) in Toronto, Canada purchased the *Fade Resistance* collection from Lee. AGO staff have catalogued, rehoused, and partially digitized the collection. You can view images from the *Fade Resistance* collection online at ago.ca/collection/faderesistance.

If you recognize yourself or someone you know in any of the photographs, we would like to hear from you: faderesistance@ago.ca.

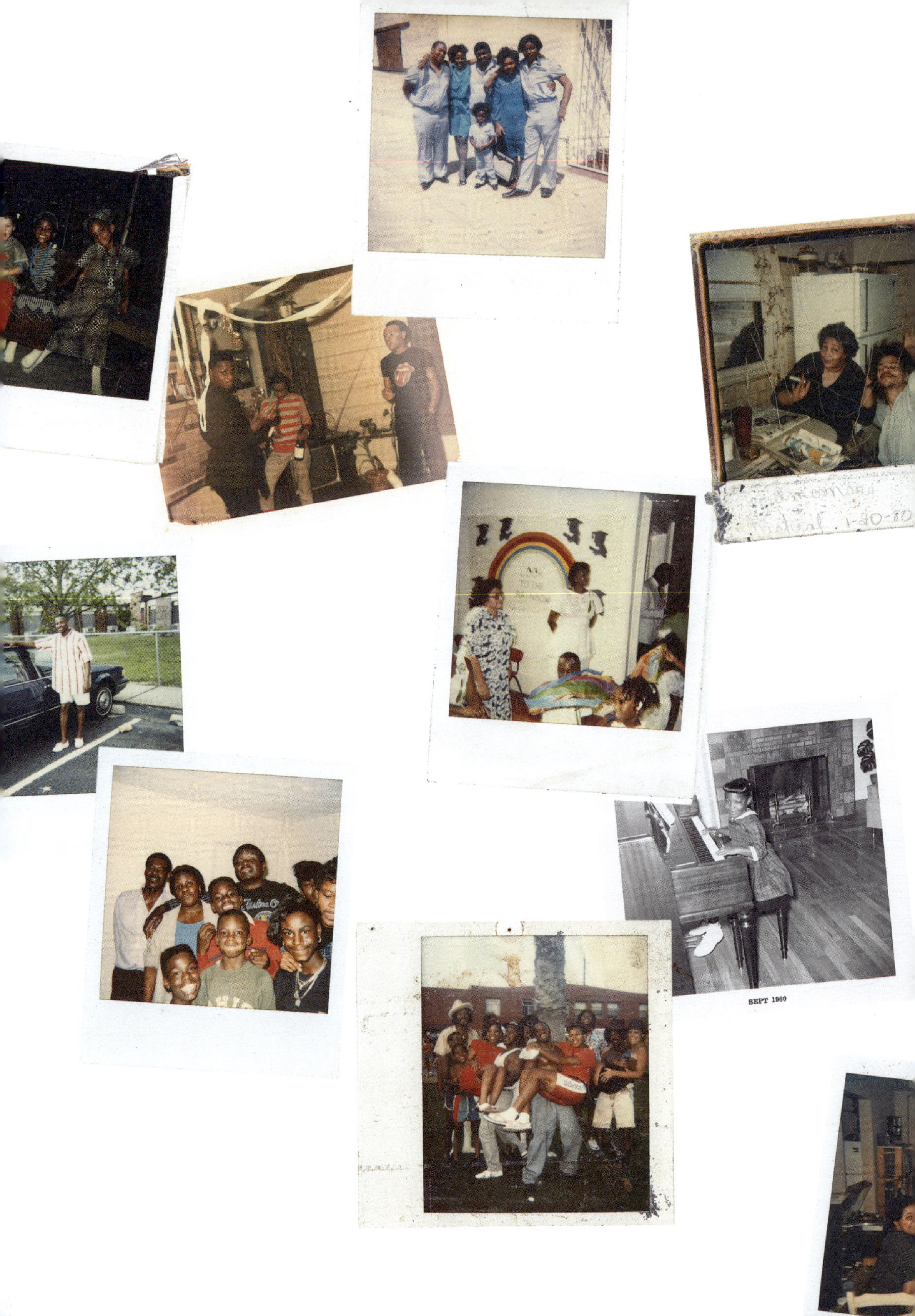

SEPT 1960